The Films of the Fifties

The Films of
Sunset Boulevard

the Fifties
to On the Beach

by Douglas Brode

A Citadel Press Book   Published by Carol Publishing Group

For My Father
Who taught me, at an early age,
that movies are not an escape from reality
but a means of comprehending it

Carol Publishing Group Edition - 1992

A Citadel Press Book
Published by Carol Publishing Group
Citadel Press is a registered trademark of Carol Communications, Inc.

Editorial Offices: 600 Madison Avenue, New York, NY 10022
Sales & Distribution Offices: 120 Enterprise Avenue, Secaucus, NJ 07094
In Canada: Canadian Manda Group, P.O. Box 920, Station U, Toronto,
Ontario, M8Z 5P9, Canada

Queries regarding rights and permissions should be addressed to:
Carol Publishing Group, 600 Madison Avenue, New York, NY 10022

Manufactured in the United States of America
ISBN 0-8065-0621-0

ACKNOWLEDGMENTS

With grateful thanks to all those
people and institutions who helped
me on this project: my wife Sue,
Charles Bernard Bornstein, Richard
Brown, Viola Thaxter, Norman
Keim, Jann Schlesinger, Doretta
Settineri of WHEN, Jane Field of
WYNS, Shane Johnson Brode and
Mark Ricci and The Memory Shop;
also, Allied Artists, Archway Films,
Buena Vista, Cinerama, Columbia,
Joseph Burnstyn Inc., Kingsley-Inter-
national, Lippert Pictures, Inc., Metro-
Goldwyn-Mayer, Paramount Pictures,
Republic Pictures, RKO Radio Pic-
tures, Inc., Trans-Lux Films, Twen-
tieth Century-Fox, United Artists,
Universal, Universal-International,
and Warner Brothers.

Contents

Lure of The Fifties

The dictionary defines nostalgia as a wistful, excessively sentimental yearning for a return to some past period or irrecoverable condition. But Webster fails to explain why even the most difficult of periods later become attractive. A great American humorist once wrote that the past always looks better than the present because it "ain't here" anymore, and that touches close to the heart of the matter. Nostalgia seems to be an inherent element of the human condition.

Take the fifties, that period for which everyone has grown so nostalgic in recent years. Like every other decade in our history, it did not exist in isolation but was part of the total time-continuum, as unconditionally connected to the late forties out of which it grew as it was to the early sixties which were, fundamentally, a reaction against the fifties. Just as our choice of Eisenhower marked a turning away from the Roosevelt/Truman era, so was our choice of John Kennedy one decade later a symbolic statement of our readiness to try a different approach, a different tone, a different mood. It's a basic rule of science that every force creates its equal but antithetical force; the same is true with periods of time. The relaxed, trustworthy, moderate Eisenhower represented exactly the way we wanted—and, perhaps, needed—to view ourselves in the fifties. It was reassuring to think we were mirrored in the fundamental decency of his image. But even then we knew that this was only part of the story. For if Eisenhower reflected our Dr. Jekyll face—the way we were on the surface—surely Senator Joseph McCarthy simultaneously mirrored and helped create our Mr. Hyde alter-ego, the way we feared ourselves to be down deep: rabid, ruthless, and reckless in our disillusionment with what our world had become.

In the early fifties, things were so difficult that we waxed nostalgic for—amazingly enough—the thirties, that terrible period when our economy was so racked with the Great Depression that almost everyone went hungry. In the late fifties we looked back with fondness at the forties, when women and children had to make do alone while the men risked their lives in combat. A depression and a war—hardly the sort of eras it makes sense to recall with fondness.

But in the thirties we had something fundamental and important; a faith in the individual, and his ability to change things for the better. Writer John Steinbeck brilliantly captured that feeling with his characterization of Tom Joad in *The Grapes of Wrath*; a simple ex-farmer/ex-convict who becomes radicalized after experiencing first-hand the inhumanity around him and who sets out to do something about it. And in the forties, we shared some-

thing very different but every bit as reassuring: a faith in "the group," in ourselves as a community of people, and the sense that we were fundamentally good and right and therefore would eventually overcome. We left World War II with the belief that, with the dragon slain, we could go on to create a wonderful and peaceful world.

But that dream went sour more quickly than anyone would have guessed possible, and we entered the fifties without either of those great faiths that had formerly seen us through. Trust either in the individual or the group was replaced by a general sense of suspicion. The growing fear that we might eventually have to fight yet another war against the newly powerful communist countries led to lethargy and defeatism. But that was mild compared to the hysteria that gripped us when we suddenly seized on the notion that every tenth person we passed on the street was, secretly, a communist.

In many respects, the first significant event of the decade took place on February 9, 1950, when Senator McCarthy of Wisconsin addressed a presumably routine Republican Party dinner-meeting in Wheeling, West Virginia. He was catapulted onto the front pages of the nation's newspapers when he whisked out a piece of paper and announced to his shocked audience that he had in his possession a list of over 200 members of the State Department who were known to be registered members of the Communist Party. In subsequent speeches the number dwindled down to 81 and the charge was reduced from "card-carrying conspirators" to "security risks"; eventually it was disclosed that the list was a total fraud and that no clear investigation into such matters had ever been undertaken.

McCarthy ultimately fell from grace in 1954, when the televised hearings of his debate with the United States Army presented an at-first amazed and then outraged nation of over twenty million home viewers with a portrait of a man who was clearly more an ambitious demagogue than a patriotic crusader. But the damage had been done. During the four years of McCarthyism, everyone in Washington—including two presidents, one a Democrat and the other a Republican—lived in constant fear of the man. The nation had become so certain we'd been infiltrated by dangerous enemies that numerous concentration camps were actually readied, at the order of the U.S. Attorney General, in which the conspirators were to be interned. But the clearest example of the country's mood became apparent when Hollywood—which had only a few years earlier cranked out numerous propaganda pictures to aid the war cause—was accused of being pro-communist.

SCREEN COMEDY: The decade began with such innocuous fare as *Francis, The Talking Mule* (1950) with Donald O'Connor

What transpired could have been avoided if we had only been wise enough to heed President Roosevelt's advice of two decades earlier: we had nothing to fear but fear itself. Whatever harm the handful of Russian sympathizers, saboteurs or spies did to America was dwarfed by what we did to ourselves. We became paranoid and, thus, significantly altered the direction of our cultural mainstream.

The Bomb emerged as the symbol of the era, and it literally decimated many people's faith in the immortality of man and the universe. There had been a nagging sense of guilt ever since Hiroshima. But when it became obvious that the Russians had nuclear weapons to equal ours, the fear they would use them to take over the world weighed heavily on the country's consciousness. Since the beginning of the century, we had been steadily forced into embracing a new role in world politics. Instead of a largely self-contained little world of our own, relating to the great macrocosm of the globe in peripheral ways, we emerged in the fifties as the spokesmen—and the muscle—for half the world. It was a role we had trouble adjusting to. Although fighting Hitler had been physically costly, we were the good guys and they were the bad guys; we had seen enough of our own westerns to know that peace is to be desired but villains are defeated only through violence.

But the fifties presented us with a whole new ball game. When a communist fighting force from North Korea tried to overrun the lower sector of that divided country in 1951, we responded in the highly controversial manner of entering a "limited war" that cost the lives of thousands of our boys even though it quickly became apparent that, under the circumstances, it was an involvement we could never decisively win. As a people, we like things simple and clearcut; this situation was unpleasantly complex. In our new lexicon, it was a "police action" or a "conflict," not a "war." So we never completely accepted it, not in the sense that we accepted World War II—lock, stock and barrel. Instead of allowing Korea to enter every aspect of our lives, we blocked it out as best we could.

But we were unable to forget about the Cold War, and the escalating bad relations between us and the Russians. As the notion of an all-out nuclear confrontation became a viable possibility, we began to live our daily lives under the invisible shadow of the mushroom-shaped cloud. In public schools, students were furnished with elaborate descriptions of the accidental ways in which such a global holocaust might come about and were told in detail the effects that atomic fallout would have on their bodies. Atomic air raid drills were instituted in many schools, and students were taught a whole series of physical positions to help them survive the initial bomb blasts. Instruction kits were distributed to be taken home in hopes that parents might be persuaded to build air raid shelters in their backyards or cellars.

In some ways, the cure was worse than the illness. The precautions, though certainly justified, failed to take into account the effect of such experiences on the adolescent mind. Though there was no clear proof of a correlation, the term "juvenile delinquency" was virtually created out of the postwar mentality. Previously every school had had its troublemaker; now, the troublemakers were the rule rather than the exception. Stranger still, there was a degree to which these students were no longer the heavies, but the heroes—or the anti-heroes, to use a fifties term. The country's youth had become alienated; parents grew hysterical, while teachers and guidance counselors shrugged at their inability to control the problem. Something had clearly disappeared from the framework of our society—a faith in the rightness of our institutions and our way of life—and impressionable youth, unable to adjust to the moral complexity of the age, rebelled against the insane possibility of total annihilation by "going wild."

Their new styles of dress and grooming clearly illustrated a desire to break away from the mainstream and to antagonize their parents. The "greaser look" emerged: the duck-tail haircut, the black leather jacket, the T-shirt with a sleeve rolled high to carry a pack of cigarettes, the garrison belt easily accessible for use in a violent confrontation. Even the emphasis on black-and-white clothing demonstrated an unconscious desire to find some basic simplicities in an ever more intolerably complex world. In lower-class tenement neighborhoods, youthful street gangs sprang up, who adorned their black leather jackets with ironically archaic crests loudly announcing their loyalty to some particular "club"—with names like The Lords, The Dukes, The Viceroys. When hostilities erupted between gangs a new word entered the language: the "rumble." "Cool" became synonymous with stylish disinterest, "hood" (short for hoodlum) was a juvenile delinquent while a "chick" was his girl, and "hip" came to mean street-wise. The jump in the juvenile crime rate was astounding, but the problem did not hit home to many Americans until it reached into middle and then upper-class neighborhoods. Kids who had been given the best of everything turned up at police stations under arrest, and their embarrassed, astounded parents had to leave their fashionable homes to bail them out.

Still, for every juvenile delinquent there were ten

Tab Hunter

Robert Wagner

Tony Curtis

"clean-cut" kids. The boys wore their hair in crew cuts or flat-tops and sported sweaters like the Kingston Trio wore. For formal dates madras sports jackets were in order and thin ties like *Peter Gunn* wore on TV; for casual dates bermuda shorts were the rule, with pink shirts and saddle shoes or penny loafers. The girls wore their hair in ponytails or had it "teased," reversed their cardigan sweaters so the buttons ran up the back, lounged around in pedalpushers and sneakers.

Even the *"nice* kids" were in a world of their own and, like the hoods, developed their own jargon. Treating your steady bad was "dumping" on him. Punching a fellow who tried to "move in" on your girl was "feeding him a knuckle sandwich." Having fun was "getting your kicks."

But in reflecting the attitudes of our adolescents, nothing could compare to the music they listened to in distinguishing between their values and their parents'. At the beginning of the decade, pop music meant the "mood music" sound found on the newly popular, longplaying 33⅓ RPM albums. Frank Sinatra experienced a comeback as a mature crooner, Liberace serenaded matrons with his soft piano playing, Harry Belafonte added just the right calypso beat, and Eddie Fisher jumped on the bandwagon to give younger women a pop singer more their age. The females were torchy, sophisticated women of the world such as Julie London, Peggy Lee and Patti Page, who sang their hearts out about sad, sordid love affairs, or else pleasant, bubbly young ladies like Teresa Brewer, Debbie Rynolds, and Dorothy Collins.

Suddenly, though, the music of the street gangs monopolized the charts. Disc jockey Alan Freed introduced the new music to New York as the Big Beat and then changed its title to rock 'n' roll. At mid-decade this frenetic combination of country-western, be-bop jazz, and rhythm and blues underwent an extreme surge of popularity; within one year the cheaply produced little 45 RPM discs were selling like hotcakes. Johnnie Ray, Kay Starr and Errol Garner's latest albums had trouble getting air time. Disc jockeys became youth-oriented in order to stay successful and played the latest smash hits of Jerry Lee Lewis, Chuck Berry and Bobby Darin. The lyrics were often raunchy, the dance styles that developed (including the Shimmy, the Stroll and the Slop) looked dangerously wild to many adults, and the new breed of singers were practically indistinguishable from the juvenile delinquents themselves—unruly hair, greasy sideburns, tight-fitting black pants. They wiggled and shook when they sang, and held their guitars as though they considered them weapons or lovers. Elvis Presley's body contortions were considered so obscene that one newspaper columnist nicknamed him "Elvis the Pelvis"; when

he appeared on TV the cameramen received strict orders to photograph him only from the waist up. But his rare television appearances served only to whet the appetites of frantic teenage girls who wanted to see Elvis in totality. Shortly, they were waiting in long lines to catch a glimpse of him —larger than life—on a movie screen, and shrieked hysterically (and in perfect unison) at every swivel of the hips.

Quickly, a backlash set in. Angered parents, committed clergymen, worried educators and ambitious politicians delivered serious sermons on the evils of rock 'n' roll, chastizing it as everything from the work of the devil to the direct cause of juvenile delinquency. But that was a case of putting the cart before the horse. Rock 'n' roll grew out of, rather than caused, the changed attitudes on the part of youth about their parents and their world. The loud volume and powerful beat caught the spirit of the times—or, at least, the spirit of one important segment of our population.

And caught their spending money as well. In the latter half of the decade, marketers and distributors of goods realized that youth had become affluent. Some of the kids worked hard to get their money; others got a weekly allowance from the "old man" who wanted his kid to have "all the benefits" he never had. Either way, teenagers had money to spend and were quick to spend it. Some kept a savings account for college from the time they were ten, but just as many others let it slip through their fingers on everything from egg creams to movie magazines to *Classics Illustrated* to 45 RPM records to youth-oriented movies (*Rumble on the Docks, Rock Around the Clock*).

The youth of America (or at least a sizable portion of it) had money because their parents had, since the war, become more comfortably situated. Some of the vets took advantage of the GI Bill and went directly into schooling programs designed to prepare them for bright futures in new fields like electronics engineering or advertising; others worked their way up to positions as junior executives or vice-presidents in the burgeoning corporations. They prided themselves on their new affluence and developed a whole series of status symbols to display it. The mark of a successful young businessman was his gray flannel suit. He shared his success with his family (and announced it to the world) by moving into suburbia. That broad term encompassed everything from a $5,000, no-down-payment, identical-to-everyone-else's house in the sprawl of Long Island, to a $50,000, landscaped, original dream-house in fashionable Connecticut. Every price bracket on the ladder between the two extremes had its particular status within the new order of things, as well as its own clearly defined series of social do's and don't's for the inhabitants.

THE CHANGING FACE OF THE WESTERN: The interest in youth and juvenile delinquency led to "teenage westerns" in which legendary westerners were now conceived of as troubled adolescents, including Hope Lange and Robert Wagner in *The True Story of Jesse James* (1957) and Paul Newman as Billy the Kid in *The Left-Handed Gun* (1958)

But certain elements soon proved common to almost every sub-class of suburbia. As people left country farms and city tenements, meeting halfway and making up what became the great American middle class, they adopted patterns of behavior that reflected their values. Father drove a station-wagon big enough to carry all the kids to their Saturday morning appointments—the boys to Little League practice, the girls to dance class—and afterwards he stopped by the A & P to pick up the week's groceries. The big social events were the Friday night cocktail party for everyone on the block and the Sunday afternoon barbecue for a few close friends. On week days the men commuted to the city by train or car, while the wives involved themselves with civic groups, the luncheon circuit, or just became addicted to the TV soaps. The babysitter became a Saturday night ritual so that the adults could catch a movie—preferably one with Marilyn Monroe or Marlon Brando.

As the kids grew older they joined the Cub Scouts and the Brownies, and their parents became "den mothers" or "pack leaders"; when the kids reached adolescence they turned to the Methodist Youth Foundation (topic of debate: "Does the Bomb make religion obsolete?") or Young Judaeans (topic of debate: "If Israel went to war with the United States, which side would you support?"). The suburbanites were dead serious about their responsibilities. They joined the P.T.A. and took a stance on educational issues: a crucial decision was whether the dependable *Encyclopedia Americana* or the innovative *World Book* would, in the long run, prove the best buy for the children's needs. They found time for leisure, too: the bowling team on Tuesday nights was every bit as important a ritual as the one-week family vacation in June. On quiet evenings the family curled up around the new TV set to watch Milton Berle, Jackie Gleason or *Your Hit Parade*.

Yet with all the newfound affluence, there was clearly something wrong. Alcoholism grew at an alarming rate, as did the number of divorces. We all, Thoreau wrote, lead lives of quiet desperation—but never were they so quietly desperate as in the fifties. Despite the new deluge of consumer commodities—plastic toys and frozen foods in aluminum foil, instant coffee, filtertip cigarettes and transistor radios, many people found themselves experiencing a gnawing dissatisfaction, yet had no conception as to why that should be the case.

But a group of people emerged who felt they did grasp both the nature and the cause of society's problems—and, what's more, had the solution to it. The failure of our post-

LOVE AND MARRIAGE: As the screen grew more mature, it presented honest and explicit views of marital problems, including Elizabeth Taylor and Paul Newman in *Cat on a Hot Tin Roof* (1958) and the British import *Room at the Top* (1959) with Laurence Harvey and Heather Sears

war society to create any kind of lasting peace so disillusioned a number of artists and intellectuals that they felt a need to drop out of the mainstream entirely, abandoning the financial-success orientation of the old American Dream and settling instead for the achievement of inner peace with one's self and personal—rather than social—satisfaction with one's work. The movement was fragmentary and loose until Jack Kerouac immortalized it in a rambling, poetic novel that combined the styles of Thomas Wolfe and Dylan Thomas. Titled simply *On the Road*, it delivered a romanticized vision of the alienated, footloose poet/prophets and gave them a title as well as a self-conception: the Beat Generation. The name was soon corrupted by the media to "beatnik"—but to the true beats, the ultimate mark of shame was "selling out to Madison Avenue."

Instead, the beats created their *own* art galleries and literary magazines. One beat poet, Lawrence Ferlinghetti, ran a small press and opened his own book store in San Francisco so that his highly irregular volumes of poetry—as well as those of his contemporaries like Greg Corso, Kenneth Rexroth and Allen Ginsberg—could reach the public "uncorrupted" by middlemen. "Coney Island of the Mind" and "Howl" were sensations with readers who saw themselves —or, at least, an image of themselves they could favorably respond to—mirrored in the wild mélange of words splashed colorfully on the page. But the beat poets incurred the wrath of local authorities who tried to have the controversial language judged obscene. Mostly in San Francisco and New York's Greenwich Village—but also in other major cities and, occasionally, in some small towns across the nation—an underground counter-culture quietly developed. The males wore bulky sweaters, faded jeans, leather sandals, and sported goatees; the women favored black leotards and no lipstick.

Like the juvenile street gangs, the beats were alienated from society. But unlike them, they rejected violence and began a protest movement against America's involvement in future wars. They lived in inexpensive "pads" where they could write, paint, dance, drink, smoke pot and meditate, and frequented coffee houses that featured progressive jazz and authentic folk music, as well as open readings of their own poetry. And while they firmly rejected Middle America's notions about formal education, they were nonetheless highly intellectual in orientation. Studying Zen Buddhism and French existentialism was a must; other creative outlets included inexpensively produced (and often sexually explicit) "underground" movies, expressive dance in the Isa-

13

RICHARD WIDMARK, ANTI-HERO: Though his cynical demeanor forced him into gangster roles in the late forties, it helped him become one of the decade's major stars, playing a man who unwittingly becomes involved with communist Jean Peters in *Pickup on South Street* (1953) and a drill instructor who readies men for the Korean conflict in *Take the High Ground* (1953)

dora Duncan style, modern abstract painting and Theatre of the Absurd plays by people like Jack Gelber and the young Edward Albee. The beats also lent a new artistic respectability to such formerly disdained professions as the stand-up comic, lavishing serious attention on such performers as Mike Nichols and Elaine May, Mort Sahl, and later, Woody Allen and Lenny Bruce.

The beats simultaneously fascinated and frightened the "squares in the suburbs." It became a popular hobby of Long Island high school students to "play beatnik" for a weekend. Wearing leotards and sweaters, couples would journey into Manhattan and spend an evening trying to pass themselves off as real beats along the Greenwich Village coffee-house circuit.

Though they provided society with one of the decade's more flagrantly fascinating fads, the beats failed to influence the mainstream of everyday life. Beat fashions and styles were certainly visible: every college campus had its small pocket of bohemians. Students might sift with mild interest through an "underground classic" such as Herman Hesse's *Sidhartha* or Kahlil Gibran's *The Prophet*, while a relatively "straight" guy might temporarily try sporting a goatee. But the college scene was mostly a quiet one. Occasional "Ban the Bomb" demonstrations failed to attract many of the ex-GI's and callow teenagers who were interested in getting their degrees and then finding a high paying job. College still meant fraternities and sororities, senior proms, spring vacations in Fort Lauderdale and summer jobs as camp counselors, cramming for final exams and strict obeyance of the campus code of conduct. A girl could lose a full semester's privileges if she entered the dormitory after the 10:30 lights-out signal, while a guy could find himself on "social probation" if an unopened beer can was discovered in his dorm. But very few of the students challenged these rules.

No, it was not on the campuses that the tenets of beatdom were significantly felt. Rather, it was serious culture that reflected the attitudes of emotional alienation and artistic experimentation that were part and parcel of the bohemian sub-culture. Painters like Jackson Pollock and others of the "abstract" school created wild, fragmented visions of reality on canvas. Actors like Brando, Montgomery Clift and James Dean popularized "The Method," a reinterpretation of the Russian master Stanislavski's ideas which flourished at Lee Strasberg's Actor's Studio in New York, creating a new style of performance—intense, emotional and sometimes almost inarticulate—that seemed peculiarly (and perversely) suited to the times. Playwrights such as Arthur Miller and William Inge turned out dramas that caught the country's mood: *The Crucible*, ostensibly a study of the witch trials in Salem, actually offered a thinly disguised indictment of McCarthyism, while *Picnic* stripped away all our romantic illusions about small-town America.

The postwar novelists were likewise second cousins of the beats. Norman Mailer's *The Naked and the Dead*, Irwin Shaw's *The Young Lions*, and James Jones' *From Here to Eternity* all criticized that most formidable of American institutions, the Armed Services. Moreover, they shocked readers with a new explicitness in sexual descriptions and four-letter words. Grace Metalious' *Peyton Place* became a best seller with adults by offering one woman's viewpoint on the moral hypocrisy and sexual maladjustment of Middle America. J. D. Salinger impressed the more intelligent and aware adolescents with his creation of Holden Caulfield in *Catcher in the Rye*, an inwardly troubled youth whose desire to retain his childhood innocence in the wake of experiences with the phoniness of society eventually sends him to a psychiatrist's couch.

Society made its way there, too. It was in the fifties that we first discovered psychoanalysis as a means by which the average person might release his pent-up anxieties. Living daily with the threat of instant obliteration and a communist under every bed had affected us more deeply than was at first apparent. "Neurosis" ceased to be a label indicating a rare disorder and came to stand for the semi-depressed state of millions of ordinary people. The term "nervous breakdown" soon became over-used; going to the "shrink" became a strange sort of status symbol in some quarters. Movies featured neurotic heroines like Joanne Woodward in *The Three Faces of Eve* or transferred the "Grand Hotel" type of multi-character soap opera to an insane asylum, as in *The Cobweb*. "Sick humor"—any kind of joke that tried to make us well again by poking fun at the sickness of our society—flourished. Juvenile humor magazines now had names like *Mad* and *Sick*, while Jules Feiffer offered a sophisticated readership more subtle but equally satiric attacks on our social pretension and personal problems.

Still, our paranoia continued. In the first half of the decade millions of people convinced themselves that we were truly on the eve of an invasion from outer space. In fact, the sightings of "unidentified flying objects" and "flying saucers" became so frequent that the Air Force had to create an entire department just to investigate and study the accumulating reports. In the decade's waning years the fear of being invaded was replaced by the startling realization that we were, truly, on the verge of invading the stars ourselves —and that the Russians looked likely to beat us to it. In 1957 they launched Sputnik, and the American people felt mortified that in the race for space we were playing sec-

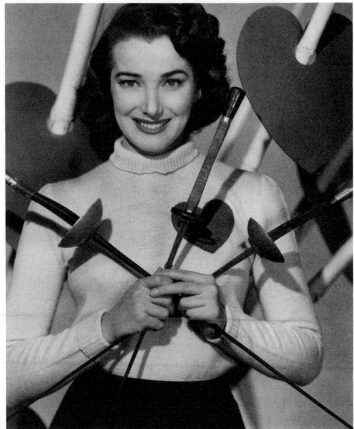

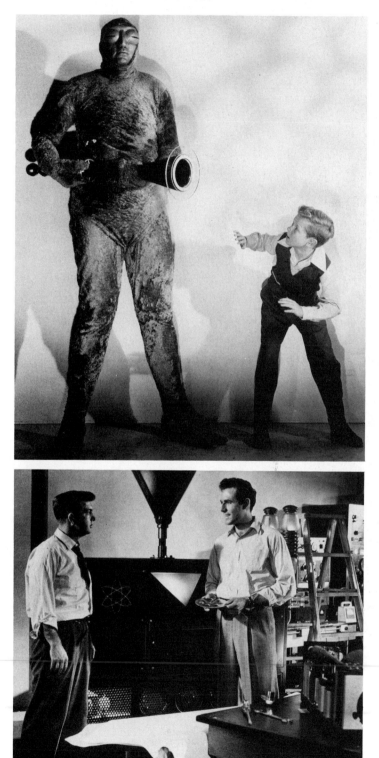

A RENAISSANCE FOR SCIENCE FICTION: The fear of invaders and the possibilities of exploring outer space revitalized interest in the genre, including kiddie films like *Invaders From Mars* (1953) and more adult pictures such as *This Island Earth* (1955)

ond-fiddle to our most feared enemy. Quickly, educational programs were drastically changed; the emphasis was shifted from liberal arts to science programs and an increasing number of scholarships and grants were offered to high school students willing to enter our scientific ranks.

High schools were in the spotlight in other respects. At mid-decade, the fact that the white high schools in the South were better equipped to educate students than those serving Negroes caught the public eye. Civil rights spokesmen in the North crusaded against the situation with a vitriolic vehemence unheard of in our century. Desegregation became the cause célébre of the fifties and reached into all aspects of American life including sports, where Jackie Robinson and Willie Mays became baseball folk heroes. Young, charismatic Martin Luther King emerged as the primary spokesman for the non-violent movement when in 1955 he urged the Negro population of Montgomery, Alabama, to boycott that city's transportation system in order to break the "back of the bus" rules for black riders. When the white power structure tried to curb the movement it escalated and attracted the attention of numerous college students in the North, who were soon streaming into the South as "protest marchers."

With such serious concerns, people needed to relax—and they had more leisure time to do it in, as well as more money to spend, than ever before. The weighty problems of the day inspired us to find more extreme forms of entertainment. In the fifties, the American male discovered "the bosom." First there was Marilyn Monroe, amply enough endowed to make her the reigning sex symbol of the day. But even her impressive proportions were eclipsed by some of the bosomy blondes that followed: Marie Wilson, Jayne Mansfield, Anita Ekberg, Dagmar, Joi Lansing, Diana Dors and, finally, the greatest sex symbol since Monroe, Brigitte Bardot—who at least brought sex completely into the open by appearing nude in her pictures. *Playboy*, the first girlie magazine with class, was born and flourished in this newly liberalized atmosphere. So did paperback books, those tawdry, pulpy potboilers by authors like Mickey Spillane and Harold Robbins. They featured scandalously explicit cover illustrations that often equalled anything inside. Even comic books became, for a while, carried away with sex and violence—the nearly naked *Sheena, Queen of the Jungle* offered twelve-year-old boys some pretty lurid fantasies until parents and teachers banded together to form pressure groups which eventually cleaned up the comic book industry—and took away most of the fun. There were gentler, more reassuring volumes as well: for adults, Norman Vin-

A RECURRING POSE: As the power of the Production Code ebbed, producers allowed their sex goddesses to display themselves in previously impossible positions, as Lana Turner in *The Prodigal* (1955) and Carroll Baker in *Baby Doll* (1956) clearly illustrated

cent Peale's *The Power of Positive Thinking* and, for adolescents, Pat Boone's *Twixt Twelve and Twenty.* On Broadway there was high-class escapist entertainment in the form of ever more elaborate musicals—*My Fair Lady, Guys and Dolls, Pajama Game, The Music Man* and even one powerful message-musical, *West Side Story.*

But the unique entertainment challenge of the fifties was television. Aside from the Bomb, it quickly became the most important element in our lives. The potential of TV to turn into, as one optimist hopefully predicted, a window on our world, was made clear when Senator Estes Kefauver and his Committee to Investigate Organized Crime allowed their open hearings to be telecast; interviews with suspected mobsters like Frank Costello and talkative, colorful molls such as Virginia Hill Hauser attracted millions of home viewers. Politicians were equally quick to seize on the new medium's power over the public mentality: when Richard Nixon found himself in hot water for accepting illegal campaign contributions he performed his famous "Checkers speech," sentimentally appealing to the people for their forgiveness.

TV certainly began with the highest of aspirations. On *See It Now* Edward R. Murrow offered his no-nonsense, highly personalized style of electronic journalism as he sought out interesting subjects and important issues; *Omnibus'* Sunday afternoon series of diverse specials touched on every aspect of culture, popular and classic alike; *Playhouse 90* and various other "live" dramatic anthologies presented both new interpretations of the classics and original plays written expressly for television. Even the entertainment shows started out on a promisingly high level: Dave Garroway gave early morning viewers a touch of intellectual wit while casual, charming Steve Allen perfected the format of the late-night talk show and Jack Paar popularized it. On *Your Show of Shows* Sid Caesar and his remarkable stock company weekly produced inventive satire of the world around us, while on *Toast of the Town* Ed Sullivan presented a striking assortment of acts that spanned the entire spectrum of the entertainment world.

But it became increasingly clear as the decade wore on that TV was turning into a mere time killer. The success of *Gunsmoke,* a weekly half-hour variation of the adult western movies, led to over thirty other cowboy series in the next three years; cops and robbers were plentiful, too, from the hard-nosed, tough-guy style of Jack Webb's *Dragnet* to the sophisticated sleuths of *77 Sunset Strip.* In the after-

noons there were giveaways like *Queen for a Day* and *The Big Payoff;* in the evenings, mind-boggling quiz shows such as *The $64,000 Question* and *Twenty-One*—which were destroyed by scandal when one brainy contestant, Charles Van Doren, admitted he'd been furnished with the questions before going on the air. The undisputed first ladies of television were Dinah Shore, the honey-blonde singing hostess and comedienne Lucille Ball. George Gobel and Arthur Godfrey were soon thought of as members of every American family. Mothers discovered that "the box" could be an effective babysitter as children gathered to watch *Howdy Doody, Kukla, Fran and Ollie* and, eventually, *The Mickey Mouse Club.* More than anything else, though, TV meant old movies. One New York City show, *Million Dollar Movie,* presented the same old feature twice every night for an entire Monday-through-Friday week, and then ran it six more times over the weekend.

In spite of it all—or, perhaps, because of it—we found time to go out to the movies. We were, in fact, the last great mass audience for motion pictures, and formed a transition between the golden days of the film business—when movies were a central part of every American's weekly experience—and the very different situation of the sixties, when many people stopped going out entirely. The 100 films that follow include some of the most memorable made during that decade. But this volume is not primarily intended as a compilation of the outstanding screen entertainments of the fifties—such films as *The King and I* and *South Pacific* would surely fit into that category, but they are not included.

These, rather, are the films *of* the fifties—ranging from the sublime *Sunset Boulevard* all the way down the spectrum to the silly *High School Confidential*—that most clearly caught the spirit of the times. They are the films which did not *happen* to be made in the fifties but, in fact, could *only* have been made in the fifties; they mirrored our world in that decade which, more than any other, has seized hold of our propensity for nostalgia. To paraphrase William Blake, the films of the thirties and forties are our songs of innocence; those of the sixties and seventies are our songs of experience. Looking back over the films of the fifties, we can be moved to an emotion greater than pure nostalgia: we can catch a glimpse of ourselves when, as a people, we were in the process of adjusting to the most important changes of the century.

Policemen fish the body of Joe Gillis (William Holden) out of Norma Desmond's pool: "Poor devil—he always wanted a pool!"

Sunset Boulevard

Paramount (1950)

Produced by Charles Brackett; directed by Billy Wilder; screenplay by Mr. Brackett, Mr. Wilder and D. M. Marshman, Jr.

CAST: *Joe Gillis* (William Holden); ·*Norma Desmond* (Gloria Swanson); *Max Von Mayerling* (Erich von Stroheim); *Betty Schaefer* (Nancy Olson); *Sheldrake* (Fred Clark); *Morino* (Lloyd Gough); *Artie Green* (Jack Webb); *Undertaker* (Franklyn Barnum); *First Finance Man* (Larry Blake); *Second Finance Man* (Charles Dayton); *Themselves* (Cecil B. De Mille, Hedda Hopper, Buster Keaton, Anna Q. Nilsson, H. B. Warner, Ray Evans, Jay Livingston)

The films of the fifties properly begin with *Sunset Boulevard,* which simultaneously depicted in its story and symbolized in its style the transition from the already decaying old glamour of the movie capital to a world-wise "new Hollywood." This was clear from the opening sequence in which we view the body of Joe Gillis (William Holden) floating face downward in a swimming pool, as the dead man's voice directly addresses us ("Poor devil—he always wanted a pool!") as though viewing himself from a distance. In 1950, psychological melodrama mixed with dark comedy for the first time, as Joe carried us back to the beginning of the strange series of events that led to his own demise.

Joe is a down-and-out Hollywood hack writer, who left his comfortable spot on a Dayton newspaper in the naive belief he'd make it big in California. Now, he has to fast-talk the men from the collection agency (Larry Blake and Charles Dayton) in order to keep his car, and beg his contact (Fred Clark) at Paramount Pictures to get him a third-rate job as script doctor. He does meet an idealistic young would-be writer, Betty Schaefer (Nancy Olson) who believes he has talent, but before their relationship can develop he finds himself pursued by bill collectors and makes his getaway by hiding on the grounds of a seemingly abandoned mansion. Then a voice from inside the house calls to him, and Joe finds a garish, middle-aged woman (Gloria Swanson) readying a funeral for a recently deceased chimpanzee. "I know you," he exclaims. "You're Norma Desmond—you used to be *big*!" "I am big," she insists. "It's the *pictures* that got small!"

Out of sheer desperation, Joe accepts her absurd offer to help prepare a "comeback script" which would have Norma playing the youthful Salome. The money is good, but Norma insists that Joe move into her house—a shift that symbolizes the manner in which he gradually becomes possessed by her. For in all respects the house, filled with mementos of her career, *is* Norma Desmond—still statuesque and impressive from a distance but, on closer scrutiny, cracked, faded, and wrinkled. The swimming pool where Clara Bow once relaxed is filled with rats (though Norma has it repaired for Joe). Guarding both the mansion and the faded star is Max Von Mayerling (Erich von Stroheim), once Norma's director and husband, now an oafish waiter/valet/chauffeur dressed up in a monkey suit.

Former movie greats Buster Keaton, H. B. Warner, and Anna Q. Nillson appear as what Joe snidely refers to as "the waxworks," Hollywood has-beens who visit on bridge night. Yet the focus remains on Norma's decadently fascinating love–hate relationship with the wisecracking writer. In the film's central scene, Max shows old Desmond movies as Norma and Joe sit on the couch and watch. "We didn't need dialogue in those days," she sighs wistfully. "We had *faces* then!" At an elaborate New Year's Eve party that Norma throws just for the two of them (complete with violinists) Joe tries to break off the relationship by abruptly leaving to move in with his old buddy, bohemian writer Artie Green (Jack Webb), the screen's first suggestion of the fifties beatnik. But Norma's attempted suicide brings him back.

Finally, Max gets out the old limousine and escorts Norma to the Paramount lot, where she visits with old friend Cecil B. De Mille and tries to persuade the embar-

Betty (Nancy Olson) offers Joe (William Holden) an escape into purity on a deserted Paramount back lot

rassed director to do her picture. Shortly thereafter, she learns that Joe is secretly meeting Betty in the deserted studio at night to work on a screenplay and that the girl, though engaged to Artie, has fallen in love with Joe. Betty's freshness and talent represent Joe's possible redemption both as a writer and as a man. But when he finds Norma making cruel phone calls to the girl he drives her back to Artie by revealing to her precisely what he is; when he tries to walk out on Norma, she fires the fatal shots and the picture comes full cycle.

Norma finally gets her wish. As she is escorted out of the house by police, the Paramount news cameras are rolling, and she makes her exit as a grotesque caricature of an old-time star. Gloria Swanson brought Norma so completely to life that people refused to believe it could be anything but an autobiographical picture; Holden, formerly an undistinguished leading man, emerged as the first significant example of a new kind of star. Billy Wilder and Charles Brackett experimented with innovative styles in dialogue and camera work, but the greatness of *Sunset Boulevard* is as inherent in the film's timing as in the art of moviemaking displayed throughout. Coming when it did, the love/death struggle of Norma Desmond and Joe Gillis articulated for American audiences the divided, self-destructive mood of Hollywood as it entered a new and uncertain decade.

(overleaf) Gloria Swanson and William Holden

Anne Baxter, Marilyn Monroe, Bette Davis

Bette Davis, Hugh Marlowe, and Celeste Holm

24

Thelma Ritter and Bette Davis

All About Eve

20th Century-Fox (1950)

Produced by Darryl F. Zanuck; directed by Joseph L. Mankiewicz; screenplay by Mr. Mankiewicz, adapted from a short story and radio play by Mary Orr.

CAST: *Margo* (Bette Davis); *Eve* (Anne Baxter); *Addison DeWitt* (George Sanders); *Karen* (Celeste Holm); *Bill Simpson* (Gary Merrill); *Lloyd Richards* (Hugh Marlowe); *Birdie* (Thelma Ritter); *Miss Casswell* (Marilyn Monroe); *Max Fabian* (Gregory Ratoff); *Phoebe* (Barbara Bates); *Aged Actor* (Walter Hampden); *Girl* (Randy Stuart); *Leading Man* (Craig Hill); *Doorman* (Leland Harris); *Autograph Seeker* (Barbara White); *Stage Manager* (Eddie Fisher); *Pianist* (Claude Stroud)

While Billy Wilder was analyzing and satirizing the movie business and its mythology in *Sunset Boulevard* another gifted writer-director turned his attentions to the previously sacrosanct world of live theater. In so doing, Joseph L. Mankiewicz came up with the film which swept the year's Academy Awards, including the top honors for Best Picture of the Year. Perhaps the number of honors *All About Eve* received was a bit excessive: though one of the great "sophisticated" film entertainments of all time, it hardly ranks as one of the great films. But the Academy's reaction can certainly be justified. For years, Broadway enjoyed a reputation as being more intelligent, worldly, and socially conscious than that childish purveyor of mass-audience fantasies, Hollywood.

Bette Davis, Gary Merrill, Anne Baxter

granted, while its string of Oscars attested to the fact that the Hollywood Establishment strongly favored their "new respectability."

Anne Baxter played the title character, an arrogantly beautiful, ambitiously bitchy young actress out to steal the star from the dressing-room door, as well as the men from the boudoir, of Margo (Bette Davis), a no-longer-young "great lady" of the legitimate stage. Mankiewicz breathed life into a number of "types" which non-New Yorkers readily accepted as the people who inhabit the world of Broadway: the lecherous drama critic Addison DeWitt (George Sanders), soft-spoken and creative director Bill Simpson (Gary Merrill), clever but uninspired playwright Lloyd Richards (Hugh Marlowe), and a half dozen others. Since each bore a strong resemblance to one or more existing people, audiences enjoyed a guessing game as to just who each was "really" supposed to be.

The focus, however, remained on Eve's rise from wide-eyed stargazer to top-billed star and Margo's concurrent fall from grace, as well as the catty, clawing way in which the younger artist must destroy the life and reputation of the older one in order to "make it." In a sense, the syndrome was an East Coast reenactment of *Sunset Boulevard*, only in reverse. And while the older and younger generations have always had their differences, it was in the fifties that a serious threat of a communication breakdown began, along with a fierce enmity that had never been known before. If the film had a single serious flaw, it was that Anne Baxter never radiated sufficiently to convince viewers that Eve could ever compete with Bette Davis' Margo (the age difference notwithstanding) for parts or for men. The role might better have been played (and the conflict memorably heightened) had Marilyn Monroe, lost in a small role, been cast as Eve.

For in Margo Channing, Bette Davis found what may very well be her most memorable role. Like so many other great stars of the thirties and forties, she necessarily had to either adjust to new, older parts or retire—and Bette Davis had no intention of fading from sight. She endured a brief period of difficulty in the late forties when she attempted to cling to the youthful roles her aging features could no longer substantiate. But in the highly theatrical part of a great stage actress who is inevitably, almost tragically brought down by fate, flaws in her own personality, and an epic antagonist named Eve, she reintroduced herself to moviegoers as a fascinating older woman. It was as impossible to conceive of anyone but Bette Davis playing Margo Channing as it was unthinkable that someone other than Gloria Swanson could have created Norma Desmond.

But 1950 was the year in which all that began to change. Even the most serious actors—who only a year before had scoffed at the thought of coming to Hollywood—made the move when, suddenly, they were offered more demanding scripts. Shortly people would look at Broadway and ask the question that eventually haunted the decade: "Is the theater really dead?" Films, on the other hand, received an ever greater amount of serious attention. With its endless sexual innuendos *Eve* was one of the first films to hint that movie audiences might be ready for the kind of adult interplay between characters that New York theatergoers took for

The Generation Gap: Spencer Tracy and Don Taylor

Father of the Bride

Metro-Goldwyn-Mayer (1950)

Produced by Pandro S. Berman; directed by Vincente Minnelli; screenplay by Frances Goodrich and Albert Hackett, based on the novel by Edward Streeter.

CAST: *Stanley T. Banks* (Spencer Tracy); *Ellie Banks* (Joan Bennett); *Kay Banks* (Elizabeth Taylor); *Buckley Dunstan* (Don Taylor); *Doris Dunstan* (Billie Burke); *Mr. Massoula* (Leo G. Carroll); *Herbert Dunstan* (Moroni Olsen); *Mr. Tringle* (Melville Cooper); *Warner* (Taylor Holmes); *Reverend Galsworthy* (Paul Harvey); *Joe* (Frank Orth); *Tommy Banks* (Rusty Tamblyn); *Ban Banks* (Tom Irish); *Delilah* (Marietta Canty)

1950 proved the crucial year of transition both for Hollywood stars and Hollywood styles. Even as ideas about what sort of subjects movies should concern themselves with emerged as a highly debatable issue, a wide array of brash new performers began to steal the spotlight—to which both *Sunset Boulevard* and *All About Eve* readily attested. *Father of the Bride*, one of the most likable little movies of all time, is usually written off as merely a marvelous bit of fluff, an enjoyably innocuous time-killer. But coming when it did, the film created a bridge between the old Hollywood and the new in more ways than one.

The American Family: Elizabeth Taylor and Joan Bennett show Spencer Tracy how they've been spending his money

While it concerned itself with the lifestyles of the average, everyday Americans and did so with the warmth and charm of *Life With Father* and any number of Andy Hardy films, there were distinctive differences. It was the first American film to be set, quite clearly, in suburbia—rather than a big city or small town. The characters studied were modestly successful, middle-class Americans—the very people who had begun to make themselves heard following the war. In terms of setting and characters, then, *Father of the Bride* set the pace for many films that followed. But it did so also in terms of tone, for while the film lovingly portrayed the people and their foibles, it mixed that tenderness with a satiric point of view on middle-class customs that, at moments, was almost savage.

The film begins as Stanley T. Banks (Spencer Tracy) collapses in his chair, surrounded by the leftovers of a wedding festivity. Gazing out at the audience, his facial expression a combination of consternation and pride, Stanley carries us back to the events that brought him to his present state. From the moment that his flirtatious social-gadfly daughter (Elizabeth Taylor) arrives home one night and suddenly announces her plans to marry one of the horde of suitors knocking at their door, Stanley and his demure wife Ellie (Joan Bennett) are thrust into an endless series of comically uncomfortable situations. Father must have a "man-to-man" talk with Buckley (Don Taylor) to determine if the lad is even able to support Kay, and then both parents must make an effort to get to know—and, hopefully, learn to like—Buckley's folks, Doris (Billie Burke) and Herbert Dunstan (Moroni Olsen). But is is the father and mother of the bride who must make all the arrangements for the ceremony, and as the events are cinematically catalogued for us, director Vincente Minnelli handles each with such a strong combination of authenticity and wit that *Father of the Bride* undergoes a quiet metamorphosis from lightweight entertainment into a critical study of the new suburban lifestyle.

The film also allowed two major stars the opportunity to gracefully move into new roles. Spencer Tracy—the gruff, roguishly clever bumpkin of the past two decades—tried on the middle-aged character he would perfect during the remainder of his career. Elizabeth Taylor—the almost too-perfect child of *National Velvet*, *Little Women* and *Lassie Come Home*—took her first important steps toward more mature roles and, eventually, superstardom. *Father of the Bride* insured their future in films by helping them do the necessary redefining of their screen images.

The Great American Ritual: Elizabeth Taylor and Spencer Tracy

Humphrey Bogart and Martha Stewart

In a Lonely Place
Columbia (1950)

A Santana Production, produced by Robert Lord; directed by Nicholas Ray; screenplay by Andrew Solt, based on a story by Dorothy B. Hughes and an adaptation by Edmund H. North.

CAST: *Dixon Steele* (Humphrey Bogart); *Laurel Gray* (Gloria Grahame); *Brub Nicolai* (Frank Lovejoy); *Captain Lochner* (Carl Benton Reid); *Mel Lippman* (Art Smith) *Sylvia Nicolai* (Jeff Donnell); *Mildred Atkinson* (Martha Stewart); *Charlie Waterman* (Robert Warwick); *Lloyd Barnes* (Morris Ankrum); *Ted Barton* (William Ching); *Paul* (Steven Geray); *Singer* (Hadda Brooks); *Frances Randolph* (Alice Talton); *Henry Kesler* (Jack Reynolds); *Effie* (Ruth Warren); *Martha* (Ruth Gillette); *Swan* (Guy Beach); *Junior* (Lewis Howard)

In the years following World War II, communism emerged as America's greatest threat. But it was not the take-overs of Czechoslovakia and the division of Berlin that frightened people most. Far worse than the Cold War was the growing suspicion of communist infiltration at home. During Washington's period of witch-hunting, Hollywood was harder hit than anyplace else. The House Committee on Un-American Activities held hearings in which it attempted to prove that the movie business was being overrun with communists who planned to use films to propagandize their cause. Some "friendly witnesses" from the movie colony provided the Committee with lists of friends who expressed offbeat ideas; studio bosses, fearing that the stigma might destroy Hollywood altogether, loudly announced their intentions to "clean house." Everyone knew that a vast secret blacklist

had been assembled, naming people who had something in their past that caused them to be viewed with suspicion. But no one knew who was on the list or who had access to it. Immediately, an unparalleled sense of paranoia swept through the industry.

Even though the terms "blacklisting" and "communism" were never mentioned, *In a Lonely Place* captured perfectly the mood of Hollywood at that moment. The story follows Dixon Steele (Humphrey Bogart), in many ways a second cousin to *Sunset Boulevard's* Joe Gillis: a cynical but compassionate scriptwriter. Assigned to adapt a third-rate novel to the screen, Steele wanders into a bar to drink away his frustrations. While flirting with Mildred (Martha Stewart) the hat-check girl, he mentions his latest job and she admits she's read the book. Steele asks her to join him at his place after work, tell him the story—and save him the trouble of reading it himself. She accepts, but the next day is found murdered. Laurel Gray (Gloria Grahame), the lady who

lives in the next apartment, saves Steele's neck when she tells policeman Brub Nicolai (Frank Lovejoy) that she saw Mildred leave the apartment alone. The chance involvement strikes up a romance between the two neighbors. However, Steele soon realizes that the police are nonetheless relentlessly hounding him—because of a past record for violence.

Steele only wants to finish his screenplay, which is going well, and pursue his affair with Laurel, who gives him the inspiration to write again (and closely resembles the Nancy Olson-William Holden relationship in *Sunset Boulevard*). But even though Laurel is sure Steele's the "right man," she is assaulted from all sides by both the police and old friends of Steele, who warn her about his propensity for violence. Finally, she begins to wonder if he is indeed guilty.

Realizing that the one good thing in his life is being poisoned by unsubstantiated whispers, Steele reacts by becoming as violent as he is claimed to be; Laurel cannot discriminate whether the others were right all along or if they have

(Left), Dixon Steele (Bogart) has to be restrained when, after constant pressure, he actually becomes the violent man everyone claims he is (from the left Morris Ankrum, Bogart, Robert Warwick, Steven Geray and Art Smith)

The final confrontation: Humphrey Bogart and Gloria Grahame

driven him into becoming exactly what they claimed by their constant pressure. When Steele learns that she is planning on leaving him because she doesn't know what to believe anymore, he is finally forced by the situation into becoming exactly the kind of murderer they insisted he is—he grabs Laurel by the neck and attempts to strangle her. At that moment, the police arrive with evidence that Mildred was killed by someone else. Laurel sees that she allowed rumor to destroy their beautiful feelings, but the harm has been done and they are finished as a couple.

The investigation-for-murder story clearly represented the harassment, on a grander scale, of the Hollywood Ten and the hundreds of other motion picture people who found themselves condemned without a trial. Moviemakers desiring to film anti-communist tracts found no opposition; those wishing to explore in depth the dangers of mass hysteria had to fearfully disguise their statements as inconsequential crime melodramas. *In a Lonely Place* was the best such film.

Humphrey Bogart as Dixon Steele, a Hollywood scriptwriter who finds himself condemned without a trial—with Carl Benton Reid

31

James Stewart enters the Apache Nation

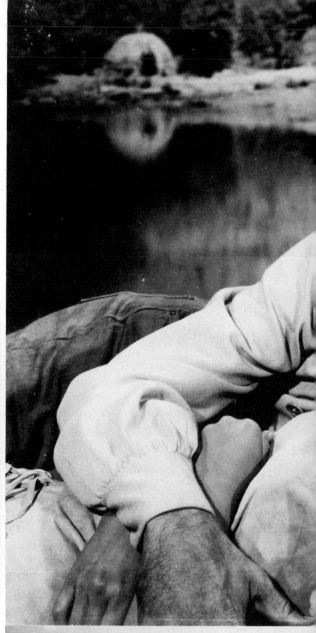

Jeff Chandler as Cochise

James Stewart and Debra Paget

Broken Arrow

20th Century-Fox (1950)

Produced by Julian Blaustein; directed by Delmer Daves; screenplay by Michael Blankfort, based on the novel *Blood Brother*, by Elliott Arnold.

CAST: *Tom Jeffords* (James Stewart); *Cochise* (Jeff Chandler); *Sonseeahray* (Debra Paget); *General Howard* (Basil Ruysdael); *Ben Slade* (Will Geer); *Terry* (Joyce MacKenzie); *Duffield* (Arthur Hunnicutt); *Colonel Bernall* (Raymond Bramley); *Gokila* (Jay Silverheels); *Nalikadeya* (Argentina Brunetti); *Boucher* (Jack Lee); *Lonergan* (Robert Adler); *Miner* (Harry Carter); *Lowrie* (Robert Griffin); *Juan* (Bill Wilkerson); *Chip Slade* (Mickey Kuhn); *Nochalo* (Chris Willow Bird)

In 1948 John Ford, the master craftsman of the western genre who often employed Indians as nameless villains or moving targets, demonstrated Hollywood's sudden and significant shift in attitude: his *Fort Apache* presented John Wayne as a cavalry officer attempting, against all odds, to make peace with well-meaning Chief Cochise, yet finally defeated by the corruption of money-hungry government bureaucrats and the incompetence of glory-seeking military men. Though the film signaled a more sympathetic portrait of the American Indian than the screen had formerly offered, it was still unintentionally condescending—the good white man must take notice of the poor unfortunates. But

gle-handed and wins the respect of Cochise (Jeff Chandler). To his surprise, he learns that these are peaceful people with a lifestyle highly preferable to that of the white community—living close to the land and near to their gods. He is impressed enough to want to drop out of his own society (a theme that would be picked up and developed often in the fifties, in both westerns and contemporary stories). Jeffords attempts to join them by becoming blood brothers with Cochise, and marrying a comely Indian princess, Sonseeahray (Debra Paget).

They enjoy an idyllic honeymoon in the panoramic privacy of a lake located under the Indians' spiritual mountain. But when some marauding whites kill the girl, Jeffords becomes the single element that keeps open hostilities from breaking out. As a result, the government names him the area's official "Indian agent."

There were built-in compromises, most obviously the contrived death of the Indian princess—with its implication that someone in the script department feared the mass audience might not be quite ready to accept miscegenation. But it eventually came: six years later in *Run of the Arrow*, an equally fine western if a lesser-known one, Rod Steiger also crossed racial barriers to marry an Indian princess who did not die. Without *Broken Arrow* to pave the way, such a thing might not have been possible.

Encouraging Jeff Chandler to portray Cochise as a soft-spoken, dignified, intelligent man—in comparison to James Stewart's charmingly irascible characterization—director Delmer Daves succeeded in reversing the usual racial stereotypes. Previously, upstanding white western heroes were occasionally followed around by a colorful Indian sidekick, but by reversing those preconceptions *Broken Arrow* proved audiences would willingly accept an Indian of heroic stature. It quickly set a trend into motion: Burt Lancaster played Massai, a noble and misunderstood warrior, in Robert Aldrich's *Apache* (1954), and countless other Hollywood stars followed suit. Most important, filmmakers found a means of dealing with the evils of racism while also providing an outdoor entertainment film in handsome color. Ostensibly just a western, *Broken Arrow* grew directly out of the sudden concern over civil rights for minority groups, and served to strengthen such convictions. For years, young children viewing westerns had been inadvertently brainwashed into thinking of the cowboys as the good guys and Indians as the bad guys. *Broken Arrow* satisfied action lovers by providing a strong conflict between both groups, but this time some of the good guys were Indians, some cowboys; some of the bad guys were cowboys, some Indians. Moral values on screen were at last becoming complex.

An idyll in the wilderness: Debra Paget and James Stewart attempt a mixed marriage

only two years later, the figure of Cochise was revived—this time as the screen's first Indian epic hero, a figure that would recur again and again in the upcoming decade.

Broken Arrow is set near Tucson, Arizona, following the Civil War—a time when numerous whites were invading the territorial lands the government had set aside for the Chiricahua Apaches. An easygoing ex-Union officer, Tom Jeffords (James Stewart) senses the growing hostilities between the Indians and whites, as well as the need for someone to take the initiative and do something about the situation. Courageously, he rides into the Indians' domains sin-

Gregory Peck as the Gunfighter

The Gunfighter

20th Century-Fox (1950)

Produced by Nunnally Johnson; directed by Henry King; screenplay by William Bowers and William Sellers, from a story by Mr. Bowers and André de Toth.

CAST: *Jimmy Ringo* (Gregory Peck); *Peggy Walsh* (Helen Westcott); *Sheriff Mark Street* (Millard Mitchell); *Molly* (Jean Parker); *Mac* (Karl Malden); *Hunt Bromley* (Skip Homeier); *Charlie* (Anthony Ross); *Mrs. Penny-feather* (Verna Felton); *Mrs. Devlin* (Ellen Corby); *Eddie* (Richard Jaeckel); *First Brother* (Alan Hale, Jr.); *Second Brother* (David Clarke); *Third Brother* (John Pickard); *Jimmie* (D. G. Norman); *Mac's Wife* (Angela Clarke); *Jerry Marlowe* (Cliff Clark); *Alice Marlowe* (Jean Inness); *Archie* (Eddie Ehrhart); *Pablo* (Albert Morin)

In the fifties, westerns became what critics liked to call "adult"; that is, either socially conscious or anti-romantic. *Broken Arrow* suggested one manner, in which the handsome locales and vibrant color of traditional westerns could be retained with significant alterations in attitude. *The Gunfighter* initiated an entirely different mode of procedure: filmed in a cold, downbeat black-and-white style, it introduced an image of the legendary western badman as a psychologically troubled character, desiring only to escape from his own mythic persona but haunted by his legendary status. Though hardly popular at the box office, the film nonetheless exerted an immeasurable effect on future westerns of the decade; in fact, the figure of the aging and alienated gunfighter became so mercilessly overused a cliché

A punk kid in every town: Gregory Peck and Richard Jaeckel

Gregory Peck as Ringo, a lonely man in a hostile world

that today it's difficult to believe he is such a relatively recent conception.

Essentially tragic in its outlook, the film is framed by Ringo's (Gregory Peck) confrontations with two younger men—the first he is forced to kill, the second manages to kill him. In addition to carrying over the startling new theme of the older and younger generations locked in a fatal struggle (which was just then also finding expression in such non-westerns as *Sunset Boulevard* and *All About Eve*), *The Gunfighter* was distinctively "internal" in more ways than one. More scenes took place indoors than in the wide open spaces that, in the past, graced the western with its sense of mute poetry, and the film contains almost no physical action to speak of—most of the fireworks take place inside the characters' minds. The story is almost Aristotelian in its sense of time and place, beginning as Jimmy Ringo wanders into an isolated frontier bar one night, where he is forced into a gunfight with a "punk" kid Eddie (Richard Jaeckel), then following Ringo's flight to a nearby town where he spends the last few hours of his life.

In comparison to John Ford's warm, colorful western villages, *The Gunfighter* offers an unpleasant vision of the American community. This is a special town for Ringo, we learn—his one-time partner in crime, Mark Street (Millard Mitchell) is the law-and-order sheriff, a wry comment on the thin line between the criminals and the authorities; the quiet schoolmarm, Peggy Walsh (Helen Westcott) is actually Ringo's wife, bringing up their young son Jimmie (D. G. Norman) far away from his father's violence. As Ringo sits glumly in a bar presided over by the wisecracking Mac (Karl Malden) and taunted on occasion by yet another punk, Hunt Bromley (Skip Homeier), the camera cuts continuously to an image of Eddie's three brothers (David Clarke, John Pickard, and Alan Hale, Jr.) moving inexorably toward the town.

Ringo encourages Molly (Jean Parker), the widow of an old gang member, to beg an audience with his wife and child. Peg finally agrees to it, and swears that if Ringo can disappear for one year without being involved in another killing, she will go away with him and reveal to the child that Ringo is his father. As Ringo mounts to leave and hide out, the sheriff's deputies apprehend Eddie's brothers, who have just arrived. But Hunt Bromley forces Ringo into a fight and the older gunman, knowing his hopes for the future are defeated even if he wins, allows himself to be killed.

While setting their story safely in a remote period of time, the filmmakers inserted many criticisms of modern America. The two punk kids are clearly patterned on the

The Death of Ringo: "Now *you're* the fastest gun alive!"; Karl Malden, Gregory Peck, Jean Parker, Millard Mitchell, and Skip Homeier

problematic youth of the postwar period who were just then winning the title "juvenile delinquents." But the old order comes under just as scathing a criticism: in a marvelously comic sequence, the town's old busybody and self-appointed guardian of respectability, Mrs. Pennyfeather (Verna Felton) leads her ardent flock of followers to the jailhouse, where she demands that the "nice young man" they meet there do something about the terrible killer at the saloon. They are, unknowingly, confronting Ringo—who tries, with little success, to convince them that the fellow's reputation may be far worse than he really is. In its sharp satire, *The Gunfighter* was taking a jab at the witch-hunting mood that had seized the country.

But the real key to the film's success was Peck's lean, sombre, incisive portrait of Ringo. Astonishingly, Peck was only 33 at the time of filming, but he created such an authentic aura of a man old before his time that the viewer literally becomes exhausted watching his world-weary face. The character he created would often be imitated, but never equalled.

As Angela, Marilyn Monroe opened the door to stardom

The Asphalt Jungle

Metro-Goldwyn-Mayer (1950)

Produced by Arthur Hornblower, Jr.; screenplay by Ben Maddow and John Huston, from the novel by W. R. Burnett; photography by Harold Rosson; musical score by Miklos Rozsa; directed by John Huston.

CAST: *Doc Riedenschneider* (Sam Jaffe); *Dix Handley* (Sterling Hayden); *Gus Minissi* (James Whitmore); *Alonzo D. Emmerich* (Louis Calhern); *Cobby* (Marc Lawrence); *Doll Conovan* (Jean Hagen); *Angela Phinlay* (Marilyn Monroe); *Louis Ciavelli* (Anthony Caruso)

When *The Asphalt Jungle* arrived on theatre screens in 1950, it changed forever both the style and substance of crime films in America. Previously, the hoodlum had been depicted as a cocky young punk (*The Public Enemy*), a victim of society (*Scarface*), or a modern tragic hero (*Little Caesar*). But in the post-war era, he emerged as an antihero, beginning with James Cagney's mother-dominated gangster in *White Heat*. Clearly, our value system had changed. So the blacks and whites disappeared from cops-and-robbers films; there were no good guys or bad guys any-

Louis Calhern and Sam Jaffe

Jean Hagen and Sterling Hayden

more, only shades of grey as self-serving men played out their minor passions. Now, the single difference between police and criminals seemed to be that one group had society's sanction to bless their violent acts. Essentially, this was a nightmare vision of the modern city as a place where primitive emotions erupted amidst an industrial landscape. It is a point of view that has persisted, and *A Clockwork Orange* represents its logical conclusion. But the frightening vision came into being during the fifties, and had its initial screen expression in *The Asphalt Jungle*.

Ostensibly, the story relates a case study of a single crime gone sour, perpetrated by a small band of minor league hoodlums who come together almost by accident. The aging Doc Riedenschnieder (Sam Jaffe), recently released from prison, masterminds a plan for the daring robbery of a jewelry store; the influential lawyer Alonzo D. Emmerich (Louis Calhern) agrees in advance to buy everything they can steal. But from the beginning, it is a fixed deck: behind his showy facade of success, Emmerich is flat broke and knows full well he must doublecross the thieves. The audi-

ence is aware of the coming betrayal as it watches the careful planning of the crime, presented in a naturalistic, semi-documentary fashion. From the first scene, the viewer is thrust into the strategy sessions of the criminals and their unpleasant milieu, made to feel almost an active participant in the robbery. The police, and indeed the entire outside world, is sensed as an antagonistic force, both to the characters and to us. So we doggedly follow Riedenschnieder's gang, though our advance knowledge of Emmerich's plans leaves little doubt as to the final outcome.

In the role of Dix Handley, Sterling Hayden created a memorable early portrait of a fifties anti-hero. He takes part in the robbery only to finance his return to the place that gave him his nickname. In the city, Dix feels cut off from his roots and is unable to respond properly. Unfortunately, he has never read (or heard of) Thomas Wolfe, and doesn't realize you can't go home again, since the values he associates with his rural Kentucky boyhood no longer exist. Dix is modern alienated man personified, afraid to show any emotion to Doll Conovan (Jean Hagen), the young

The Lonely Crowd: Sam Jaffe, Sterling Hayden, Anthony Caruso and (standing) James Whitmore

woman who wants desperately to love him, and unable to feel any sense of community with his henchmen. The necessary failure of the scheme is not so much due to Emmerich's betrayal of the men as their own subtler, more sinister betrayal of themselves: a group venture cannot succeed without a group, and this is but a lonely crowd of isolated individualists, scrambling in the shadows for personal survival.

In his New York *Times* review, Bosley Crowther praised the picture for its "ruthless authority," admitting that director John Huston "filmed a straight crime story about as cleverly and graphically as it could be filmed" while insisting the picture was essentially "corrupt" since it enjoined "the hypnotized audience to hobnob with a bunch of crooks . . . and actually sympathize with their personal griefs." Others were less restrained in their praise. Archer Winsten of the New York *Post* hailed it as a masterpiece of the genre: "The crime picture of this decade . . . maybe the best one ever made." And at least a few critics joined audiences in singling out a lithesome, leggy young lady who had a small but showy part as Emmerich's "niece" Angela. Though restrictions of the time made it impossible for the dialogue to acknowledge Marilyn Monroe as the man's mistress, Huston's able direction left little doubt in viewers' minds as to their real relationship. After cataloging the film's many impressive features, Liza Wilson of *Photoplay* added, almost as an afterthought: "There's a beautiful blonde, too, named Marilyn Monroe, who . . . makes the most of her footage." Indeed she did! In her fifth film, Marilyn radiated that very special glow—a combination of innocence and experience—which would soon catapult her to superstardom in a decade ripe for her unique brand of sensuality.

Eduard Franz (left) supervises the search for The Thing

The Thing

RKO (1951)

Produced by Howard Hawks and presented by Winchester Pictures Corporation; directed by Christian Nyby; screenplay by Charles Lederer, based on the story "Who Goes There," by John W. Campbell, Jr.

CAST: *Nikki* (Margaret Sheridan); *Captain Patrick Hendry* (Kenneth Tobey); *Dr. Carrington* (Robert Cornthwaite); *Skeely* (Douglas Spencer); *Lieutenant Eddie Dykes* (James Young); *Crew Chief* (Dewey Martin); *Lieutenant Ken Erickson* (Robert Nichols); *Corporal Barnes* (William Self); *Dr. Stern* (Eduard Franz); *Mrs. Chapman* (Sally Creighton); *"The Thing"* (James Arness)

One night in 1947, a pilot flying over the state of Washington reported an entire fleet of flying craft moving at a speed which he estimated as well over a thousand miles an hour. The man referred to them as "saucer shaped," though the authorities preferred the more officious title, "unidentified flying objects." Both terms caught the public's fancy, and immediately hundreds of similar sightings made the newspapers across the country. Though the government seemingly treated the whole thing as either a passing fad or a case of mass hysteria, the air force nonetheless spent hundreds of thousands of dollars attempting to determine whether or not the "flying saucers" existed. Popular

Dewey Martin, Kenneth Tobey, Robert Cornthwaite, John Dierkes

magazines had a field day exploiting the phenomenon and, a few years later, the somewhat slower-moving world of movies caught up. There were literally dozens of flying saucer films during the early fifties, but none quite as good as the first.

In *The Thing*, old-time Hollywood hand Howard Hawks created a compact little yarn that progressed believably and intelligently along a premise that never once strained the viewer's credibility. Following a major magnetic disturbance at the North Pole, an expedition is dispatched to study the source. In the frozen wilderness a combination of soldiers commanded by Captain Patrick Hendry (Kenneth Tobey) and civilian scientists under the leadership of Nobel Prize winner Dr. Carrington (Robert Cornthwaite) encounter a great saucer-like object almost buried beneath the sheet of ice it apparently crashed into. While trying to extricate the craft they inadvertently destroy it. Momentarily though, they discover a survivor—a being that looks vaguely human and is frozen in a block of ice.

From that point on, Hawks builds a growing sense of terror. The group carries the body back to their isolated outpost. While the military men break into an argument with the intellectuals as to whose jurisdiction "the thing" ultimately falls under, one soldier is left to keep an eye on what they kiddingly call a "man from Mars." Hawks effectively cuts from a shot of the ice melting around the creature, to the guard distractedly looking away, and finally to the meeting in the next room—interrupted by screams from just beyond the door.

The battle between men and monster is complicated by the interesting argument among the men themselves. The soldiers want to find a way to kill the creature, while the scientists insist on taking him alive so that they can study him. Discovering that guns are quite useless, they barricade themselves in a room and, in a gesture that reveals much about the time, survive by pooling their knowledge. Deciding that the thing must be a human form of vegetable, they realize that electricity may do the trick. And, in the final face-to-face confrontation with the creature, they destroy it thanks to their cooperation with one another.

The film works masterfully as science fiction because of its perfect pacing: director Christian Nyby learned about such techniques while working as Hawks' film editor over the years. Just as crucial was Hawks' decision to put off showing "the thing" as long as possible; there is a split-second view of him early in the film, but it comes so suddenly and unexpectedly we barely get a glimpse before he's gone. The monster's unseen presence creates an aura of escalating fear that elevates the picture into a classic exercise in suspense rather than a mere "monster movie." At the same time, it works as the personal expression of Mr. Hawks: in films as diverse as westerns, war stories, and racing car epics he concentrated on the relationships within a predominantly male community, as individuals experience self-knowledge and communication with others by fighting a powerful adversary. In *The Thing*, he brought that singular point of view strikingly in line with the interests of the fifties.

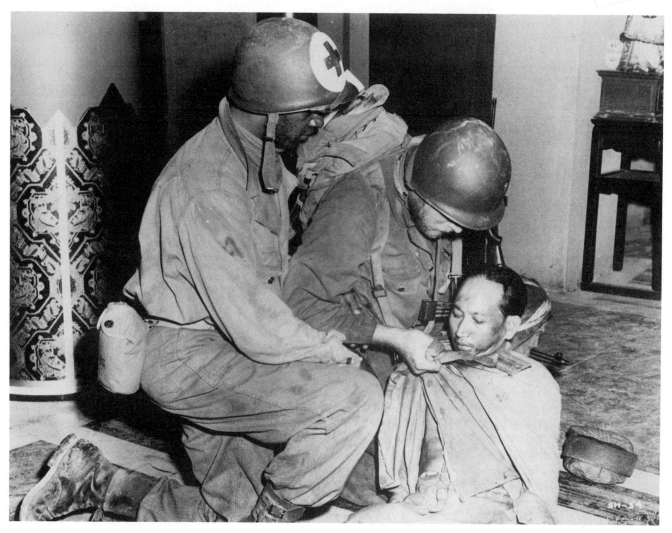

James Edwards, Gene Evans, player. A bleak view of combat

The Steel Helmet

Lippert Pictures, Inc. (1951)

Produced, directed and written by Samuel Fuller.

CAST: *Sergeant Zack* (Gene Evans); *Short Round* (William Chun); *Corporal Thompson* (James Edwards); *Private Bronte* (Robert Hutton); *Lieutenant Driscoll* (Steve Brodie); *Sergeant Tanaka* (Richard Loo); *Second GI* (Sid Melton); *Private Baldy* (Richard Monahan); *The Red* (Harold Fong); *First GI* (Neyle Morrow); *Second Lieutenant* (Lynn Stallmaster)

Throughout the fifties, the most fascinating maverick in the movie industry was Samuel Fuller. He worked as an independent who wrote, produced, and directed low-budget films which often were big box-office hits. Fuller's style was more sensational than sensitive in the treatment of his subjects. But he possessed the shrewd sense of a yellow journalist (which, in fact, he once was) as to the contemporary

Gene Evans as Sgt. Zack. A new kind of war hero for a new kind of war

issues that would seize the public's imagination. So his pictures always predated the big studio releases in touching on controversies of the day.

On June 25, 1950, the country's newfound fears of communist aggression were suddenly substantiated when North Korean troops slammed across the border into South Korea, resulting in American and United Nations forces being brought into the combat zone within the week. Fuller sensed the significance of the event: on the one hand the escalating terror of communism, and on the other a growing defeatism about entering into combat so quickly after the *second* war-to-end-all-wars. Fuller prepared a script in one week, shot a picture in ten days, and only months later presented the first fictional film dealing with the Korean conflict to the American public.

The story retained the outer shell of typical World War II movies and, as in every such combat tale from the early *Bataan* to the late *A Walk in the Sun,* focused on some highly diverse American prototypes on a dangerous mission. The difference was that, in films of the early forties, the group managed to get "the job" done against great odds. In *The Steel Helmet* the men bicker among themselves and eventually betray one another. When they die, it is not only without glory but also without reason. Their central emotion is not patriotism, but apathy.

As Sergeant Zack, Gene Evans created a forceful yet frightening portrait of a leader who, unlike John Wayne or Errol Flynn in the films of only a few years before, drove his men on more through bullying force than firm control. But this, we sense, is the only way in which the leader can operate in the nightmarish war-world of the fifties. Fuller's

vision is unrelentingly dark: in the opening sequence, Zack is seen crawling on his belly through a battlefield literally layered with corpses. He encounters a small patrol wandering, quite significantly, without any sense of direction in a foggy stretch of jungle. They have no conception where the enemy is or, symbolically enough, where their own lines are. In addition, they are being killed off one by one by a hidden sniper, a fact they accept with lethargic fatalism.

Zack agrees to lead the patrol to an ancient temple they were (for reasons that now seem to make little sense) supposed to find. But he does so only for the most mercenary of motivations—he wants a box of cigars one of the men has. When Zack finally shows some emotion to a little South Korean boy, Short Round (William Chun) who saves his life, the child is killed by a stray shot a moment later—and Zack hurriedly retreats back into himself. When the dead body of an American GI is discovered, a soldier decides to remove the dog tags. "Leave him be," Zack calls. "A dead man is a dead man, and nobody cares." The soldier sneers at Zack's callousness, begins to remove them anyway, and is instantaneously killed by a booby trap planted on the body.

While major moviemakers carefully backed off to decide how they felt about the touchy situation in Korea, Fuller jumped in immediately. His treatment suggested (and perhaps, to a degree, helped determine) the very different attitudes Americans would assume toward this new conflict: in World War II we had demonstrated self-assuredness and solidarity; this time, the feelings would run from divisiveness to cynicism.

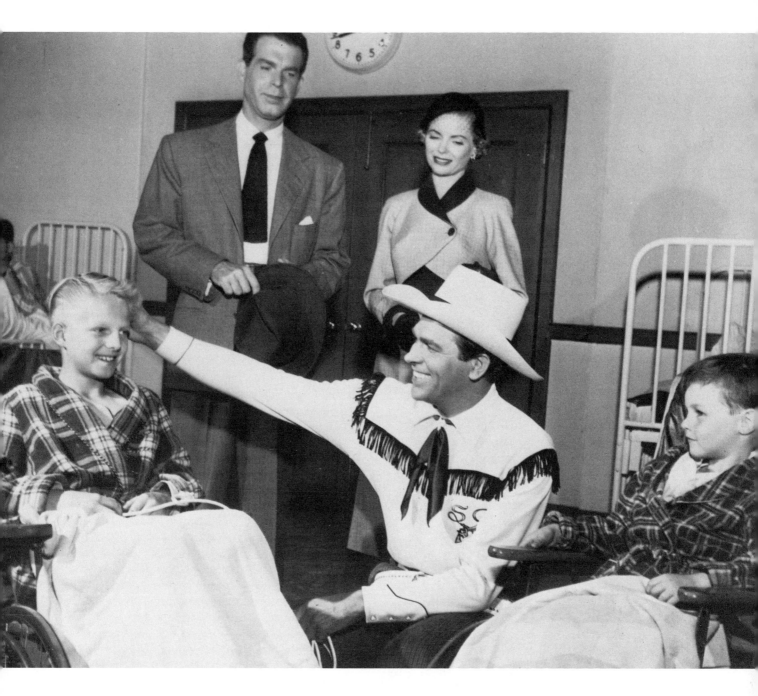

Callaway Went Thataway

Metro-Goldwyn-Mayer (1951)

Produced, directed and written by Norman Panama and Melvin Frank.

CAST: *Mike Frye* (Fred MacMurray); *Deborah Patterson* (Dorothy McGuire); *"Smoky" Callaway, "Stretch" Barnes* (Howard Keel); *Georgie Markham* (Jesse White); *Tom Lorrison* (Fay Roope); *Martha Lorrison* (Natalie Schafer); *The Drunk* (Douglas Kennedy); *Marie* (Elizabeth Fraser); *Johnny Terrento* (Johnny Indrisano); *Marvin* (Stan Freberg); *Director* (Don Haggerty)

Television immediately established itself as the most significant force of the new decade, much to the chagrin of moviemakers—who often soothed bruised egos by taking potshots at the competition. One widespread TV trend was that, in order to fill up the afternoon kiddie hour, grade C cowboy pictures cranked out a decade earlier for Saturday morning double bills were hauled from the vaults, dusted off, and repeated endlessly. Because of the new medium's

The hypocrisy of the junior executives: As Fred Mac-Murray sifts through fan mail for Smokey, Dorothy McGuire uses one of his advertisements for a dart board

unpredictable impact, these features quickly became so popular with a huge new baby-boom audience of children that a host of actors, including William Boyd, Roy Rogers and Gene Autry—some long-since retired—found themselves national figures on a far greater scale than they had previously known—or imagined possible!

This early-fifties syndrome was deftly satirized in *Callaway Went Thataway*, which laced light situation comedy-romance with barbed attacks on TV's tendency to exploit both its programs and its public. Mike Frye (Fred Mac-Murray) and Deborah Patterson (Dorothy McGuire), a team of television advertising executives (and, significantly, the first film appearance of what would soon become fifties stock figures) search frantically for a means of boosting their station's highly popular series of old "Smoky" Callaway films. The kiddie idol was, it turns out, never the upstanding hero he'd been passed off as a few years back; Callaway quickly drank away all his earnings, then disappeared.

While on vacation at a Colorado dude ranch, the couple encounter "Stretch" Barnes (Howard Keel), a real cowboy who bears an uncanny physical resemblance to the long-absent movie star. They cart the boy back to Hollywood, where he's carefully schooled to imitate the image Smoky presented. But in so programming Stretch, Mike and Deborah unwittingly destroy the boy's authentic American innocence—replacing it with media-created hypocrisy.

In essence, they succeed in turning the likable Stretch into the despicable Smoky; watching the unpleasant transformation, we bear witness to an archetypal example of the media's frightening powers. Complicating matters (and keeping the film from growing too serious), the *real* Smoky (also played by Keel) shows up from the South America saloon where he's been languishing, and threatens to expose their farce unless given a cut of the profits. His deus-ex-machina appearance allows MacMurray and McGuire—perfectly cast as the bright young urban-sophisticates—ample opportunity to begin comprehending the essential corruptness of the kind of work they do.

Dorothy McGuire, Howard Keel and Fred MacMurray

Hugh Marlowe and Patricia Neal

The Day the Earth Stood Still

20th Century-Fox (1951)

Produced by Julian Blaustein; directed by Robert Wise; screenplay by Edmund H. North, from a story by Harry Bates.

CAST: *Klaatu* (Michael Rennie); *Helen Benson* (Patricia Neal); *Tom Stevens* (Hugh Marlowe); *Dr. Barnhardt* (Sam Jaffe); *Bobby Benson* (Billy Gray); *Mrs. Barley* (Frances Bavier); *Gort* (Lock Martin); *Drew Pearson* (Himself); *Harley* (Frank Conroy); *Colonel* (Carlton Young); *Major General* (Fay Roope); *Mrs. Crockett* (Edith Evanson); *Major White* (Robert Osterloh); *Brady* (Tyler McVey); *Government Man* (James Seay); *Mr. Barley* (John Brown); *Hilda* (Marjorie Grossland); *Interviewer* (Glenn Hardy)

The atomic bomb, which at first seemed to be our saviour by bringing the war to a speedy end, soon changed into a modern Frankenstein's monster with immense powers far beyond our control. Panic spread at the disclosure that some scientists had leaked information to the Russians and they now had the Bomb, too. Before long, "atomic" movies were every bit as popular as "invasion" movies; *The Day the Earth Stood Still* was an interesting hybrid between the two and resulted in a surprisingly satisfying and adult film.

It unfolds in the manner of a moral fable that combines elements both of monster pictures and message movies. Klaatu (Michael Rennie), an emissary from Mars, lands his spacecraft near Washington, D.C., and checks into a boardinghouse where he listens, at the dinner table, to a

Michael Rennie, Patricia Neal and friend

cross-section of the American public. The people express their views on the two great fears of the day: invaders from outer space and an atomic war with Russia. An attractive widow, Helen Benson (Patricia Neal) and her young son, Bobby (Billy Gray) take a special interest in this charming, educated, understanding fellow, who at once becomes a father figure to the boy and, in time, a love interest for the woman. Her boyfriend Tom Stevens (Hugh Marlowe) resents the intrusion of this stranger, and continually speaks against his highly unorthodox behavior.

Helen eventually grows suspicious of Klaaton's continuous discussion of the need for peace, and approaches an eminent scientist, Dr. Barnhardt (Sam Jaffe). Together they discover that Klaatu is indeed an alien—but that his only mission is to warn earthlings away from their dangerous preoccupation with nuclear weapons. In order to prove to all that there are powers in the universe far beyond our new atomic toys, he mysteriously stops the flow of all electricity on earth for a frightening thirty minutes, then leaves as quietly as he came.

Devoid of the usual horror picture excesses and gimmicks (save for some occasional obligatory appearances by Klaatu's robot companion) the picture works instead on a psychological level: Helen's torment between instinctive loyalty not only to her country but to her very planet, against her clear sense that this man from Mars really does know what's best. The film is most interesting, however, as an historical footnote. It records the fact that, as early as 1951, our brave new world had already reached a frightening extremity; in one of our fantasy solutions, we could readily envision invaders from another world as saving, rather than menacing, our earth.

The military and the scientists often clashed in fifties science fiction films: Sam Jaffe and players

John Garfield and Shelley Winters

Shelley Winters, John Garfield, Wallace Ford and Bobby Hyatt

He Ran All the Way

United Artists (1951)

Produced by Bob Roberts; directed by John Berry; screenplay by Hugo Butler and Guy Endore, based on the Sam Ross novel of the same name.

CAST: *Nick* (John Garfield); *Peg* (Shelley Winters); *Mr. Dobbs* (Wallace Ford); *Mrs. Dobbs* (Selena Royle); *Mrs. Robey* (Gladys George); *Al Molin* (Norman Lloyd); *Tommy Dobbs* (Bobby Hyatt)

John Garfield's last important screen role came in 1950 when he was cast as the anti-hero of *The Breaking Point*, a classy remake of the Bogart hit *To Have and Have Not*. Garfield played Ernest Hemingway's Harry Morgan, an honest and independent cargo skipper fighting to maintain individuality and integrity in a world of corruption and conformity. More by fate than luck, that same year saw him play in another Hemingway story, *Under My Skin*, as a

Selena Royle and John Garfield: the anti-hero as Mama's boy

that end. We experience the sense of watching a predestined tale, a fate that rang as true for the film's star as it did for its hero. Nick, like Garfield himself, is a man who could have been anything but got the wrong breaks and turned out to be a magnificent loser. After a brutal argument with his mother, Nick goes along on a poorly planned small-time robbery. But everything goes wrong, his cronies desert him, and in desperation to make a getaway he holds a frightened family captive. The old man (Wallace Ford) fears the tough character but soon comes to like his strange brand of courage; the young boy (Bobby Hyatt) is awed by the man's grit; the girl Peg (Shelley Winters) quickly falls in love, attracted by the vulnerability she senses beneath the tough exterior. But though he burns to enjoy a normal life with just such a woman, his awareness of his own doom forbids it.

Every element of the film, right down to the title itself, expressed perfectly the Garfield myth: anxious and uncertain, a surface cool hiding a mass of repressed hysteria. The screen's new psychological style took an interestingly fresh look at his stock character. But he belonged too exclusively to a world that had passed to make the successful transition into the fifties as had some of his old colleagues like Bette Davis and Humphrey Bogart. In *Body and Soul*, he had scoffed at the gangsters threatening his life with a sullen smile and the words: "What're you gonna do? *Kill* me? *Everybody* dies!" In a sense, Garfield had spoken for himself and the less than adequate treatment he had received; when on May 20, 1952 he died suddenly of a heart attack at age 39, many knowledgeable people insisted his condition had been aggravated by deep-rooted anxieties over Hollywood's mishandling of him. Certainly, though, he paved the way for more offbeat styles in screen heroes, and while his death left a vacuum, it was quickly filled by such fifties anti-heroes as Marlon Brando, Montgomery Clift and James Dean.

tough, uncompromising jockey pushed by forces beyond his control into violating his own code by throwing a race. The two pictures were not so much early films of the new decade as the final ones of an era that was ending. For Garfield—more than Bogart, or any other star—was the film equivalent of the Lost Generation's rootless romantics that Hemingway had immortalized in his novels.

But there was something strangely proper about the fact that his last film was a dark, confused, inexpensively made little potboiler. Garfield had, since his first starring role in *Four Daughters* (1938) proved a most difficult figure, a man happy neither in the socially conscious Group Theatre, where he learned his craft, nor in the tinsel-town world of the Hollywood studios, where he earned his fame. The fact that he was never allowed to play the single role he felt born for—the violinist who must turn to boxing for money in *Golden Boy*—in the film version of that story, evidences the tragic misuse of this most enigmatic figure. He nonetheless carved for himself a Hollywood legend, but most often had to do so in pictures clearly beneath his talents. *He Ran All the Way* was the last such venture.

Yet, "Nick" is not only the last but in many respects the most perfect of the Garfield characterizations. The film begins with Nick's eerie, almost surreal nightmare vision of his own destruction and then, from the moment he wakes, dutifully follows a series of events that lead directly to just

Elizabeth Taylor, Montgomery Clift, Shelley Winters

A Place in the Sun

Paramount (1951)

Produced and directed by George Stevens; screenplay by Michael Wilson and Harry Brown, based on the novel *An American Tragedy,* by Theodore Dreiser and Patrick Kearny's play.

CAST: *George Eastman* (Montgomery Clift); *Angela Vickers* (Elizabeth Taylor); *Alice Tripp* (Shelley Winters); *Hannah Eastman* (Anne Revere); *Marlowe* (Raymond Burr); *Charles Eastman* (Herbert Heyes); *Earl Eastman* (Keefe Brasselle); *Anthony Vickers* (Shepperd Strudwick); *Mrs. Vickers* (Frieda Inescort); *Dr. Wyeland* (Ian Wolfe); *Marcia Eastman* (Lois Chartrand); *Bellows (Defense Attorney)* (Fred Clark); *Jansan* (Walter Sande); *Boatkeeper* (Douglas Spencer); *Coroner* (John Ridgley); *Mrs. Louise Eastman* (Kathryn Givney); *Judge* (Ted de Corsia); *Kelly* (Charles Dayton); *Reverend Morrison* (Paul Frees); *Mr. Whiting* (William R. Murphy)

Though the credits stated that the screenplay was "based on the novel *An American Tragedy,*" George Stevens' decision to change both the work's title and the characters' names was hardly fortuitous. Although the basic plot devices of Theodore Dreiser's book were followed closely, Stevens so completely made over the work in terms of attitude and meaning that the new title and names were nearly a necessity.

The picture begins with the shot of a young man walking along a busy highway with his back to us, trying to thumb a ride. As the credits slip by, he moves slowly closer to the screen; at the end of the sequence, a beautiful young girl (Elizabeth Taylor) rides past, beeps the horn of her sports car, and waves to him in a semi-friendly, semi-flirtatious gesture. As he turns to watch her drive on, we have our first clear view of his face: awed by her glamour and beauty, ambitious enough to want to attain her for himself.

Montgomery Clift, Walter Sande, Fred Clark, Raymond Burr

Frieda Inescort, Elizabeth Taylor

When Geoge learns that Alice is pregnant, his frenzied attempts to marry his romantic ideal without actually deserting the girl of his own class culminates with Alice's death in a boating accident. George tries to cover his own involvement, but when it is discovered he is forced to stand trial. Marlowe (Raymond Burr), an unsparing prosecution lawyer, brings the actual boat into court and demands that George sit in it and explain the incident in vivid detail. While the boy insists that he did not bring Alice onto the lake with plans for a murder, he finally admits that he doesn't know himself whether or not he could have saved her. At that point, his fate is sealed: the jury returns a "guilty" verdict and he is sentenced to be executed.

Dreiser, who had himself borrowed the idea from newspaper headlines of his day, employed the story for purposes of muckraking—radicalizing his twenties readers against a callous class structure. The focus of *An American Tragedy* was on the social system that could drive any man to such extremities. Stevens effectively updated the tale for an entirely different purpose, making his version the first clearcut masterpiece of the screen's new psychological realism: *A Place in the Sun* is centered on the hero's complex search for himself. Dreiser's protagonist, an unpleasant street punk, emerged at the hands of Montgomery Clift as a likably innocent, inwardly confused victim of circumstances—and, as such, the first full-blown appearance of the definitive fifties hero. Clift was certainly the first of the decades' "loners," and a direct descendant of Garfield. Significantly, then, like Garfield's last characterzation in *He Ran All the Way*, Clift is pictured as a mama's boy whose wrong-headed approach to life grows directly out of an unsatisfying, difficult early relationship with that parent. But the differences between Garfield and Clift tell us as much as the similarities: the former was the cocky, wise-talking climber, the latter incarnated the internal, intense outsider.

For both its top-billed females, *A Place in the Sun* signaled career milestones. Shelley Winters, previously a lackluster (and often overweight) leading lady, emerged as a character actress to be reckoned with, creating in a few short scenes a convincing portrait of pathos and mediocrity. Elizabeth Taylor, formerly a notable juvenile and then an impressive ingenue, at last forced audiences to deal with her as a "serious" actress: the simple-sweet girl goddess, rich but unspoiled, vulnerable despite her irresistability. In the film's most remembered sequence she and Clift kiss briefly, desperately, in a partially darkened room. The image of their doomed passion idealized all the old notions of star-crossed romance for a whole new generation of moviegoers.

George Eastman (Montgomery Clift), a poor slum boy, journeys to the town where his rich uncle Charles (Herbert Heyes) owns a factory; George is shocked to learn that the lovely girl he saw on the highway is his own cousin Angela. But the family is a bit embarrassed at the arrival of their country cousin, and put him on at the plant in a relatively menial position. Frustrated and lonely, he strikes up an affair with a fellow factory worker, Alice Tripp (Shelley Winters). But when his relatives gradually begin to accept him into the family, going so far as to indicate they would view him as a match for Angela, he desperately wants to get out of the sordid affair.

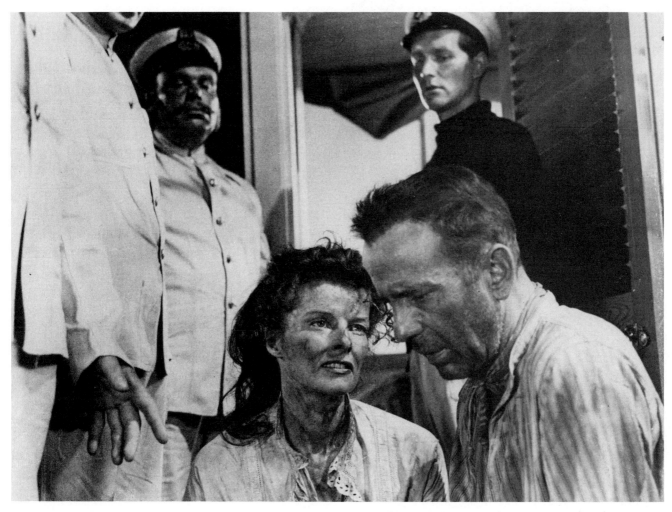

Peter Bull (standing), Katharine Hepburn, and Humphrey Bogart

The African Queen

United Artists (1951)

A Horizon-Romulus production, produced by S. P. Eagle; directed by John Huston; adapted for the screen by James Agee and Mr. Huston, from the novel *The African Queen,* by C. S. Forester.

CAST: *Charlie Allnut* (Humphrey Bogart); *Rose Sayer* (Katharine Hepburn); *Reverend Samuel Sayer* (Robert Morley); *Captain of the "Louisa"* (Peter Bull); *First Officer of the "Louisa"* (Theodore Bikel); *German Army Officer* (Peter Swanick)

Despite the proliferation of psychological themes and arresting new styles, Hollywood had by no means suddenly lost its sense of fun, its spirit of adventure, or its ability to produce pure escapism. And though *The African Queen* was filmed largely on location thousands of miles away from any sound stages, it stands proudly as the final great example of the traditional "Hollywood movie"—a species which gradually disappeared somewhere between the slow death of the studio system and the rapid birth of an expanded film consciousness. Rarely would a provocatively masculine indi-

ing Christianity to the natives. The shock of the experience kills Sayer, and Rose has no idea how she will survive. Then their usual once-a-month visitor, Charlie Allnut (Humphrey Bogart) putters up to the landing on his dirty, cluttered tug *The African Queen*.

The earthy man and the aristocratic woman are uneasy allies at first: since he has plenty of booze to drink and butts to smoke, Charlie suggests that they hide in the backwaters and sit out the war. But Rose, ever the high-minded Englishwoman, insists they do their patriotic duty by navigating their launch all the way downriver where a huge German gunboat, the *Louisa*, patrols the waters—then blast it sky high by ramming it with *The African Queen* and a load of explosives.

Essentially the film tells the story of two simultaneous "educations." For while Charlie gradually succeeds in awakening the cold-fish "Rose" by turning her into the sensual, fun-loving "Rosie," she also manages to change him over completely from the gin-soaked isolationist to a rip-roaring man of dedication who wants to see the *Louisa* and its arrogant officers (Peter Bull and Theodore Bikel) go up in smoke every bit as much as she does. At the beginning, they are antithetical caricatures but grow, through their intense physical suffering, interesting interpersonal relationship, and eventual love, into full-blown, highly likable human beings.

Their comic repartee is interrupted by sequences of unforgettable power, including a sudden attack by deadly mosquitoes and some blood-sucking leeches that have to be burned off Charlie's body. Yet the humor in no way reduces the suspense or believability of the dangerous situations. In fact, the two merge strikingly when their small craft is swept over the wildest of rapids. After the ordeal Rosie, her face flushed with a sensual arousal and her eyes aglow with near-carnal pleasure, throws back her head and purrs: "*That*, Mr. Allnut, was the most exhilarating experience of my life!" And when their beloved sunken boat rams into the *Louisa* at the very moment when the two are to be hanged by the Germans, enabling Charlie and Rosie to escape and swim off into the sunet, audiences who had recently experienced the unpleasant execution of the hero in *A Place in the Sun* were reminded of just how delightful a "dream factory" happy ending can be.

vidualist like "Bogie" be pitted against a frigid, strong-willed female adversary such as "Kate," if only because so many of the old-fashioned superstars retired or passed away in the following years, while the rising younger ones were interested in different (ostensibly more "honest") movies. Just as significant was that, in the fifties, film drama and film comedy grew ever farther apart, whereas the unique appeal of thirties and forties films—from *Gunga Din* to *Boom Town*—had been their ability to work on three levels simultaneously: as romances, for women; as action yarns, for men; and as spoofs, for everybody.

Such was the case with *The African Queen*, written "straight" by James Agee but directed with tongue-in-cheek by John Huston. In German East Africa at the outset of World War I, British Reverend Samuel Sayer (Robert Morley) and his haughty sister Rose (Katharine Hepburn) are taken totally by surprise when a detachment of German soldiers destroys the little village where they have been teach-

Dorothy Hart, Frank Lovejoy

I Was a Communist for the FBI

Warner Bros. (1951)

Produced by Bryan Foy; directed by Gordon Douglas; screenplay by Crane Wilbur, based on the story of Matt Cvetic, as told to Pete Martin.

CAST: *Matt Cvetic* (Frank Lovejoy); *Eve Merrick* (Dorothy Hart); *Mason* (Philip Carey); *Jim Blandon* (James Millican); *Crowley* (Richard Webb); *Gerhardt Eisler* (Konstantin Shayne); *Joe Cvetic* (Paul Picerni); *Father Novac* (Roy Roberts); *Harmon* (Eddie Norris); *Dick Cvetic* (Ron Hagerty); *Garson* (Hugh Sanders); *Ruth Cvetic* (Hope Kramer)

The anticommunist films all shared certain fundamental positions. Clearly, they were calculated to convince the House Committee on Un-American Activities that even if a few communists did turn up in Hollywood, the movie industry itself was certainly as patriotic as ever. But a number of distinct film styles were tried as frames on which the propaganda could be hung. While *The Woman on Pier 13* was the first definitive example of a conventional "woman's picture" being altered ever so slightly to express these attitudes, *I Was a Communist for the FBI* paved the way for films that would do the same job from a man's point of

Frank Lovejoy attends a meeting of the Pittsburgh Steel Union and discovers it is a hot-bed of communist sympathizers

Loyal Americans break up an anti-Fascist (and, supposedly anti-American) strike

view, combining elements of the Nazi spy films that flourished briefly just before the outbreak of the last war with situations from stock underworld yarns.

Early in the story, a young man attends his first major communist convention. A simple Pittsburgh steelworker, Matt Cvetic (Frank Lovejoy) appears astonished to find that his supposedly idealistic "common man" comrades hold

their banquet for Gerhardt Eisler in a plush hotel suite, where they stuff themselves on caviar and guzzle bottles of expensive wine. But when Cvetic complains to one of the ringleaders that this is a far cry from the dedicated speeches which brought him into the organization, the man snaps back: "This is the way we're *all* gonna live after we take over the country!" The implication, of course, is that communism—besides being an incorrect approach to the problems of America and the world—lacks even the saving grace of sincerity, as its leaders are cynically living off the work of those naive fools who labor for their cause. But Cvetic hardly needs to hear this; he is, in fact, an FBI plant.

The picture was more "inspired by" than "based on" the actual experiences of the real Matt Cvetic, as reported in several magazine articles he penned after his guise was eventually dropped. But that veneer of "truth" only made this highly fictionalized and simplistically manipulative film all the more dangerous. Certainly, there were communist groups in the country that needed to be stopped by men like Cvetic. But by depicting their leaders as cartoon villains, the film did little damage other than to make such figures look grotesquely stupid and easy to defeat; unfortunately, they were neither. The big danger, though, came in some of the film's casual implications.

It suggested that intellectuals in general and teachers in particular were more susceptible to communism than "ordinary" people. As Cvetic enters the communist cell, they are just in the process of initiating a confused young teacher, Eve Merrick (Dorothy Hart). A comrade tells Cvetic that this is precisely the type of person most receptive to their master plan, and by the picture's end the audience has been led to believe that anyone who questions the government's policies on anything is a possible "pinko."

But the communists in the film save their most savage remarks for people of liberal political leanings. They sarcastically explain that such well-meaning "bleeding hearts" can easily be exploited to cause economic problems because of their belief in causes like the civil rights movement. Negroes in particular are depicted as being an easy mark, as well as laborers and union members—especially those who would under any circumstances consider a strike.

The film made Cvetic a lonely figure by insisting he could not reveal his true identity even to his family, who turn away from him in disgust. His exploits were so popular that a similar secret agent, Herbert Philbrick, became the protagonist of a long-running weekly TV series, *I Led Three Lives*, in which week after week, he uncovered some liberal, laborer or teacher selling his soul to the dreaded social disease.

A mother's tragedy: Robert Walker and Helen Hayes

My Son John
Paramount (1952)

Produced and directed by Leo McCarey; screenplay by Myles Connolly and Leo McCarey; adapted by John Lee Mahin from a story by Mr. McCarey.

CAST: *Lucille Jefferson* (Helen Hayes); *John Jefferson* (Robert Walker); *Mr. Stedman* (Van Heflin); *Dan Jefferson* (Dean Jagger); *Dr. Carver* (Minor Watson); *Father O'Dowd* (Frank McHugh); *Ruth Carlin* (Irene Winston); *Ben Jefferson* (James Young); *Chuck Jefferson* (Richard Jaeckel); *Bedford* (Tod Karns)

Helen Hayes is more than just an actress, or even a star. She is an American institution, and that fact must certainly have influenced Leo McCarey when he cast her as a down-to-earth American mother and housewife who begins to suspect that her beloved son may be a communist sympathizer. The stature this great lady of film and theatre (who, in addition, had been absent from the screen for close to twenty years) brought with her to the role transformed this tale from just a minor story about one woman's traumatic experience into a major statement about The

Van Heflin and Robert Walker

American Mother. However, instead of exploring the dramatic possibilities inherent in such a woman's plight, the moviemakers only served up another helping of propaganda.

The story, presented straight-faced as a portrait of courageous action, offered viewers the frightening assertions that guilt by association is a correct mode of procedure, that offbeat and original approaches necessarily indicate the holder of such ideas is inclined toward communism, and that liberals and intellectuals are clearly the most dangerous elements in society. When Ben (James Young) and Chuck (Richard Jaeckel) Jefferson, two clean-cut, football-playing youths, happily sign up for the Korean War and promptly go off to do their patriotic chore, their mother Lucille (Helen Hayes) suspects something is amiss, since her oldest son, John (Robert Walker), fails to fly home from Washington (where he holds an important but mysterious job) for the send-off party. He does eventually return for a visit, and Lucille is shocked to hear him scoff at his father's (Dean Jagger) steadfast loyalty to the American Legion. Later, he argues that perhaps Bible stories should be taken on a symbolic rather than literal level of truth. For Lucille, this is the last straw.

Unable to control her emotions, she forces the young man to swear on the Bible that he is not and never has been a communist—an oath he readily agrees to. But after he returns to his job, word reaches Lucille that John is being investigated by the F.B.I. as a possible security leak. She at once treats that information—the *possibility* that he's involved in something underhanded—as proof positive that her darkest suspicions were correct. When she learns John is

dating a young woman (Irene Winston) who is suspected of being a spy, Lucille assumes her son is also guilty of just such actions.

It isn't difficult to believe that, in such trying times, a mother could do such things. What is both frightening and reprehensible is the picture's implication that her course of procedure is precisely the right one, that it would be a waste of time to wait and see what the F.B.I. investigation turns up. Being investigated becomes synonymous with being guilty; by ending the film with John's confession that he is indeed a communist, the picture legitimizes the woman's hysteria and suggests any real American would, and should, follow her example.

My Son John represented a drastic departure from the normal style of filmmaker Leo McCarey, and he never fully recovered from the critical lambasting he received after the film's release. Generally regarded as one of the finest directors of the thirties, he had worked with the Marx Brothers in *Duck Soup* and Mae West in *Belle of the Nineties*. But he is best remembered for a string of charming comedies—at once satiric and sentimental—that includes *The Awful Truth* (1937) and *Going My Way* (1944); he won the Best Director Oscar for each of those pictures. After *My Son John*, though, his career came to a virtual standstill.

Bosley Crowther, in his *New York Times* review, summarized the critical reaction when he labelled this a ". . . picture so strongly dedicated to the purpose of the American anti-Communist purge that it seethes with the sort of emotionalism and illogic that is characteristic of so much thinking these days. . . . In the present confused national climate, *My Son John* may add heat and wind, but it may also startle some people into making a new and sober estimate of things."

"What do you do it for, Will? You do it for a tin star!" Lon Chaney Jr. and Gary Cooper

High Noon

United Artists (1952)

A Stanley Kramer Production, produced by Stanley Kramer; directed by Fred Zinnemann; screenplay by Carl Foreman.

CAST: *Will Kane* (Gary Cooper); *Jonas Henderson* (Thomas Mitchell); *Harvey Pell* (Lloyd Bridges); *Helen Ramirez* (Katy Jurado); *Amy Kane* (Grace Kelly); *Percy Mettrick* (Otto Kruger); *Martin Howe* (Lon Chaney); *William Fuller* (Henry Morgan); *Frank Miller* (Ian MacDonald); *Mildred Fuller* (Eve McVeagh); *Cooper* (Harry Shannon); *Jack Colby* (Lee Van Cleef); *James Pierce* (Bob Wilke); *Ben Miller* (Sheb Woolley); *Sam* (Tom London); *Station Master* (Ted Stanhope); *Gillis* (Larry Blake); *Barber* (William Phillips)

If *The Gunfighter* presented the public with an adult western before they were quite ready for it, *High Noon*'s timing was perfect. In terms of style, the film was a direct descendant of that earlier picture; the sombre, unromantic black-and-white photography, the drab, colorless workman's town, the physical action disappearing almost entirely in favor of a concentration on the psychological state of a believable figure, more human than hero. Gary Cooper's Oscar-winning performance undercut several decades of mythic stature, achieving for the western lawman what Gregory Peck had already accomplished for the lone outlaw.

The film begins as three desperadoes meet beneath the dead branches of an isolated tree, exchange wordless recog-

"You have big shoulders, Harvey, but you are not a man!"; Katy Jurado and Lloyd Bridges

The Lawman and the Pacifist: Gary Cooper and Grace Kelly

Ian MacDonald and Grace Kelly: An Attack on the American Community?

nition, then ride arrogantly into a small town—while the titles glide by and Tex Ritter warbles the western ballad, "Do not forsake me, oh my darlin' . . ." It is 10:30 on a quiet Sunday morning, and retiring marshal Will Kane (Cooper) is in the process of getting married to a young Quaker, Amy (Grace Kelly). But the wedding ceremony is shortened when the telegraph man runs in with a message that Frank Miller (Ian MacDonald), a killer Kane arrested some years before, has been released from jail and may be arriving on the noon train. As Miller's three former gang members make camp at the train station, Kane cancels his plans to leave town and begins making arrangements to face the man if and when he arrives. But in the ensuing ninety minutes his old friends encourage him to run, and turn their backs when he refuses. His pacifist wife walks out on him for breaking his promise never to take up a gun again, and Will Kane finds himself, at high noon, standing alone in the deserted streets.

High Noon was so unexpectedly popular that it created a whole new set of anti-romantic clichés, which were picked up and repeated in dozens of downbeat "adult" westerns. Cooper's character was a far cry from his own earlier western heroes in *The Virginian* and *The Plainsman*—just a simple, decent man trying to live by his ideals but not above breaking out in tears upon realizing that he will get no help from his friends—an action heretofore unheard of in the stereotype world of dime-novel cowboys. Even the time scheme was a shocker: the story takes place in exactly the same block of time it takes the picture to run its course, a concept rendered extremely difficult by the fact that al-

most every scene contains a clock somewhere in the background.

But the most striking thing in the film is the depiction of the typical American town, Hadleyville, which offers a clear mirror of the unpleasant way in which we had come to view ourselves in the new decade. Some people refuse to help out of cowardice, like the sly judge (Otto Kruger) who had just performed Kane's wedding service. Others like the deputy, Harvey Pell (Lloyd Bridges), have been harboring unspoken resentments for some time. Others feel betrayed by him, like his former Mexican lover (Katy Jurado). Ultimately, though, those who would risk their lives to help the man who so often risked his for them are discouraged from doing so by Kane's best friend (Thomas Mitchell), who convinces them that the Northern money interests will refuse to invest in Hadleyville if they hear the people are not above engaging in shoot-outs in the streets.

Kane is an American version of Dr. Stockmann, the hero of Henrik Ibsen's *An Enemy of the People*, a good man deserted by his community out of dark fear, petty ambition, and overwhelming greed. Hadleyville is not so much a depiction of America as it was in the Old West as one of America in the early fifties. Writer Carl Foreman was quickly blacklisted as a communist, perhaps for providing a final image that many people took as a rejection of American society: having survived the ordeal, Kane drops his badge in the dust, turns his back on the populace, and leaves. *High Noon* offered us our first complete vision of the hero as dropout from society. It was not to be the last.

Donald O'Connor, Debbie Reynolds, King Donovan, Gene Kelly, Jean Hagen, Millard Mitchell

Singin' in the Rain

Metro-Goldwyn-Mayer (1952)

Produced by Arthur Freed; directed by Gene Kelly and Stanley Donen; screenplay and story by Adolph Green and Betty Comden.

CAST: *Don Lockwood* (Gene Kelly); *Cosmo Brown* (Donald O'Connor); *Kathy Selden* (Debbie Reynolds); *Linda Lamont* (Jean Hagen); *R. F. Simpson* (Millard Mitchell); *Guest Artist* (Cyd Charisse); *Zelda Zanders* (Rita Moreno); *Roscoe Dexter* (Douglas Fowley); *Dora Bailey* (Madge Blake)

The immense success of *Sunset Boulevard*, especially its nostalgia for the sudden decline of the old Hollywood, helped shape one of the major movie preoccupations of the early fifties. For as film styles, stars and subjects began to change drastically, the manner in which the legendary "dream factory" products of the past had been made took on increasing interest. Most often this lead to classy, trashy soap operas like *The Barefoot Contessa* or moody melodramas such as *The Big Knife*. An entertaining exception was *Singin' in the Rain*, a colored fountain of music and movement.

Gene Kelly in one of the film's fabulous production numbers

Donald O'Connor, Gene Kelly and Debbie Reynolds

The picture begins at one of those glamorous Hollywood premieres, as the starstruck fans push forward eagerly for a quick glance at two of their idols. The big stars are Don Lockwood (Gene Kelly), a dashing if slightly conceited leading man of the silent screen, and Linda Lamont (Jean Hagen), a moronic, ego-oriented but highly popular blonde bombshell. Don and his old pal Cosmo Brown (Donald O'Connor) tolerate Linda but laugh at her endless efforts to land Don as a husband. But just as Don finds himself taken with a brash and bubbly newcomer, Kathy Selden (Debbie Reynolds), a new problem arises: talking pictures.

Their gruff but understanding producer, R. F. Simpson (Millard Mitchell) quickly makes them realize that if they are going to survive what he believes will be no mere momentary gimmick, they had better adjust fast. When Linda's voice proves to be an earsore, the trio save her career by dubbing in Kathy's—an act which eclipses the young talent but temporarily saves the obnoxious star. After a successful showing of the film, Linda proudly parades live onstage, forgetting that the creation was synthetic. Don encourages the audience into demanding a song from her; after she has made a fool of herself he introduces the exciting new talent, Kathy Selden.

ald O'Connor and Gene Kelly

Cyd Charisse displays her magnificent legs in a "specialty number" with Gene Kelly

The film's plot is often near-nonsensical. As with so many of the early musicals *Singin' in the Rain* lovingly satirizes, its makers threw in any idea they came up with; because of their professionalism, imagination, genuine wit and obvious sense of love for what they were doing, every last one worked. The film's title, and its title song, give a good indication as to the mood: it has absolutely nothing to do with the story.

It was no mere accident that this was an M-G-M movie. Every one of the great studios had its own special genre that it handled better than anyone else; with M-G-M, it was most certainly the musical. That studio turned out more of them than any other company, and while none were totally without charm, many were near-classic in stature. *Singin' in the Rain* was far from the last, but it was in many ways their pivotal musical: it contained the broadest spectrum of songs and most eclectic combination of choreographed styles within a single picture.

At the very moment when motion pictures were becoming less romanticized in their visions of life, Gene Kelly and Stanley Donen cast wistful eyes backward from their vantage point to gently kid Hollywood history in a manner that, just a few years earlier, would have been quite impossible. However, in a decade as involved in social concerns as the fifties, serious attention was paid only to musicals which had "something to say"—and this was quite obviously not one of them. Most of those pictures have dated badly, and some are unwatchable today. *Singin' in the Rain* has done more than merely survive. It has, over the years, gained a reputation as the most inventive movie musical of all time.

Lana Turner and Kirk Douglas

The Bad and the Beautiful

Metro-Goldwyn-Mayer (1952)

Produced by John Houseman; directed by Vincente Minnelli; screenplay by Charles Schnee, based on a story by George Bradshaw.

CAST: *Georgia* (Lana Turner); *Jonathan* (Kirk Douglas); *Harry Pebbel* (Walter Pidgeon); *James Lee* (Dick Powell); *Fred* (Barry Sullivan); *Rosemary* (Gloria Grahame); *"Gaucho"* (Gilbert Roland); *Henry Whitfield* (Leo G. Carroll); *Kay* (Vanessa Brown); *Syd* (Paul Stewart); *Gus* (Sammy White); *Lila* (Elaine Stewart); *Von Ellstein* (Ivan Triesault)

There have always been movies about the making of movies. But even the best of them, including the original *A Star Is Born* (1937), proved unsatisfying. Though they catalogued the elements of the moviemaking process and provided interesting melodrama, something intangible was missing. Such films did not come entirely into their own until the advent of the fifties. This was, from the onset, the "psychologizing" decade: although Freud had written his works years before, it was not until the unstable era when we all lived under the mushroom shadow of instant obliv-

Lana Turner and Kirk Douglas

Dick Powell, Barry Sullivan and Lana Turner

James Lee (Dick Powell), a dedicated Scott Fitzgerald-ish writer whose neurotically oversexed southern belle wife (Gloria Grahame) is parlayed into an affair with the stupid but seductive actor "Gaucho" (Gilbert Roland) so that her husband will be left alone to work on his scripts; Fred (Barry Sullivan), a trusted friend and talented director tricked by Jonathan into compromising himself; and Harry Pebbel (Walter Pidgeon), the sage old studio head who watches over all and dutifully comments on everything he sees.

Jonathan is the first great example of a fifties prototype: the heel as hero. Kirk Douglas virtually carved out a career for himself by portraying just such figures—superficially attractive but rotten to the core: his Jonathan looks like a lumberjack, acts like an emotional storm trooper, and talks like Noel Coward. The film even provided him with the kind of pat, predictable motivation for his ruthlessness that would become imitated in countless fifties films, in which the neurotic became firmly established as the American anti-hero: Jonathan is mean and callous because his father, a great movie pioneer, died penniless and forgotten.

The film is impressive because, technically speaking, it is consummately well crafted in all respects; it is trash because, while pretending to be an uncompromising attack on Hollywood's corruption, it actually allows audiences to wallow in that corruption. It pretends to provide us with an insider's view of the modern Babylon: included is every Hollywood "type," from available starlets to sleazy agents to "Yes!"—men to gossip columnists. It whisks us from the top to the bottom of the Hollywood world, from cheap rooming houses a few blocks off Sunset Boulevard to magnificent mansions in Beverly Hills. It contains endless movie jargon about "clearing the set" and "shooting on location." But *The Bad and the Beautiful* is as simplistic and garish as its title; and what it actually offers is an amalgam of fact and fantasy in which bits of truth and incredible distortions are inseparably welded into an elaborate cinematic artifice.

The Hollywood-on-Hollywood films grew directly out of the transitional trauma state of the fifties. And though they did not disappear at decade's end (there were *Harlow, The Carpetbaggers,* and *The Oscar* in the mid-sixties), subsequent attempts at the genre were just as grotesque but not nearly as much fun. Houseman, Minnelli and Douglas got together in 1962 to do it all over again by filming *Two Weeks in Another Town* but while the resultant picture proved just as trashy as the first, it lacked the perverse charm. Ironically, though, in that later picture a number of filmmakers study clips from one of the great old films —and the picture they view is *The Bad and the Beautiful.*

ion that society embraced his tenets. And such psychologizing at once proved the missing ingredient in films about film. The vacuum filled, they flourished In keeping with the sudden craze for intimate behind-the-scenes glimpses of the disappearing "old Hollywood" (which had already provided us with two great films, *Sunset Boulevard* and *Singin' in the Rain*) veteran producer John Houseman assembled a striking entourage—ranging from the gifted director Vincente Minnelli to an all-star cast—for what became the first of a series of "trash masterpieces" about life in the movie capital.

The plot centers around the "bad" Jonathan (Kirk Douglas), a powerful film producer and charmingly ruthless fellow. We witness his casual supervision of a vast movie lot and the various people (all bearing titillating resemblances to real-life personalities) whose lives he manipulates. There is the "beautiful" Georgia (Lana Turner), an alcoholic extra whom, to satisfy a capricious whim, he seduces, builds into a superstar, and then casually destroys;

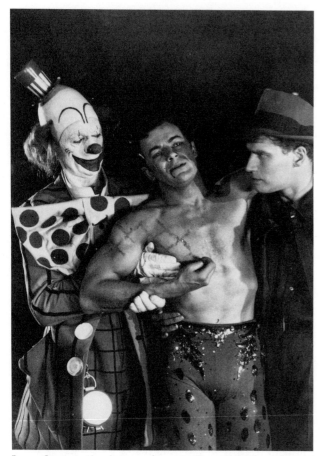

James Stewart (in clown make-up), Cornel Wilde and Charlton Heston

Gloria Grahame

Betty, Hutton, Charlton Heston, Cornel Wilde

The Greatest Show on Earth

Paramount (1952)

Produced and directed by Cecil B. De Mille; screenplay by Fredric M. Frank, Barre Lyndon and Theodore St. John, from a story by Frank Cavett and Messrs. Frank and St. John.

CAST: *Holly* (Betty Hutton); *Sebastian* (Cornel Wilde); *Brad* (Charlton Heston); *Phyllis* (Dorothy Lamour); *Angel* (Gloria Grahame); *"Buttons," a Clown* (James Stewart); *Detective* (Henry Wilcoxon); *Klaus* (Lyle Bettger); *Henderson* (Lawrence Tierney); *Emmett Kelly* (Himself); *Cucciola* (Himself); *Antoinette Concello* (Herself); *John Ringling North* (Himself); *Harry* (John Kellogg); *Assistant Manager* (John Ridgely); *Circus Doctor* (Frank Wilcox); *Ringmaster* (Bob Carson); *Buttons' Mother* (Lillian Albertson); *Birdie* (Julie Faye)

To no one's surprise Cecil B. De Mille's *The Greatest Show on Earth* won the Best Picture of the Year Oscar. Considering some of the important and innovative films released, the Academy's decision appears, at least in retrospect, questionable. Yet the movie's merits—the quality of the filmmaking as well as its value as a pop-culture testament—legitimately demand close attention. The matching of De Mille's unique style—skillfully crafted epics with a wide spectrum of entertainment, perfectly calculated to engage the entire American family—found itself precisely suited to the circus in general and the Ringling Brothers and Barnum & Bailey in particular. Form and content have rarely been so perfectly in tune, as one American institution commented on another.

The story-line was a grand-scale soap opera. Brad (Charlton Heston), a tough but fair big-top boss, herds his

Cornel Wilde, Betty Hutton

"mixed shows" across country on a picturesque circus train, trying to solve the personal problems of his various colorful stars. Holly (Betty Hutton), a beautiful "flyer" who loves the boss, must learn to understand that his primary commitment is to keep the show rolling. Sebastian (Cornel Wilde), an arrogant, egotistical aerialist is out for a big fall. Klaus (Lyle Bettger), the elephant trainer, hopelessly loves the beautiful but manipulative Angel (Gloria Grahame) and is treated with great insensitivity by her. Buttons (James Stewart), the clown, employs his makeup and putty nose to hide his real identity from a suspicious police detective (Henry Wilcoxon).

By the final curtain all the plot ends are, in classic De Mille style, sufficiently resolved. The good are generally rewarded, the bad punished. But not before each performer runs through his act, the entire train undergoes a spectacular wreck, and moments of considerable passion are sparked between competing personalities.

Like *All About Eve, The Bad and the Beautiful*, and numerous other films of the era, this De Mille extravaganza catered to twin desires that filmmakers at once sensed were particularly strong with fifties audiences. Viewers wanted "the real thing" rather than a studio fabrication of it, as well as an insider's view, a behind-the-scenes glimpse into the worlds of show business—movies, the theatre, even the circus. To achieve those ends, De Mille deserted his back lot at the Paramount studios (where, in *Sunset Boulevard*, he had been depicted working) in favor of taking his camera crew on location and capturing the essential atmosphere of sawdust and tinsel. At the same time, he peopled the story with real-life circus personalities doing cameo roles as themselves, from the country's greatest clown, Emmett Kelly, to the world's most highly-respected circus manager, John Ringling North.

Previously, De Mille had created fantasy epics out of great periods of the past—the Bible, American history—but the glorious escapism of the circus world provided him with material for a modern epic as entertaining as any of his earlier pictures yet strikingly more realistic than any of them. The opening sequence in which the circus folk make a mass exodus from their winter quarters in Florida, journey for miles by train, and then finally set up the tents for a show would appear almost a documentary study of circus life were it not for the inclusion of Charlton Heston and the other stars.

The Greatest Show on Earth stands as the prime example of the immense full-color, all-star spectaculars moviemakers would necessarily mount to lure their patrons away from the now substantial threat of television.

Though *This Is Cinerama* treated viewers to many sights and scenes, the one they remembered was the Coney Island roller coaster ride.

This Is Cinerama

Cinerama (1952)

Developed by Fred Waller; stereophonic sound concept by Hazard Reeves; produced by Merian C. Cooper and Robert L. Bendick; narrated by Lowell Thomas.

As the popularity of television blossomed, the motion picture industry's need to offer audiences something the new medium couldn't, quickly became a necessity. For a number of years, Fred Waller had been developing a projection system with a more natural viewing range than ordinary films, and as pressures grew within the industry to find a means of preventing moton pictures from being overshadowed, Waller's Cinerama seemed less and less an oddball project, more and more a possible salvation. Assisted by veteran producer Merian C. Cooper (no stranger to bigness, he'd been responsible for *King Kong* twenty years earlier) and Robert

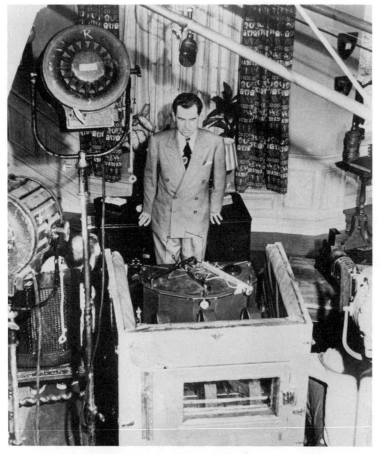

Lowell Thomas explains the Cinerama process in the film's opening sequence.

major breakthrough, allowing for the peripheral vision experiences we encounter in everyday life. The sound system developed to accompany Cinerama was stereophonic in nature, creating the illusion that voices and music originated from different positions on the screen.

The film began with an introduction (in a normal, single projector image) by Lowell Thomas, chairman of Cinerama's board of directors, explaining the history and development of man's desire to communicate in such a way that sounded as if everything done since cave paintings were part of some master plan leading directly to Cinerama! Then, Thomas disappeared as the entire, enormous tri-panel image filled the screen. The first sequence was the one everybody remembers best: a breathtaking roller coaster ride, shot entirely from the point of view of a front seat rider, which became famous for making many in the audience as nauseous as if they had actually taken the ride.

Following sequences all presented on-screen experiences that would have been impossible to record in totality with ordinary motion picture cameras: a ballet from the La Scala Theatre in Milan, all of Niagara Falls filmed from an aerial view, Handel's *Messiah* as performed by a robed choir of young people, a gondola ride in Venice's Grand Canal, a bagpipe parade at a castle in the Scottish Highlands, a garden performance by the Vienna Boys' Choir, a full-scale bullfight in a Madrid arena, Act II of the opera *Aida*, a water sports festival in Florida's Cypress Gardens, and finally a stirring aerial journey over various sections of America—from the Great Plains to New York City.

In its combination of pop and classical culture, with equal weight given to each, Cinerama was largely regarded as a kitsch art creation. An even more serious problem was that Cinerama did not readily lend itself to telling a story, and later attempts to use it in such a manner were less than successful. Because of the awesome possibilities for panoramic effects, sequences that made use of that potential had to be fitted, or rather forced, in continuously.

No subsequent Cinerama project ever equalled the original in its ability to interest the public, and movies had to look elsewhere for some source of bigness that would impress viewers but still support a narrative.

L. Bendick, he perfected his technique and assisted in making the film that, more than any other, came to represent the desire for hugeness in motion picture entertainment that dominated the decade.

The Cinerama system utilized a screen greater in size than any previously employed, stretching in a wide angle arc of 146 degrees across the width of the theatre. Three motion picture projectors simultaneously shot forth separate "panels" of the image which, together on screen, made up the total panoramic view. Though film purists were quick to argue that this wreaked havoc on the film artist's necessity to organize a limited space artistically, realists hailed it as a

Burt Lancaster and Nick Cravat, former acrobatic partners in a circus, used their years of training in the film's many action sequences

The Crimson Pirate

Warner Bros. (1952)

A Norma Production, produced by Harold Hecht; directed by Robert Siodmak; written by Roland Kibbee.

CAST: *Vallo* (Burt Lancaster); *Ojo* (Nick Cravat); *Consuelo* (Eva Bartok); *Humble Bellows* (Torin Thatcher); *Professor Prudence* (James Hayter); *Baron Gruda* (Leslie Bradley); *Bianca* (Margot Grahame); *Pablo Murphy* (Noel Purcell); *El Libre* (Frederick Leicester); *Governor* (Eliot Makeham); *Colonel* (Frank Pettingill); *La Signorita* (Dana Wynter); *Attaché* (Christopher Lee)

There was never any question that Burt Lancaster was born to stardom: he enjoyed that rare privilege by playing the leading role in his very first film, *The Killers* (1946). The problem was that while producers were thoroughly aware of his potential, they weren't quite sure what sort of stardom he was meant for. Attempts to turn him into a younger variation of the tight-lipped Bogart hero in *Rope of Sand* fared no better than a stab at casting him as one of the new, postwar neurotic heroes in *Kiss the Blood Off My Hands*. Almost in desperation, Warner Brothers dumped him into a

daughter Consuelo (Eva Bartok) and through her influence, becomes a dedicated follower of their humane cause.

Though the film is designed purely as entertainment, it does contain one character who foreshadowed a most important type in films of the fifties. Professor Prudence (James Hayter) is an early screen incarnation of the well-intentioned but frightfully dangerous man of science, whose efforts to aid his friends by perfecting a superweapon almost annihilates them on several occasions. Prudence devises a bomb of previously unknown power, with which they can blow up their enemy's otherwise unconquerable fort—and which leaves a residue that looks suspiciously like a mushroom cloud. One of the film's running dark-humor gags is the possibility that he will slip and destroy his friends.

Lancaster gave his lines the consciously unemotional readings that would become his chief trademark as a screen personality. But whenever his monotone stopped and he began to move, the picture went right along with him in a flourish of razzle-dazzle color that reminded many of the golden days of Doug Fairbanks, Sr. Rather than align himself permanently with Warner Brothers and become a regular member of their stock company, Lancaster chose a startlingly new route. He began the association of Hecht-Hill-Lancaster, and with it the totally original conception of the star as a corporation unto himself, surrounded by a pair of writer–producers dedicated to helping him pick and choose the right vehicles while molding his popular image into a marketable commodity. Kirk Douglas quickly followed suit and formed Brynaprod; after that it was the rule rather than the exception. This was a move from which the major studios never fully recovered, as actors became creative forces rather than colorful birds in the gilded cages of a carefully controlled star system. At the same time, though, it heralded an end to the old glamour: one could hardly imagine a Clark Gable or a John Garfield presiding over corporate meetings in which he himself was the exploitable object of discussion. As the stars began turning into executives, they simultaneously ceased being our gods and goddesses.

second-rate costume epic, *The Flame and the Arrow,* only to discover that Lancaster's toothy grin gave an unexpectedly enjoyable tongue-in-cheek quality to the otherwise routine film. The studio immediately planned a more elaborate adventure yarn, tailored for Lancaster's talents and making full use of his background as a circus performer. The result was *The Crimson Pirate* which, while hardly one of the decade's most distinguished films, was surely one of its most entertaining.

Vallo (Lancaster) is the captain of a scurvy crew of buccaneers, among whom he can trust only his silent sidekick Ojo (Nick Cravat, Lancaster's acrobatic partner in his pre-Hollywood big-top days). A merchant ship they overtake and capture carries an emissary to the king of France, with word of a plot to overthrow a revolution on a Caribbean Island. Planning to play each side against the other, the pirates set sail to contact the revolutionary leader El Libre (Frederick Leicester). But their plot becomes a shambles when Vallo falls madly in love with the man's lovely young

Marlon Brando and Mary Murphy

The Wild One
Columbia (1953)

A Stanley Kramer Production; directed by Laslo Benedek; screenplay by John Paxton, based on a story by Frank Rooney.

CAST: *Johnny* (Marlon Brando); *Kathie* (Mary Murphy); *Harry Bleeker* (Robert Keith); *Chino* (Lee Marvin); *Sheriff Singer* (Jay C. Flippen); *Mildred* (Peggy Maley); *Charlie Thomas* (Hugh Sanders); *Frank Bleeker* (Ray Teal); *Bill Hannegan* (John Brown); *Art Kleiner* (Will Wright); *Ben* (Robert Osterloh); *Wilson* (Robert Bice); *Jimmy* (William Vedder); *Britches* (Yvonne Doughty)

In the late summer of 1947, a wandering motorcycle gang descended on the quiet town of Hollister, California. At first they were satisfied to drink beer and perpetrate small acts of vandalism. But before they finally left, the town had been ransacked and serious acts of violence had broken out. When the story broke the national newspapers, screenwriter John Paxton seized on it as an idea for a socially commentative motion picture that would raise the question of why nomadic, alienated youth cults had popped up with such frequency in the few years following the war's end. He presented a script to the single producer who made a point of seeking out projects that were controversial and contemporary, Stanley Kramer. When *The Wild One* became the film's working title, there was clearly only one choice for the role of Johnny—the rebellious, drifting leader of the cyclists—and that was the new decade's most exciting dramatic find, Marlon Brando.

The film opens with a long shot of an empty road. Gradually, the tiny figures of cyclists appear far in the distance. The camera holds the shot until they come roaring up to it, decked out in black leather jackets and tearing across the road in a frightfully tight-knit squadron. Johnny's voice-over narration casually confides to us that this is a story he won't soon forget: we then follow his gang into a legitimate motorcycle competition, where they are quickly thrown out but manage to steal the first-prize trophy on their way. The gang then roars into the sleepy little town of Wrightsville, where they stop to rest and soon begin causing havoc. The town policeman (Robert Keith) is ineffective at stopping the escalating destruction, though Johnny decides to keep things in control after he realizes the man is the father of Kathie (Mary Murphy), a young café waitress he is drawn to. But all hell breaks loose when another gang, led by Johnny's rival Chino (Lee Marvin), arrives on the scene, looking for a rumble.

The Wild One was intended as a study of a new phenomenon, but unwittingly created a romantic aura around it. There was an undeniable mystique to the black leather jackets, the jive talk, and the swaggering arrogance of these alienated troublemakers. The picture was at once criticized for adding to the brand-new problem by glorifying its leaders. In fact, the film does not set out to attack or defend the hoodlum–hipsters but only to depict their lifestyle—as juxtaposed against the depressing daily routine of the small-town residents. At one point the clean-cut Kathie, having thus far resisted Johnny's advances, allows him (under the spell of the moonlight) to lift her up behind him on his huge bike. As they roar out of town together, she clasps her arms around his chest while her hair blows wildly, and we see that he has saved her from the ennui of her existence.

In the film's most telling exchange of dialogue, Johnny is asked as he and his boys guzzle beer at a roadside tavern, "What are you rebelling against?" With a superbly nonchalant shrug of the shoulders, he replies, "What've you

Marlon Brando and Yvonne Doughty

got?" By delivering that phrase, Brando unwittingly became the spokesman for what would, in time, come to be called the "Beat Generation": beaten before they even had a chance to get started, by the ever-present insane possibility of a push-button war that could wipe all life off the face of the planet in a matter of minutes.

Brando himself was less than happy about his own identification with the character of Johnny. He had accepted it as just another role and complained when people assumed he was inseparable from the motorcycle punk he had played. He was doomed to play the sensitive, inarticulate hero of his age, but would do so with considerably more dignity and subtlety in subsequent films.

The Big Heat

Columbia (1953)

Produced by Robert Arthur; directed by Fritz Lang; screenplay by Sydney Boehm, based on a story by William P. McGivern.

CAST: *Dave Bannion* (Glenn Ford); *Debby Marsh* (Gloria Grahame); *Katie Bannion* (Jocelyn Brando); *Mike Lagana* (Alexander Scourby); *Vince Stone* (Lee Marvin); *Bertha Duncan* (Jeanette Nolan); *Tierney* (Peter Whitney); *Lieutenant Wilkes* (Willis Bouchey); *Gus Burke* (Robert Burton); *Larry Gordon* (Adam Williams); *Commissioner Higgins* (Howard Wendell); *George Rose* (Cris Alcaide); *Hugo* (Michael Granger); *Lucy Chapman* (Dorothy Green); *Doris* (Carolyn Jones)

In May of 1950, a special Committee to Investigate Organized Crime, headed by Tennessee's Senator Estes Kefauver, initiated its probes of grand-scale criminal infiltration into America's business and political worlds. The crusaders swept through six major cities, beginning in Miami and ending in New York; their open hearings were televised, and as interest in their work grew the viewing audience spiralled from a few hundred thousand loyal fans at the onset to over twenty million by the time the investigation reached its climax and brought Frank Costello to the stand. Angered gangsters and nervous politicians were questioned, and the impact of the event was unfathomable: television emerged as a medium with potential beyond anyone's wildest imagination.

The moment of climax: Glenn Ford, Lee Marvin, Alexander Scourby

Gloria Grahame and Glenn Ford

Beauty and The Beast, circa 1953: Lee Marvin and Gloria Grahame

Gloria Grahame and Lee Marvin

As a result, Americans grew more conscious of organized crime than they had been since the early thirties, when newspaper accounts of figures like Al Capone inspired such films as *Scarface, Little Caesar* and *The Public Enemy*. No sooner did the Kefauver Committee hit the airwaves than "the crime film" enjoyed a renaissance. Typical examples were *Hoodlum Empire*, with Brian Donlevy as a United States senator heading up a crime investigation and *Captive City*, in which John Forsythe portrayed a crusading newspaper editor uncovering layer upon layer of corruption behind the façade of his seemingly pleasant small town. But the best of them all was *The Big Heat*, directed by the great German filmmaker Fritz Lang. As early as 1932, he had demonstrated a striking talent for dealing with evil and perversity in *M* with Peter Lorre. Following the rise of Hitler, Lang migrated to Hollywood, where his talents at dealing with the dark side of life were put to good use in offbeat thrillers.

The Big Heat opens with the announced suicide of a policeman named Duncan. Fellow detective Dave Bannion (Glenn Ford) cannot understand why such a highly respected and well-liked man would take his own life, and why everyone else on the force is so quick to close the books on the incident. He decides to do some digging on his own, and uncovers a number of irregularities. However, when he tells his superiors, they dissuade him from taking his search further. Angered, he continues; a few mornings later his wife Katie (Jocelyn Brando) goes outside to start

his car and is killed in an explosion—obviously meant for Bannion.

Rather than be intimidated by her death, Bannion is all the more committed to learning the truth. And when evidence turns up that causes him to publicly announce his contention that Duncan was murdered, he is stripped of his plainclothesman's badge. Angry and embittered, he continues—learning that Duncan was mixed up in a terrible conspiracy that encompassed important politicians, high-ranking members of the police department, and the most powerful of underworld elements in the country. Mob boss Mike Lagana (Alexander Scourby) sends his toughest hoods after Bannion, but the steadfast loner continues to fight—and eventually discloses the conspiracy to the public.

Under less able hands, *The Big Heat* might have been a routine crime melodrama. But Lang made the film a classic of its kind through his strikingly unique style, so well suited to the night-world he took as his subject, and an ability to let us share the hero's gradual realization that, under the surface of respectable American life, unfathomable corruption could lurk. In the film's most flagrantly frightening moment, killer Lee Marvin expresses a temper tantrum by flinging a pot of scalding coffee into the face of his beautiful mistress (Gloria Grahame). It was one of the most graphic acts of violence viewers had ever experienced and one that became a vivid movie memory for all who saw it.

A growing awareness of love: Marcellus Gallio (Richard Burton) embraces Diana (Jean Simmons)

The Robe

20th Century-Fox (1953)

Produced by Frank Ross; directed by Henry Koster in the CinemaScope process; screenplay by Philip Dunne, adapted by Gina Kaus, from the novel by Lloyd C. Douglas.

CAST: *Marcellus Gallio* (Richard Burton); *Diana* (Jean Simmons); *Demetrius* (Victor Mature); *Peter* (Michael Rennie); *Caligula* (Jay Robinson); *Justus* (Dean Jagger); *Senator Gallio* (Torin Thatcher); *Pilate* (Richard Boone); *Miriam* (Betta St. John); *Paulos* (Jeff Morrow); *Emperor Tiberius* (Ernest Thesiger); *Junia* (Dawn Addams); *Abidor* (Leon Askin); *Rebecca* (Helen Beverley); *Quintus* (Frank Pulaski)

Less than a full year after the gigantic tour de force of *This Is Cinerama*, Twentieth Century-Fox introduced its own answer to the challenge of television: CinemaScope. Like Cinerama, it offered a wider, more natural image than the traditional one, projected on a 68 x 24 foot screen. However, in CinemaScope the effect was achieved with a single projector, so that none of the annoying panel divisions so often in evidence in Cinerama were present. And while the projected image was considerably more panoramic than in ordinary films, it was not oppressively so. Thus, CinemaScope was able to extend the range of vision yet still function in the telling of a story—though it certainly helped,

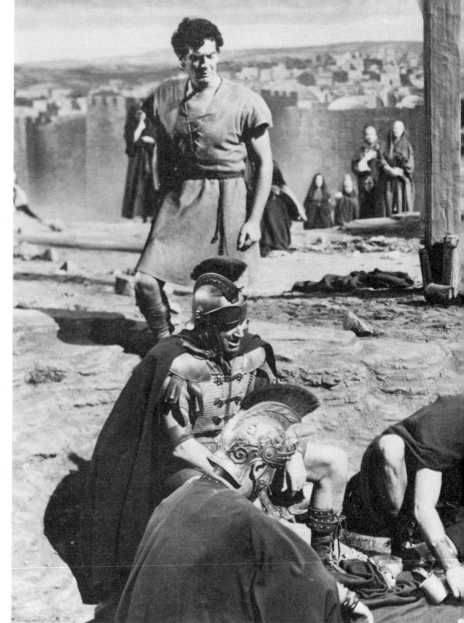

A growing awareness of religion: Demetrius (Victor Mature) confronts Peter (Michael Rennie)

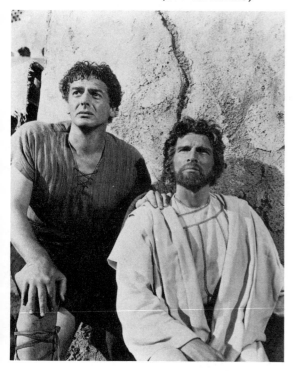

Caligula (Jay Robinson) menaces Diana (Jean Simmons)

The Crucifixion: Victor Mature (standing) watches Richard Burton (seated) gamble with the guards

due to the extreme magnitude, if the story happened to be epic in nature.

The Robe was the first contact audiences had with this new technique, and it did prove enough of a stimulant to lure them away from their television sets. Though it covered a section of history already familiar from four decades of Cecil B. De Mille epics—the thrills and tortures of ancient Rome—the wide screen made everything appear new, different, and thus worth seeing again. The story itself was strictly conventional, a combination of religious morality play and grand-scale costume drama, with a few action sequences thrown in to keep the kids awake. Marcellus Gallio (Richard Burton) is the young, self-assured Roman officer placed in charge of the crucifixion of Christ. His Greek slave, Demetrius (Victor Mature) rescues Jesus' robe afterwards and carries it with him, ultimately converting to Christianity under the influence of The Big Fisherman, Simon Called Peter (Michael Rennie). In the meantime his earthier master falls in love with Diana (Jean Simmons) and eventually the two young lovers choose execution as Christians at the hands of the mad Caligula (Jay Robinson) over life as decadent Romans.

Though the film was immensely successful at the box office (and even inspired a sequel, *Demetrius and the Gladiators*) it achieved only limited artistic success in making use of CinemaScope as an integral part of the storytelling process. Since much of the film's intended force depended more on the inner torment of the characters than the outer displays of action, the vastness of the image was often not fully utilized and, indeed, was almost alien to the central conflicts of ideas and ideals. But Richard Burton did impress American audiences with his sullen, brooding style, and CinemaScope clearly demonstrated its potential as a continuing element of the moviemaking medium, rather than a virtual one-shot like Cinerama.

The effect of depth-perception added to the effect of such scenes as the great fire that destroys Jarrod's wax works. (Vincent Price)

House of Wax

Warner Bros. (1953)

Produced by Bryan Foy in Natural Vision; directed by André de Toth; screenplay by Crane Wilbur, based on a story by Charles Belden.

CAST: *Professor Henry Jarrod* (Vincent Price); *Lieutenant Tom Brennan* (Frank Lovejoy); *Sue Allen* (Phyllis Kirk); *Cathy Gray* (Carolyn Jones); *Scott Andrews* (Paul Picerni); *Matthew Burke* (Roy Roberts); *Mrs. Andrews* (Angela Clarke); *Sidney Wallace* (Paul Cavanagh); *Sergeant Jim Shane* (Dabbs Greer); *Igor* (Charles Buchinsky); *Barker* (Reggie Rymal); *Bruce Allison* (Philip Tonge)

Bwana Devil was the first 3-D film to reach the public. It was a low quality, routine potboiler—a ridiculous mélange of action, romance and melodrama set in modern Africa. But it played to packed houses ready for the biggest thrill since Cinerama: donning cardboard eyeglasses, viewers were treated to images with a stereoscope effect that imitated the depth–perception of natural sight. Not to be outdone by the Cinerama feature, *Bwana Devil* was also preceded by a short documentary explaining the process, and allowing parents the luxury of believing that the sensual excicetement of seeing "lions leap into your lap" contained some "educational" value for their children.

There was a momentary rage for 3-D films. But since they were hurriedly turned out to cash in on the boom, most were of poor quality. Then Warner Brothers released the first major feature shot in the process—*House of Wax*. In addition, the company prresented an aural equivalent to the heightened visuals in what they called "directed sound," or having different voices and noises originate from various areas of the theatre. According to the promotional material circulated by Warner Brothers, the combination of the two processes was going to revolutionize the movie industry.

The story, however, was extremely conventional, and, in fact, proved to be a rehash of their old horror film from the thirties called *Mystery of the Wax Museum*. In the new version, set in Paris during *la belle époque*, Professor Henry Jarrod (Vincent Price) is trapped in a fire that destroys his wax museum, following an argument with his crooked partner, Matthew Burke (Roy Roberts). Shortly thereafter Jarrod is busily running a new waxworks, apparently unharmed by the blaze. But when a series of strange murders hits the city, police detective Tom Brennan (Frank Lovejoy) begins to suspect something sinister. Eventually he discovers that Jarrod is now deranged, and instead of creating wax figures he achieves his lifelike displays by covering over the dead bodies of his victims, including his former partner and also innocent girls of the night like young Cathy Gray (Carolyn Jones). Pretty Sue Allen (Phyllis Kirk) spies a mannequin that looks strangely similar to a girlfriend who had disappeared, but when Jarrod tries to inflict a similar fate on her, Brennan rushes in at the last moment, and Jarrod tumbles to his death in his own vat of boiling wax.

Endless action sequences assaulting the viewer with the process had to be included to make the uncomfortable glasses (which were at first fun but soon became a nuisance) bearable. When boiling wax was poured out at the viewer in the film's climax, 3-D added to the thrills. More often, though, its inclusion seemed forced, as when for no reason whatever a man paddled a ball on the end of a string out at the audience.

Despite all the hoopla, the special effects turned out to be a one-shot. "Directed sound" was merely a distraction and disappeared at once, while the 3-D process itself followed shortly thereafter. Like Cinerama, it proved to be an elaborate gimmick rather than an effective technique. Such major productions as Alfred Hitchcock's *Dial M for Murder* and *Hondo*, a John Wayne western, were filmed in 3-D but released in "flat" versions instead.The feeling within the industry was that 3-D had died of overexposure, and its use would hinder rather than help the box-office potential of such pictures.

The camera-work of *The Little Fugitive* reflected the style of Italian Neorealism, currently the rage at the "art houses"

Joey (Richie Andrusco) turns in pop bottles and lives off the deposit money

Under the boardwalk, down by the sea: the makers of *The Little Fugitive* looked at a slice of American life from the alienated child's point of view

Little Fugitive

Joseph Burstyn, Inc. (1953)

Produced, directed and written by Ray Ashley, Morris Engel and Ruth Orkin.

CAST: *Joey* (Richie Andrusco); *Lennie* (Rickie Brewster); *The Mother* (Winnifred Cushing); *Pony Ride Man* (Jay Williams); *Photographer* (Will Lee); *Harry* (Charlie Moss); *Charlie* (Tommy De Canio)

Little Fugitive was seen by very few people, yet it proved to be a breakthrough film. Coming early in the decade, it seriously influenced people's thinking about the possibilities of independent moviemaking. Throughout the thirties and forties the American movie was virtually synonymous with the Hollywood movie. Then a small but growing number of filmgoers, mostly in New York and California but also at

Joey's brother, realizing the "joke" has gone sour, tries to contact him

Clutching his beloved harmonica, Richard Andrusco falls asleep beneath the boardwalk

university film societies across the country, discovered "underground films." In such shoestring budget features, offbeat talents dealt with unique subjects in a frank manner that was impossible within the studio system. Usually such experiments were only a few minutes in length, and the general absence of slickness made them unfit for the mass market. But it was in the fifties that such avant-garde moviemakers first began to wonder if the American public might be ready to accept something different.

Three former journalists and still photographers—Ray Ashley, Morris Engel and Ruth Orkin—pooled their talents and limited funds in order to create a full-length feature that would show a slice of life Hollywood had heretofore been unwilling (or unable) to acknowledge. Deciding to remain independent at all costs, in order to avoid being corrupted into including obligatory box-office attractions like a romantic sub-plot, they turned out an outstanding little gem that was the American equivalent of the Italian neorealist films just then showing up in the art houses, with their shot-in-the-street styles and "real" people instead of glamorous stars.

The story is simple and uncluttered, depicting life in a Brooklyn tenement as seen through the eyes of a seven-year-old boy named Joey (Richie Andrusco). The lower-middle-class lad loves the old Hopalong Cassidy and Gene Autry pictures on TV and wants to play cowboys all day long. His older brother Lennie (Rickie Brewster) runs with a gang of ten year olds, but is saddled with the job of baby-sitting. In the extreme heat of a July morning, he decides to pull a trick on Joey and free himself for the afternoon: pretending to play with the child, Lennie's gang convinces Joey that he's somehow killed his own brother by shooting him with a cap gun. At first Joey is skeptical, but when Lennie doesn't get up, he flees in terror.

Joey runs off to Coney Island, where he wanders glumly for a while. But the amusement park offers distractions for the guilt-stricken child, and soon he's spending his money on the merry-go-round and games of skill. When he runs out of cash, Joey devises a system of survival; establishing himself in a little nest under the boardwalk, he searches for discarded pop bottles to pay for hot dogs and rides on the "real live" pony. He is careful, though, to avoid policemen at all costs. Gradually, the pony ride man (Jay Williams) grows suspicious, while Joey's mother (Winnifred Cushing) is away and unaware of the situation. The child is finally restored to his family, but only after he braves out a sudden rainstorm—alone and afraid.

The essential integrity was evident in every element of the film: the unpretentiously slight story, the stark locations, the unromanticized people and the gritty photography. Yet it was clearest of all in the choice of Richie Andrusco for the lead—a totally believable incarnation of a big-city child, instead of Hollywood's misconception of one. *Little Fugitive* charmed those audiences it did reach into an understanding that there could be an American alternative to Hollywood, while inspiring other would-be filmmakers who rejected the notion of working within the existing limitations of the commercial movie business.

Montgomery Clift as Robert E. Lee Prewitt: a man who should have played taps at Arlington

From Here to Eternity

Columbia (1953)

Produced by Buddy Adler; directed by Fred Zinnemann; screenplay by Daniel Taradash, based on the novel by James Jones.

CAST: *Sergeant Milton A. Warden* (Burt Lancaster); *Private Robert E. Lee Prewitt* (Montgomery Clift); *Karen Holmes* (Deborah Kerr); *Angelo Maggio* (Frank Sinatra); *Alma (Lorene)* (Donna Reed); *Captain Dana Holmes* (Philip Ober); *Sergeant Leva* (Mickey Shaughnessy); *Mazzioli* (Harry Bellaver); *Sergeant "Fatso" Judson* (Ernest Borgnine); *Sergeant Maylon Stark* (George Reeves); *Sergeant Ike Galovitch* (John Dennis); *Sergeant Pete Karelsen* (Tim Ryan); *Mrs. Kipfer* (Barbara Morrison); *Georgette* (Kristine Miller); *Annette* (Jean Willes); *Sal Anderson* (Merle Travis); *Treadwell* (Arthur Keegan); *Sergeant Baldy Thom* (Claude Akins); *Sergeant Turp Thornhill* (Robert Karnes)

Adapting James Jones' best-selling novel to the screen sounded like a literally impossible task, at least without diluting its power. The book was nearly a thousand pages in length, contained some of the most obscene language and graphic descriptions of sexual activity to yet appear in American fiction, and launched a direct attack on the bureaucracy of our military system. But even though numerous sub-plots were eliminated, all the four-letter words dropped, and the prostitutes changed into hostesses of a friendly "conversation club," *From Here to Eternity* survived all the necessary compromises, emerging to almost everyone's surprise as a film classic.

The story line was soap opera raised to the level of grand tragedy by the social import of the characters and the symbolic significance of their fates. In the days immediately preceding the Japanese sneak attack, Private Robert E. Lee Prewitt (Montgomery Clift) is transferred into the Pearl

Ernest Borgnine, Burt Lancaster, and
Frank Sinatra

"I never knew it could be like this!"; Burt Lancaster and Deborah Kerr in the illicit beach scene which shocked many, thrilled just as many others

Harbor-based company of Captain Dana Holmes (Philip Ober), an insecure commanding officer desperately in need of asserting his masculinity by having his team win the upcoming army boxing matches. Learning that Prewitt is both an excellent bugler and a prize-winning lightweight, he offers the young soldier the position of company bugler if he'll fight on the team. Though he yearns for the position, Prewitt refuses; he once blinded a friend in the ring, and will not go against his personal promise never to box again. Holmes orders his flunkies to administer "the treatment," a brutalizing process intended to break the man; Prewitt is befriended only by Alma (Donna Reed), a B-girl who loves him but does not want to marry a common serviceman; Angelo Maggio (Frank Sinatra) a wisecracking young Italian buck-private; and Milton A. Warden (Burt Lancaster), the tough but fair-minded top sergeant who is in love with his commanding officer's wife, Karen (Deborah Kerr).

The film is actually two separate stories, connected by circumstances and coincidence: Montgomery Clift gave his consummate performance as the peculiar hero he embodied —sensitive, lonely, unyielding; Burt Lancaster complemented him as the company man, the fellow who keeps things running. Both emerged as moral men in an amoral world, expressing their integrity in different ways: one in rebellion against society and the system, the other by attempting to correct it from inside. Much of the film's im-

mense appeal rested in the fact that these had already emerged as the most popular male hero "types" of the decade, and while many films centered around either one or the other, this was the single picture which maintained a delicate balance between the two.

For the ladies, a different approach was employed: Donna Reed and Deborah Kerr had been known as cleancut types (the former middle class, the latter upper crust) and by casting them as shady ladies, the film took on an added dimension—and their careers a new direction. The film also salvaged the acting career of Frank Sinatra, who had recently staged a comeback as a singer thanks to the great popularity of the new long-playing records; as Maggio he demonstrated immense talents as an actor in his first demanding dramatic role. The film often expressed in short, strong sequences ideas it had taken hundreds of pages to communicate in the book. The classic example occurs when all of Prewitt's alienation and loneliness is made clear when he blows taps at night on a deserted quad, while the camera cuts to the faces of the soldiers as they solemnly listen, then back to a tear as it rolls down Prewitt's cheek. The film also suggested the growing strain of nostalgia America was just beginning to experience for the war years: the peacetime army is depicted as corrupt, but at the outbreak of war, the men express a sense of relief at being saved from their ennui and allowed to prove themselves in combat.

oner as hero: Montgomery Clift and Donna Reed

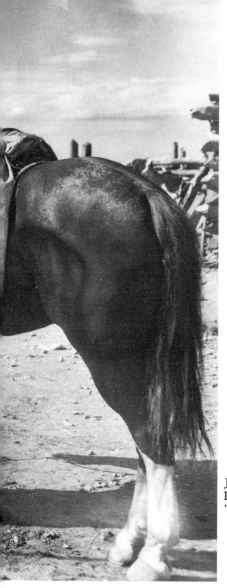

Jean Arthur (in window), Brandon
De Wilde, Van Heflin, Alan Ladd:
"Call me Shane!"

Shane

Paramount (1953)

Produced and directed by George Stevens; screenplay by A. B. Guthrie, Jr., based on the novel by Jack Schaefer, with additional dialogue by Jack Sher.

CAST: *Shane* (Alan Ladd); *Marion Starrett* (Jean Arthur); *Joe Starrett* (Van Heflin); *Joey Starrett* (Brandon de Wilde); *Wilson* (Jack Palance); *Chris* (Ben Johnson); *Lewis* (Edgar Buchanan); *Ryker* (Emile Meyer); *Torrey* (Elisha Cook, Jr.); *Mr. Shipstead* (Douglas Spencer); *Morgan* (John Dierkes); *Mrs. Torrey* (Ellen Corby); *Grafton* (Paul McVey); *Atkey* (John Miller); *Mrs. Shipstead* (Edith Evanson); *Wright* (Leonard Strong); *Johnson* (Ray Spiker); *Susan Lewis* (Janice Carroll); *Howells* (Martin Mason); *Mrs. Lewis* (Helen Brown); *Mrs. Howells* (Nancy Kulp)

Following the success of *A Place in the Sun*, George Stevens turned to the myth of the American West; dealing wih material that had been retold to the point of familiarity, he created an instantaneous classic. *Shane* retained many of the conventions of popular westerns but approached them from a slightly different perspective; instead of the well-known studio cowboy towns, the picture was shot on location beneath Wyoming's Great Teutons. While the story and dialogue often followed traditional western patterns, the readings that the actors were persuaded to give their lines—and even their facial gestures and eye movements—were highly influenced by the newly developed "adult" westerns. Thus, *Shane* was a hybrid between the classic and the contemporary fashions in movie westerns.

In the breathtaking opening sequence, a lone rider (Alan

urial on the prairie: Van Heflin, Jean Arthur,
don De Wilde, and Alan Ladd

The Cowboy as Villain: John Dierkes, Emile Meyer, and Jack Palance

stated, are communicated through the most subtle of gestures. It is at once clear that Marion Starrett loves Shane, and he just as clearly feels the same way. But nobody says or does anything about it until, near the end, when her husband is about to shoot it out with some cattlemen, he hints to her that he is "getting out of the way"; his frantic wife replies: "You talk as though I *want* you to get killed!" When Shane finally rides away in the famous final scene, Joey calls after him to come back. He insists that his father will need help with the farming, but when he finally yells, "Mother wants you, I *know* she does!" the camera cuts to a close-up of the child's face filling with tears as he suddenly realizes his mother's true feelings.

Though in most films Alan Ladd made a depressingly bland leading man, he proved far more effective in the lead than anyone could have guessed, more so than such highly respected character leads like Kirk Douglas or Richard Widmark could possibly have been. The blond Shane is eventually matched against the black outfitted and dark-complexioned gunman Wilson (Jack Palance); they step outside the gritty realism of the rest of the story to engage in a ritualistic duel between good and evil. Interesting also is the fact that nobody ever knows for sure if Shane is indeed a gunman; everyone assumes it, but his past is left fascinatingly unclear. Ladd wears the buckskin outfit only in the opening and closing sequences; during the rest of the picture he wears the workingmen's denim, as though by changing costumes he tries to divest himself of an identity he has grown to dislike.

The film avoids simplistics by making the old cattle baron a surprisingly sympathetic figure. Ryker avoids bringing in a hired killer until he has tried every other means of dislodging the homesteaders, including begging them to take top-paying jobs with him. In a powerfully played midnight meeting with Starrett, he defends his actions by explaining in lurid detail his exploits as a young man, wresting the land away from outlaws and Indians, demonstrating his confusion at the changing times and the intrusion of these dirt farmers. The conflict between Shane and Wilson is the mythic American western morality play between good and evil, but the simultaneous conflict between Starrett and Ryker is a more complex situation in which neither man is entirely in the right. Shane offers a reappraisal of American history as a conflict not between good guys and bad guys, but between incompatible groups of well-meaning, self-righteous people.

Ladd) enters a hidden valley and, after first being spied by little Joey (Brandon de Wilde) encounters the boy's parents, Marion (Jean Arthur) and Joe (Van Heflin) Starrett, dirt farmers trying to earn a living from the earth. Most often we view the stranger through the child's eyes, and his idolization of the man is effectively conveyed as the handsome figure, clad in velvety cream-colored buckskins, chases off some angry cattlemen by the simple fact of his presence. Asked his name, he replies: "Call me Shane," and before the night is over he has taken up with the family, helping them stand up to the cattle baron Ryker (Emile Myer).

Despite the old-hat quality of the homesteaders-cattlemen's conflict, the story is given uniqueness and believability. Numerous sub-conflicts, while never actually

The magnificent special effects made *Them!* more memorable than any other atomic monster movie; here, an army helicopter spots the giant ants crawling out of their desert nest

James Whitmore vs. an ant

Them!

Warner Bros. (1954)

Produced by David Weisbart; directed by Gordon Douglas; screenplay by Ted Sherdeman, adapted by Russell Hughes from a story by George Worthington Yates.

CAST: *Sergeant Ben Peterson* (James Whitmore); *Dr. Harold Medford* (Edmund Gwenn); *Dr. Patricia Medford* (Joan Weldon); *Robert Graham* (James Arness); *Brigadier General O'Brien* (Onslow Stevens); *Major Kibbee* (Sean McClory); *Ed Blackburn* (Chris Drake); *Little Girl* (Sandy Descher); *Mrs. Lodge* (Mary Ann Hokanson); *Captain of Troopers* (Don Shelton); *Crotty* (Fess Parker); *Jensen* (Olin Howland)

In addition to inspiring melodramatic thrillers like *Split Second* and offbeat comedies such as *The Atomic Kid*, the national preoccupation with the Bomb revived interest in science fiction films and created what became known as "monster movies." In such pictures the Bomb itself was never directly depicted as man's nemesis. Rather, all sorts of side-effects created by man's experimentation with nuclear weapons threatened to unexpectedly arise and wipe the human race off the face of the earth. Usually this took the form of having our scientifically sophisticated experiments awaken some prehistoric creature from its sleep, as in both the American B movie *The Beast from 20,000 Fathoms* and its highly popular Japanese counterpart, *Godzilla*. Though such films were successful enough, most were cheaply made and looked it. The significant exception was *Them!*, which featured some of the finest special effects ever created for this type of film.

The picture begins in the New Mexico desert, where state trooper Sergeant Ben Peterson (James Whitmore) discovers an entire ranch house destroyed, then finds a small child hysterically screaming: "Them!" With the aid of FBI agent Robert Graham (James Arness) and an eminent scientist, Dr. Harold Medford (Edmund Gwenn), Peterson eventually discovers that experimental atomic bomb blasts set off in the isolation of the desert have freed a large colony of giant ants, twelve to fifteen feet in length, which are now destroying everything in their path. It quickly becomes a race against time in which the trio (symbolically the necessary creation of a union between state and federal police-power figures, along with the man of science) must track down and destroy the swarming flock before the queen can mate, propagating enough new ants to cover the globe. Finally they find the ants have nested in the drainage system beneath Los Angeles and, armed with deadly high-power insect spray, they crawl down into the darkness to administer it.

A significant detail in *Them!* and other lesser films of its ilk was that the scientist figure, often harboring extreme guilt feelings about the dangers unleashed by the Bomb, absolves himself by coming up with the means to eliminate the plague he and his colleagues have been instrumental in loosing upon the world. The effect is that scientists are first criticized and then absolved by the film—and by the audience that assimilates it. *Them!* did feature one obligatory cliché, in which the scientist's headstrong but equally learned daughter (Joan Weldon) tags along and swiftly becomes a romantic interest for Arness. More often, though, the film shocked viewers with the unexpected, as when the hero, Peterson, is suddenly killed during the final fight with the ants.

The Gill-Man (Ben Chapman) abducts Kay (Julia Adams)

The most memorable of all fifties monsters was the sad-eyed gill-man

Creature from the Black Lagoon

Universal-International (1954)

Produced by William Alland; directed by Jack Arnold; screenplay by Harry Essex and Arthur Ross, from a story by Maurice Zimm.

CAST: *David Reed* (Richard Carlson); *Kay Lawrence* (Julia Adams); *Mark Williams* (Richard Denning); *Carl Maia* (Antonio Moreno); *Lucas* (Nestor Paiva); *Edwin Thompson* (Whit Bissel); *Gill Man* (Ben Chapman); *Chico* (Henry Escalante); *Zee* (Bernie Gozier); *Dr. Matos* (Sydney Mason); *Tomas* (Julio Lopez); *Louis* (Rod Redwing)

Although B westerns were in trouble in the fifties due to the competition of weekly TV series, monster movies flourished. Yet Hollywood produced almost no *memorable* horror figures, compared to such beloved creatures as Dracula, Frankenstein's monster, the Wolfman and the Mummy, all of whom had been revived in numerous pictures throughout the thirties and forties. Only one fifties monster was impressive enough to inspire such sequels, and that was the "gill man." He was introduced in *Creature from the Black Lagoon*, a low-budget science-fiction entry that gained no critical acclaim but acquired an immediate and lasting reputation with dedicated fans of the genre.

The story follows a group of scientists as they journey up the Amazon in search of the missing link between *Homo sapiens* and his prehistoric past. Mark Williams (Richard Denning), the leader, is a braggart who often intimidates the younger, quieter David Reed (Richard Carlson). Lovely Kay Lawrence (Julia Adams), Williams' fiancée and a fellow scientist, is also present.

They discover an isolated, bottomless lagoon which may be the lair of the creature they are searching for, and spend their days looking for signs. But the monster is busily watching them—and falling deeply in love with Kay. When at one point she takes a swim in a tight-fitting white bathing suit, the lonely gill man, intoxicated and awestruck at the sight of her, swims directly beneath Kay like a shadow, his every move following hers precisely.

Mark's basic ruthlessness, clearer to Kay in this isolated setting than it was back in civilization, eventually drives her closer to David, who responds by becoming more decisive. When the party suddenly realizes the gill man has no intentions of letting them leave, at least not with Kay, and is at work blocking up their points of exit, it is David who assumes command and tries to get them out. But the gill man carries Kay off to his hidden cave deep beneath the lagoon, and David must follow and fight it out with his primitive alter-ego in order to retrieve her.

In many ways, *Creature* was the definitive B picture of the era. The struggle between Richard Carlson and Richard Denning allowed audiences the opportunity of watching two "kings of the B's," rarely cast *together* in a film, fight it out. Julia (sometimes billed as "Julie") Adams emerged as one of the undisputed queens of the fifties B pictures.

But the creature himself furnished the film with its real source of fascination. Ugly in a highly original way, his loneliness and obsession for Kay (which, though terrifying, seemed more sincere than the affection of *either* of the two men) made him a highly empathetic figure, not unlike King Kong: the unchallenged god of a lost world suddenly made vulnerable by his weakness for the beauty he has never before experienced. The film ended with a shot of the dead creature floating face down in the lagoon, but his unexpected popularity caused Universal-International to revive him for two sequels, *Return of the Creature* and *The Creature Walks Among Us*—both lacking the weird charm of the original.

Richard Widmark and Bella Darvi:
The man of action meets the woman
of science

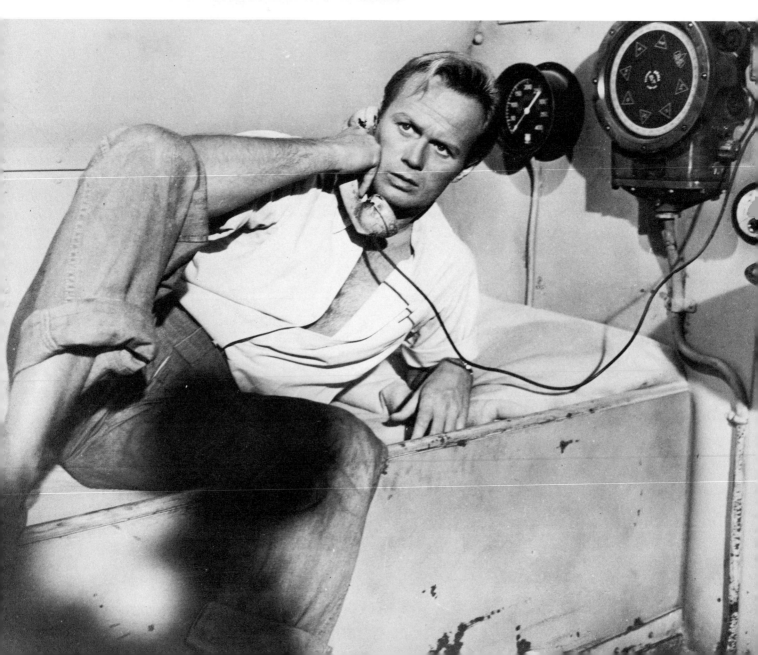

Hell and High Water

20th Century-Fox (1954)

Produced by Raymond A. Klune; directed by Samuel Fuller; screenplay by Jesse L. Lasky, Jr. and Mr. Fuller, based on a story by David Hempstead.

CAST: *Adam Jones* (Richard Widmark); *Denise* (Bella Darvi); *Professor Montel* (Victor Francen); *Ski Brodski* (Cameron Mitchell); *Chief Holter* (Gene Evans); *Dugboat Walker* (David Wayne); *Neuman* (Stephen Bekassy); *Fujimori* (Richard Loo); *Happy Mosk* (Peter Scott); *Gunner McCrossin* (Henry Kulky); *Chin Lee* (Wong Artarne); *Quartermaster* (Harry Carter); *Welles* (Robert Alder); *Carpino* (Don Orlando)

In 1953, the White House announced in a curt statement that a bomb of foreign origin had been exploded somewhere outside the United States. A mixture of hopelessness and panic gripped the country: whether or not this marked the beginning of the end became a popular discussion with everyone from high school debating teams to political caucuses. Understandably enough Samuel Fuller, the controversial writer-director who made his reputation by leaping in where others feared to tread, quickly fashioned a film that on the surface exploited the country's ugly mood and nervous interest, yet also provided an intriguingly possible explanation as to how and why a "mystery bomb" explosion could have happened.

Hell and High Water begins with a somber documentary-style narration, summarizing both the White House's official statement on the incident and the Atomic Energy Commission's later clarifications that the bomb had been exploded somewhere in the region between the north tip of the Japanese islands and the Arctic Circle. *"This,"* the voice firmly concludes, "is the story of that explosion!"

What follows, though, is a totally fictitious tale, based on the premise that a group of international scientists, led by the brilliant Professor Montel (Victor Francen), grow uncomfortable with the government's obvious inability to cope with the ever greater threat of nuclear warfare. They commission a high-powered submarine, commandeered by cynical soldier of fortune Adam Jones (Richard Widmark) and manned by a motley crew of scoundrels and refugees, to secretly journey into North Pacific waters and search for a suspected atomic arsenal they fear is being stockpiled by the communist powers. A beautiful female scientist, Denise (Bella Darvi), travels with them and finds herself falling in love with the unconventional skipper. Upon reaching their destination they discover that the communists are in fact about to launch a salvaged American B-29. The plane is loaded with an atomic bomb, which they plan to drop on North Korea, with the blame naturally to fall on the United States. In desperation, Jones has his men shoot the plane down, but the bomb explodes as the B-29 crashes—and, this, the film concludes, is the explanation of the "mystery bomb."

Upon the picture's release, the critics uniformly denounced it as being "far-fetched" as an explanation and "irresponsible" for presenting the wildest fiction as though it were proven fact. In even suggesting that this was the absolute explanation behind such an international incident rather than merely a possibility, *Hell and High Water* was certainly the most flagrant example of this kind of thing since Orson Welles' much-heralded radio-documentary version of *The War of the Worlds* two decades earlier. But the ideas in the film—that a cult of scientists might finally prefer to work independently, forsaking all government intervention for what they believed to be the good of mankind, or that a country might drop a bomb on its allies to make the United States look bad—appear, after what we have learned about world politics in the last twenty years, less open to attack as "unlikely." Instead, they seem uncannily perceptive.

Go Man, Go!

United Artists (1954)

Produced by Anton M. Leader; directed by James Wong Howe; screenplay by Arnold Becker.

CAST: *Abe Saperstein* (Dane Clark); *Sylvia Saperstein* (Pat Breslin); *Inman Jackson* (Sidney Poitier); *Zack Leader* (Edmon Ryan); *James Willoughby* (Bram Nossen); *Papa Saperstein* (Anatol Winogradoff); *Mama Saperstein* (Celia Boodkin); *Fay Saperstein* (Carol Sinclair); *Sam* (Ellsworth Wright); *Slim* (Slim Gaillard); *Ticket Seller* (Frieda Altman); *Master of Ceremonies* (Mort Marshall); *Secretary* (Jean Shore); *First Bathing Beauty* (Jule Benedic); *Second Bathing Beauty* (Jerry Hauer); *Announcers* (Marty Glickman, Bill Stern); *Appraiser* (Lew Hearn); *Irma Jackson* (Ruby Dee)

Americans love sports as dearly as they do movies but, inexplicably, movies about sports have never done particularly well. A notable exception was this independently produced little saga of The Harlem Globetrotters, who were heroes both of the sports world and the civil rights movement. For the team became a cause célèbre of that popular crusade which saw its first great impetus at mid-decade. In December of 1955, Dr. Martin Luther King would help inspire the first great non-violent demonstrations for integration. But the seeds were brewing long before that. The Globetrotters' entry into big-time basketball was a major breakthrough for all Negro athletes and this pleasant, easygoing picture turned their victory over racism into the stuff folk tales are made of.

One of the film's fascinating features is that, while essentially a drama about the evils of racism, such things are never mentioned during the course of its eighty-minute running time. The story is played as low-keyed entertainment melodrama, with occasional light comedy relief and a good deal of fine documentary footage featuring the Globetrotters sinking baskets in their unnervingly nonchalant style. But there is an undercurrent running through the piece which wordlessly communicated to the audience what the Globetrotters *really* had to overcome. And the way in which they beat the system—and, in so doing, changed it—gives the picture its heart and charm. In time, it suggested, all things were possible, so long as there were men of diligent perseverance like Abe Saperstein.

The white organizer–manager of the team was played with simplicity and a strong sense of common decency by Dane Clark, an extremely misused actor whose talents were wasted throughout the fifties. Abe and his wife Sylvia (Pat Breslin) discover some talented Negro athletes clowning with a basketball on the street corner and determine to elevate them to the status they deserve and would naturally receive, if they were white. They begin small, touring through a seemingly endless succession of small towns. But Abe's countless problems are shared by a loyal Negro associate, Inman Jackson (Sidney Poitier), and his lovely wife Irma (Ruby Dee).

Eventually they receive praise from fair-minded sports reporters like Zack Leader (Edmon Ryan). And in time James Willoughby (Bram Nossen), a big-time promoter of sporting events, takes an interest in the team. They are booked, finally, into a landmark basketball match with a white "name" team—and beat them. It is at this point that the film draws its curtain, closing with the beginning of the Globetrotters' success story.

The fact that the "name" team is *not* named in the picture only serves to remind us that racial discrimination, and the blight of being beaten by an all-Negro team, was still present—and presented a serious problem—in the Hollywood of 1954. The white team emerges as The Great White Hope, since a defeat for the Globetrotters at this crucial point would force them out of professional ball, probably for good. None of this, of course, is stated outright in the film. But viewers had little trouble in reading between the lines. The accomplishment of the athletes from Harlem symbolized the future possibilities for black talent, while the friendship of the Sapersteins and the Jacksons was just as clearly illustrative of social integration.

Victory through perseverance: Dane Clark and the Harlem Globetrotters

Patricia Breslin, Dane Clark, Sidney Poitier

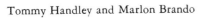
Tommy Handley and Marlon Brando

Marlon Brando and Eva Marie Saint: old-fashioned romantic love with a new realistic background

On the Waterfront

Columbia (1954)

A Horizon Picture, produced by Sam Spiegel; directed by Elia Kazan; screenplay by Budd Schulberg, based on an original story by Mr. Schulberg and suggested by the series of Pulitzer Prize-winning articles by Malcolm Johnson.

CAST: *Terry Malloy* (Marlon Brando); *Edie Doyle* (Eva Marie Saint); *Father Barry* (Karl Malden); *Johnny Friendly* (Lee J. Cobb); *Charley Malloy* (Rod Steiger); *"Pop" Doyle* (John Hamilton); *"Kayo" Dugan* (Pat Henning); *Glover* (Leif Erickson); *Big Mac* (James Westerfield); *Truck* (Tony Galento); *Tillio* (Tami Mauriello); *Barney* (Abe Simon); *Mott* (John Heldabrand)

Like *From Here to Eternity* the year before, *On the Waterfront* won immediate recognition as one of the great American films. It combined various elements (the possible corruption of labor unions, the Kefauver crime committee probes) which had already been the basis for numerous crusading melodramas. But *Waterfront* employed them as the basis for a modern epic with tragic overtones. Budd Schulberg's screenplay was the greatest example yet of Hollywood's new willingness to handle hard-hitting material; Marlon Brando's performance elevated him from gifted newcomer to the most important actor in motion pictures; Leonard Bernstein's modern symphony lent the story a clas-

sic grace while Boris Kaufmann's stunning cinematography endowed the picture with a sense of documentary-realism; finally, director Elia Kazan tied all the elements together into the most memorable example of the decade's "new maturity" in films.

Terry Malloy (Brando) is a worthless but likable loafer who hangs around New York City's docks doing small favors for union boss-racketeer Johnny Friendly (Lee J. Cobb), lavishing his affection on the pigeons he keeps caged on his tenement rooftop and dreaming of the world of professional boxing he once almost entered. One day he follows one of Friendly's orders, only to realize later that he was used to set up a man to be murdered. His guilt is compounded when he meets and falls in love with Edie (Eva Marie Saint), the dead man's sister. Unaware of Terry's involvement in the act, she asks him to help her get the people responsible.

One of those people is Terry's own brother, Charley (Rod Steiger), a crooked lawyer now reduced to running errands for Friendly. Terry ceases his relations with them and is befriended by Father Barry (Karl Malden), a tough, uncompromising waterfront priest who wants the boy to stand up against the corruption. When Friendly gets word of Terry's change of heart, he instructs Charley to see to it that the boy keeps his mouth shut. In one of the film's great moments, the two brothers sit in the darkness of a taxicab, realizing that communication between them has become impossible, moving ever further away from each other until, at last, they are alone together. When Terry suddenly realizes that Charley consciously manipulated him into losing his crucial boxing match years earlier, he mutters his most unforgettable line: "I could a been somethin', Charley. I could a been a contenda, instead of a bum. Which is what I am."

Part of the film's power is that it goes beyond the limitations of even the best realistic art. Early in the film Father Barry stands up to some longshoremen who are mocking his ministry, insisting: "If you don't think Christ is down here on the waterfront . . . you don't know nothing!" Later, when Johnny Friendly has his goons beat Terry to a pulp, the image of the bloodied man with outstretched arms is given a symbolic dimension by Barry's earlier words.

Like the great works of classical drama, *Waterfront* deals with the theme of man's eventual coming to knowledge. Terry Malloy at first seems hardly comparable to the likes of Hamlet. But Schulberg, Kazan and Brando managed to gradually, and believably, elevate him to just such a figure of greatness, at least in his own crude way. Charley's con-

The Crucifixion of Terry: Karl Malden, Marlon Brando, Eva Marie Saint

fession of his earlier betrayal of Terry, Terry's own confession to Edie of his involvement in her brother's death, and finally the revealed truth about Friendly's corruption all illustrate the premise of the search for truth as man's most glorious and frightening enterprise, while the corruption on the New York docks serves as a modern equivalent for the "poisoned city" of works like *Oedipus Rex*.

Like the earlier wave of hysterical anti-communist tracts, *Waterfront* claimed that labor unions had been infiltrated by corrupt forces. But whereas those simplistic pictures had seemingly suggested this was a good enough reason to get rid of such organizations entirely, *Waterfront* used them as a symbol for all the evolving modern bureaucracies, implying it was time to clean them up and bring them back in line with their original ideals. The film can also be read as a personal statement from Mr. Kazan, who was widely criticized by his fellow liberals for having given testimony before the Committee on Un-American Activities.

The film does have one major flaw. At the end, when the beaten Terry manages to stand and brush past Friendly, followed by all the other dock workers while the racketeer raves and rants at the loss of his power, the film simply isn't believable—on a realistic level or a symbolic one. Terry's death is as necessary for the total catharsis of the docks as Prewitt's was for the army in *From Here to Eternity*. But this was somewhat countered by the shot of a well-to-do businessman viewing the televised committee hearings, but turning off the set in the middle—suggesting that if the public was willing to close their eyes to corruption, they would create a climate in which it could continue.

James Mason and Judy Garland

A Star Is Born

Warner Bros. (1954)

Produced by Sidney Luft; directed by George Cukor; screenplay by Moss Hart, based on the Dorothy Parker, Alan Campbell, Robert Carson screenplay, from an original story by William A. Wellman and Robert Carson; music and lyrics by Harold Arlen, Ira Gershwin and Leonard Gershe.

CAST: *Esther Blodgett* (Judy Garland); *Norman Maine* (James Mason); *Libby* (Jack Carson); *Oliver Niles* (Charles Bickford); *Danny McGuire* (Tom Noonan); *A Starlet* (Lucy Marlow); *Susan* (Amanda Blake); *Graves* (Irving Bacon); *Libby's Secretary* (Hazel Shermet); *Glenn Williams* (James Brown); *Miss Markham* (Lotus Robb)

Judy Garland was more than just a singer, an actress and a show business personality: she transcended such categories and became an American legend whose life was a modern myth of a person with overabundant talent eventually destroyed by an inability to cope with personal pressures. Her numerous screen appearances were always delightful, even when the individual vehicles were clearly beneath her. But she found only two musical movies which made full use of her talents: *The Wizard of Oz*, which temporarily rescued her from the Andy Hary series in 1939, and *A Star Is Born*, her one great adult musical role. It was also her single musical for Warner Brothers rather than M-G-M, and her last movie appearance for years. There was a definite sense con-

Judy Garland, James Mason, Charles Bickford

veyed by the film that in it, Judy was completing her statement as a movie star.

Playwright Moss Hart based his screenplay on the highly regarded non-musical film of fifteen years before. But when his modernization of the classic Hollywood fable was brought to the screen by George Cukor, in CinemaScope and color and containing a host of Arlen-Gershwin-Gershe songs, it appeared to be a semi-autobiographical vehicle for Garland. She portrays Esther Blodgett, a wide-eyed Hollywood hopeful who is discovered performing in a benefit show by Norman Maine (James Mason), a big-name star just hitting the skids. Esther is unaware of this and promptly falls in love with the mature, sophisticated man, while he finds himself equally taken with her innocence and exuberance.

Norman gives Esther a few early breaks that help make her a star, something that comes quite naturally to the talented youngster. The two marry, but her growing fame depresses the ever less-successful man, until he learns to rely on alcohol and falls quickly into fits of temper. Esther finds herself torn between the two great loves of her life—her man and her career.

Fittingly, there is one show-stopping number inspired by each of her loves in which Judy sings and dances with an emotional intensity that carried over an extra dimension to the film's subsequent dramatic moments. Her "The Man That Got Away" number lent poignance to the eventual suicide of her husband, who at last fully comprehends his wife's greatness and the public's right to such a star, but is unable to face life without her constant companionship. Judy counters that eerie, torchy solo with a lavish production number, "Born in a Trunk," which recounts her early ambitions for eventual success and communicates the fated quality of her career.

Many of the film's plot devices were shopworn and creaky, yet that was rarely noticeable, so believable were the major performances. The good and the bad of Hollywood were a bit caricatured in the personages of a lovable producer (Charles Bickford) and a despicable journalist (Jack Carson). But the love story emerged as truly tragic rather than just a simple tearjerker, thanks to the whole string of poignant, powerful sequences—tender moments like their first intimations of love on a deserted sound stage, as a big microphone hangs over their heads hinting at the impossibility for privacy, and a most memorable depiction of the honeymoon as they struggle to express simple, basic love in the stifling confines of a multimillion-dollar Hollywood beach house.

In many ways, *A Star Is Born* served as an answer to *Sunset Boulevard*. Like Billy Wilder's film, it was chock full of background details of the picture business; likewise, it presented a portrait of the old Hollywood meeting the new on the transitional ground of the fifties. But whereas *Sunset Boulevard* cynically predicted that the old would devour the new in its desire to survive, *A Star Is Born* suggested it would give ground gracefully, making way for the fresh talent to arrive and reach its potential.

The mirror became a popular symbol for filmmakers in the fifties; here, it serves to convey the troubled psychological state of Shelley Winters as she confronts Paul Douglas

Executive Suite

Metro-Goldwyn-Mayer (1954)

Produced by John Houseman; directed by Robert Wise; screenplay by Ernest Lehman, from the novel by Cameron Hawley.

CAST: *McDonald Walling* (William Holden); *Mary Blemond Walling* (June Allyson); *Julia O. Tredway* (Barbara Stanwyck); *Loren Phineas Shaw* (Fredric March); *Frederick Y. Alderson* (Walter Pidgeon); *Eva Bardeman* (Shelley Winters); *Josiah Walter Dudley* (Paul Douglas); *George Nyle Caswell* (Louis Calhern); *Jessie Q. Grimm* (Dean Jagger); *Erica Martin* (Nina Foch); *Mike Walling* (Tim Considine); *Bill Lundeen* (William Phipps); *Mrs. George Nyle Caswell* (Lucille Knoch); *Julius Steigel* (Edgar Stehli); *Sara Asenath Grimm* (Mary Adams); *Edith Alderson* (Virginia Brissac); *Ed Benedeck* (Harry Shannon)

New forms of corporate power, with far-reaching complexities and legal sophistications, emerged as a ruling authority in the country. With such power came arrogance and ruthlessness, as well as a new subject for moviemakers with a serious dedication for chronicling the lifestyles of their time. For as big business took on new shapes and forms, the role of vice-president in an important corporation became a professional position of the highest status. If the anti-Establishment hero of the era was easily identifiable as "the beatnik," then the Establishment hero was just as assuredly "the executive."

Executive Suite, the first major motion picture to deal bluntly with this social phenomenon, intended to provide middle-American audiences with a realistic glimpse behind the façade of a "typical" corporation, allowing viewers a

Barbara Stanwyck casts her crucial
votes as Fredric March looks on

Walter Pidgeon and Barbara Stanwyck

greater understanding of how the modern business structures worked. The story begins with the sudden and unexpected death of the president of a furniture manufacturing concern, leading to a power struggle among the various men in line for the job.

McDonald Walling (William Holden) is clearly a representational figure for The Bright Young Man With New Ideas; but as a relative newcomer to the concern, he's considered an unlikely challenger for the top position. Loren Phineas Shaw (Fredric March) is, behind a reserved front, an ambitious schemer who discovers that sales manager Josiah Dudley (Paul Douglas) is involved with a young woman (Shelley Winters) and uses this knowledge to blackmail the hapless man into helping Shaw fight for the position, by tarnishing the reputations of all other hopefuls. Jesse Q. Grimm (Dean Jagger) is a quiet, lackluster man who has risen through hard work to head the production department, but has grown tired and anxious for retirement. And finally, the senior vice-president, Frederick Y. Alderson (Walter Pidgeon), views the situation as his last chance to achieve any importance in his chosen profession.

The film vividly recounts their melodramatic relationships with one another, as they work at their white collar jobs and wait for the crucial board of directors meeting where the next president will be chosen—and where the late president's former mistress Julia Tredway (Barbara Stanwyck) will play an important role through her large block of voting stock.

Executive Suite was nowhere near as important a work as its makers hoped for. While the four central figures did provide viable symbols of the various kinds of men inhabiting the newly created executive world, they were finally such stereotypes that viewers had trouble believing in them as human beings. Instead of revealing the complexity of the modern executive the film offered characters who were, under their sophisticated button-down business suits, the same sort of good guys and bad guys audiences found at home on television: Fredric March's villain was without a single redeeming quality while William Holden's hero displayed not one vice. This was carried to an extreme by the casting of June Allyson, by this time well-known as the symbolic all-American girl, as his wife. Which of the two men would eventually win was as easy to predict as the victor in a Dodge City shoot-out.

Nevertheless, the film partially lived up to its promise. The workings within a corporate structure were effectively illustrated and *Executive Suite* provided fifties audiences with a first peek into a world that had caught our attention and interest.

William Holden and June Allyson

The good life: Fred MacMurray, Lauren Bacall, Elliott Reed, Clifton Webb, Cornel Wilde, June Allyson, Margald Gilmore and Van Heflin

Change partners and dance: Lauren Bacall and Cornel Wilde are far more interested in their own spouses' activities than in each other

Woman's World

20th Century-Fox (1954)

Produced by Charles Brackett; directed by Jean Negulesco; screenplay by Claude Binyon, Mary Loos and Richard Sale, based on a story by Mona Williams.

CAST: *Gifford* (Clifton Webb); *Katie* (June Allyson); *Jerry* (Van Heflin); *Elizabeth* (Lauren Bacall); *Sid* (Fred MacMurray); *Carol* (Arlene Dahl); *Bill Baxter* (Cornel Wilde); *Tony* (Elliott Reid); *Evelyn* (Margalo Gillmore); *Tomaso* (Alan Reed)

Woman's World presented a second glimpse into the lifestyle already explored in *Executive Suite* but with a significant twist: its premise was that the wives behind the men ultimately prove to be more crucial in determining an executive's success or failure than the men themselves. The premise was not unlike that of the earlier film: Mr. Gifford (Clifton Webb), president of an important motors corporation, must choose which of three vice-presidents will receive the newly created position of general manager for the firm.

June Allyson and Cornel Wilde

wall-to-wall carpeting and get herself locked in the ladies' room.

The film was typical of the slick, stylish CinemaScope soap operas that had quickly become popular by offering sophisticated sneak-peeks into the fashionable world. The title, however, proved quite ironic. As Mr. Gifford runs the three couples through his elaborate games, husbands and wives come to know more about each other in a few days than they ever learned in years of normal married life. But just as Gifford gives up on his gimmick and picks Jerry because of his qualities, Carol—in her anxiety to reach New York and join the chic set—propositions the older man on the hunch that she can land the job for her uninspired husband through sex. Her meddling has the opposite effect, for Gifford immediately scratches Jerry's name and begins trying to decide between the other two. When Jerry learns of his wife's interference, he approaches Gifford with an apology explaining that he certainly didn't want the job badly enough to get it that way, and that his wife's ambitions were strictly her own.

Gifford is impressed enough by the man's integrity to offer Jerry the position after all. The decision proves best for the other couples as well: Katie and Bill can return to the Midwest where they will be more at home anyway, while Sid senses that his marriage to Elizabeth is more important than success at any cost in the business world. Only the social-climbing Carol ends up a loser: Jerry walks out on her, and his clearly indicated success does not provide the springboard to the Manhattan high life she had hoped for.

Though overly glossy and melodramatic in its treatment, *Woman's World* did provide a glimpse of the important if often invisible role wives played in the corporate structure —the single element clearly glossed over in *Executive Suite*. It also suggested that, in the complex and often amoral world of Madison Avenue, it was not the Sammy Glicks who succeeded but the honest, hard-working, old-fashioned American types—a reassuring message, if not necessarily one that always proved true in real life.

Coming to the conclusion that the men are equally qualified, he decides to pick by wife instead. Gifford invites the three couples to New York where he wines and dines them, carefully scrutinizing the women in hopes of finding the one he believes has the most potential to make her man succeed.

Carol (Arlene Dahl) is a sophisticated, experienced woman who desperately wants her husband Jerry (Van Heflin), a solid, competent but unambitious fellow, to land the job. Elizabeth (Lauren Bacall) is intelligent and strong-willed, but she would prefer that her husband Sid (Fred MacMurray), an eager-to-reach-the-top type, be passed over for the post as his total commitment to the organization is causing a rift in their marriage. Katie (June Allyson), an eager-to-please girl-next-door, wants to impress the boss for the sake of her likable, clean-cut husband Bill (Cornel Wilde), but only manages to spill her martinis on the

The Dancin' Kid meets Johnny Guitar: Scott Brady, Joan Crawford, and Sterling Hayden

Johnny Guitar

Republic (1954)

Directed by Nicholas Ray; screenplay by Philip Yordan, based on the novel by Roy Chanslor.

CAST: *Vienna* (Joan Crawford); *Johnny Guitar* (Sterling Hayden); *Emma Small* (Mercedes McCambridge); *Dancin' Kid* (Scott Brady); *John McIvers* (Ward Bond); *Turkey Ralston* (Ben Cooper); *Bart Lonergan* (Ernest Borgnine); *Old Tom* (John Carradine); *Corey* (Royal Dano); *Marshal Williams* (Frank Ferguson); *Eddie* (Paul Fix); *Mr. Andrews* (Rhys Williams); *Pete* (Ian MacDonald)

The western has always been regarded as the great American morality play, but it is nonetheless open to the ideas and fashions of the times. In the fifties there were two major departures from the traditional horse opera: the "adult western," as typified by *The Gunfighter* and *High Noon*, and the "neurotic western," most perfectly exemplified by *Johnny Guitar*. Directed by Nicholas Ray in outlandishly garish color and containing abrupt and often grotesque shifts from studio sets to on-location shots, the film was at first jeered by American critics who found it too

Vigilante justice: Denver Pyle (far left), Mercedes McCambridge

Guilt by association: Ben Cooper, Joan Crawford and Scott Brady

concluding with a shoot-out between two women as the men stand by helplessly and watch. Vienna (Joan Crawford), a handsome, hardened saloon keeper wears dresses only in the privacy of her upstairs back rooms; she appears in black, tight-fitting men's clothing when presenting herself to the world. Emma Small (Mercedes McCambridge), the cattle baroness, wants to run Vienna off the land that is directly in line for the upcoming railroad. Emma seizes the opportunity when her brother is killed in a stagecoach robbery, which everyone assumes (importantly, without proof) to have been perpetrated by the Dancin' Kid (Scott Brady) and his gang, frequent guests at Vienna's saloon. Vienna is guilty by association. After the town marshal (Frank Ferguson) is accidentally killed, Emma works the villagers into a frenzy, culminating in an attempt to lynch Vienna—but she is rescued by a wandering drifter, Johnny Guitar (Sterling Hayden).

The film bubbles over with sexual frustrations. Emma is quite obsessed with the Dancin' Kid who, in a strikingly erotic gesture, whisks her onto a dance floor, forcing her to respond to the masculine movements of his body. But the Kid is in love with Vienna—as is his young sidekick, Turkey (Ben Cooper), and a conflict erupts between the outlaws and the singing stranger, Johnny Guitar, eventually discovered to have been Vienna's lover in the past.

Director Ray, a close friend of Frank Lloyd Wright, designed the sets for the picture entirely on the great architect's premise that "a house should not be *on* a hill, but *of* a hill." Vienna's dwelling appears to rise naturally from the dusty wasteland, while the Kid's hideout looks like a natural extension of the green mountains; the townspeople's abodes, however, are obviously imposed on the land, indicating that they are people who do not understand it.

Like *High Noon, Johnny Guitar* clearly studied the horrors of McCarthyism by placing them in the relative safety of a western setting. Vienna does not pay her help but plans to share her profits equally with them; the townspeople's fear of her is, essentially, a fear of communism. She is almost lynched not because of any factual evidence against her, but strictly because of her friendship with "enemies of the people" who, it turns out, did not commit the robbery and murder for which they were blamed. Emma's inexplicable hatred for Vienna and unconscious search for something to blame on her is a clear-cut case of witch-hunting. Most frightening of all, the ordinary people allow themselves to be manipulated by Emma's terror tactics until finally they recoil in horror at their own actions. Nicholas Ray had already suggested the paranoia of Hollywood with *In a Lonely Place;* in *Johnny Guitar,* he depicted the country's.

"unrealistic" for their tastes. But that didn't blunt its popularity at the box office, or the ecstatic critical reception it received in France, where the garishness was readily accepted as a kind of calculated cinematic surrealism.

The people who love and hate the film agree on one point: *Johnny Guitar* is the weirdest western ever made,

oman They Almost Lynched: Joan Crawford, and Mercedes McCambridge

The Innocents Abroad: Jean Peters, Maggie McNamara, and Dorothy McGuire

European experience is dumbfounded by American innocence: Louis Jourdan and Maggie McNamara

Three Coins in the Fountain

20th Century-Fox (1954)

Produced by Sol C. Siegel; directed by Jean Negulesco; screenplay by John Patrick, from a novel by John H. Secondari.

CAST: *Shadwell* (Clifton Webb); *Miss Francis* (Dorothy McGuire); *Anita* (Jean Peters); *Prince Dino Di Cessi* (Louis Jourdan); *Maria* (Maggie McNamara); *Giorgio* (Rossano Brazzi); *Burgoyne* (Howard St. John); *Mrs. Burgoyne* (Kathryn Givney); *Principessa* (Cathleen Nesbitt); *Dr. Martinelli* (Vicente Padula)

In the suddenly bygone days of Hollywood's golden era, European settings were lavishly created in the confines of studio sets while the Production Code, with its endless lists of no's, rendered the depiction of adult man-woman relationships difficult indeed. But as films of the thirties and forties popped up almost nightly on television, filmmakers of the fifties sensed the need to offer viewers things they couldn't obtain comfortably, and for free, at home. Two of the more productive means producers seized on were the concepts of filming on location and dealing more frankly

Dorothy McGuire, Jean Peters, Maggie McNamara, Clifton Webb, Kathryn Givney and Howard St. John

than ever before with sex. The cinema became more colorful both visually and morally: *Three Coins in the Fountain* typified the new sophistication that grew out of the combination of these elements.

Above all else, it represents the fifties variation on the traditional "woman's picture." As the film begins three headstrong, independent, attractive young ladies arrive in Rome, discussing in tantalizingly off-hand terms their plans to search for romance. Partaking of a popular legend, they throw coins into the lovely fountain of Trevi, making silent wishes that their dream men will come along. Each girl's heartbreaking relationship with the fellow she sets her mark on is then carefully chronicled. The naive Maria (Maggie McNamara) meets a real Italian prince, Dino Di Cessi (Louis Jourdan) and, through a combination of guile and innocence, eventually wins his attentions; the sharp, chic Anita (Jean Peters), tiring of her executive job with a major American firm, surprises herself by falling for a simple, honest Italian, Giorgio (Rossano Brazzi); the stolid, quiet Miss Francis (Dorothy McGuire), secretary to an aging expatriate writer, Mr. Shadwell (Clifton Webb), gradually convinces him she has other virtues besides her excellence at taking dictation.

Ultimately the film subscribed to conventional morality,

suggesting that any truly lasting relationship was one which ended in marriage. Yet it was mildly titillating in its time, if only for restructuring the movie-going audiences' notions (especially the female portion) of how worldly young women acted, talked, and dressed—suggesting that not only femme fatales planned and schemed to get their man, but "nice" girls as well. With three distinct stereotype females presented, almost every woman in the audience could associate with one. How different from the forties concept of "the good girl" were these ladies, slightly afraid of a passionate love affair but nonetheless walking directly into it, while carefully but without malice plotting to manipulate the right man into marriage.

Three Coins in the Fountain contains almost everything that audiences had come to think of as slick, chic entertainment by mid-decade, combining Jean Negulesco's breathtaking panoramas of Rome and Venice (which looked, thanks to newly refined color processes in CinemaScope, as refreshing as if they'd never been photographed before) and screenwriter John Patrick's saucy, sophisticated dialogue. The final touch to the perfect product was the dreamily romantic title song, which became the hit love ballad of the year, and a popular standard afterwards.

A folk-hero for the fifties: Fess Parker, Buddy Ebsen and Hans Conried

Davy Crockett, King of the Wild Frontier

Buena Vista (1955)

Produced by Bill Walsh for Walt Disney; directed by Norman Foster; written by Tom Blackburn.

CAST: *Davy Crockett* (Fess Parker); *George Russell* (Buddy Ebsen); *Andrew Jackson* (Basil Ruysdael); *Thimblerig* (Hans Conried); *Tobias Norton* (William Bakewell); *Colonel Jim Bowie* (Kenneth Tobey); *Chief Red Stick* (Pat Hogan); *Polly Crockett* (Helene Stanley); *Bustedluck* (Nick Cravat); *Colonel Billy Travis* (Don Megowan); *Bigfoot Mason* (Mike Mazurki); *Charlie Two Shirts* (Jeff Thomas)

In the autumn of 1954, Walt Disney opened his lavish California amusement park and presented his first television series; both were named, appropriately enough, "Disneyland." His Wednesday evening TV hour consisted largely of ancient cartoons, plugs for new films, and one special feature that turned out to be a hit beyond anyone's wildest expectations: a three-part serial about the famous frontiersman, Davy Crockett. At once, a national cult grew up around the hero. Bill Hayes' recording of the catchy title song "The Ballad of Davy Crockett" hit the number one spot on the charts and remained there for a record-breaking

In the fifties, even the hero of a Disney family film was a civil rights crusader: Fess Parker campaigns for Indians' rights in Congress

six months, while coonskin caps—previously a lukewarm seller as Dan'l Boone hats—became a valuable commodity after being relabeled Davy Crockett merchandise.

After the Crockett films had been rerun on television and received total exposure in that medium, Disney had his craftsmen edit them into a 90-minute feature film. Never a waster of money, he had foreseen the possibility of eventual theatrical release and shot the episodes in color. The full-length picture followed Crockett (Fess Parker) and his sidekick Georgie Russell (Buddy Ebsen) from their early experiences as Indian Scouts for General Andrew Jackson (Basil Ruysdael) during the Creek War, through their pioneering and homesteading activities along the Obion River and Crockett's eventual fling with politics, to the final, eventful trip to Texas—in the company of a cagey gambler named Thimblerig (Hans Conreid) and a down-and-out Indian called Bustedluck (Nick Cravat)—culminating in their fated meeting with Colonel Jim Bowie (Kenneth Tobey) in defense of the shrine of Texas independence, the Alamo.

The popularity of the Crockett film was due to the uncannily effective "Disney-izing" of the real Crockett's life, creating a marvelous balance between integrity to the essentials of history and some purely commercial elements. In many respects the film relied on conventions of B westerns: Russell, a true associate of Crockett's, was turned by Buddy Ebsen into a typical comic-relief sidekick of the sort kids were used to, while Fess Parker was a routine embodiment of the American western hero—strong, soft-spoken, and honest. There were many such condescensions to the kiddie audience, like Crockett's comic "grinning down a b'ar," or having him single-handedly solve the Indian war by fighting a totally fictitious duel with the Creek Chief, Red Stick (Pat Hogan). But other elements were surprisingly mature, such as the presentation of Crockett as a serious family man rather than the usual wandering romantic lead, and the inclusion of immense grief at the death of his wife Polly (Helene Stanley). There was even a suggestion of Crockett's desire to work politically for Indians' rights, accompanied by at least a hint of the corrupt nature of Jacksonian politics. And finally, the film ended with the hero's death —not your usual fade-out for a kiddie western!

Though the coonskin cap had existed as long as the cowboy hat as a possible commodity, it had been waiting patiently for someone to come along and discover its marketability. With *Davy Crockett* Disney did just that, creating the most extravagant craze of an era.

Tom Ewell and Marilyn Monroe

The Seven Year Itch

20th Century-Fox (1955)

A Charles K. Feldman Group Production, produced by Charles K. Feldman and Billy Wilder; directed by Mr. Wilder; screenplay by Mr. Wilder and George Axelrod, from the play by Mr. Axelrod.

CAST: *The Girl* (Marilyn Monroe); *Richard Sherman* (Tom Ewell); *Helen Sherman* (Evelyn Keyes); *Tom McKenzie* (Sonny Tufts); *Kruhulik* (Robert Strauss); *Dr. Brubaker* (Oscar Homolka); *Miss Morris* (Marguerite Chapman); *Plumber* (Victor Moore); *Elaine* (Roxanne); *Mr. Brady* (Donald MacBride); *Miss Finch* (Carolyn Jones); *Ricky* (Butch Bernard); *Waitress* (Doro Merando); *Girl* (Dorothy Ford)

Marilyn Monroe was *Playboy* Magazine's very first centerfold girl, and it would have been a grievous error if anyone else had received that honor. For the Marilyn we saw on film was the girl without a care in the world, only partially aware of the enormous powers of her own sexuality. She was the incredibly endowed sex symbol next door, the goddess with a little girl's giggly voice. It was always difficult for her fans—and in the fifties that meant everybody—to accept the reality they kept hearing about: the broken marriages, insecurity and a self-image of worthlessness, the sensation of being packaged as a commodity for the public's consumption and finally the suicidal loneliness. All that conflicted uncomfortably with the image we saw, bigger

Marilyn Monroe and Tom Ewell

than life, on screen. For in films at least, Marilyn Monroe was the ideal girl of the day—what every man dreamed of in a woman, and what every woman secretly wanted to offer her man.

The Seven Year Itch was not her best film, but it was the most definitive portrayal of the character she played best: her own screen image. An important detail of George Axelrod's script was his decision not to give her character a name; she is referred to as "The Girl," a seemingly available but strangely untouchable female creature, without clear past or future, who miraculously moves into the apartment upstairs when Richard Sherman (Tom Ewell) finds himself alone for the summer, after his wife and children have departed for a seashore vacation. Ewell's performance stands as a perfect caricature of the era's urban executive, his button-down brain filled with sexual fantasies picked up from his occupation as a publisher of paperback books—which saw their first great surge of popularity in the early fifties.

At moments it is unclear whether we are supposed to accept M.M.'s character as an actual person or as the living embodiment of Sherman's (and ultimately, the average man of the fifties) wildest fantasies. In the film's most widely remembered scene, they leave a movie theatre and, finding the air unbearably hot, The Girl decides to cool off by standing on the vent over the subways. A train rumbles by beneath, blowing the cool air up—and her dress with it. Laughingly, she struggles (but not too hard!) to keep it down as Ewell looks on, his mouth hanging open like a hound dog's.

If we can learn anything about a period of time by studying its sex symbols, then Marilyn is the greatest source of knowledge for the fifties. Significantly, she appeared out of the oblivion of a chorus line in 1950, and her career began to wane in 1959—even though she was as lovely as ever, and had just proven herselr both an excellent light comedienne in *Some Like It Hot* and, a bit later, as a capable dramatic actress in *The Misfits.* But it was as the reigning sex symbol of the decade that she was appreciated: the childlike impish eyes almost conflicting with the erotically suggestive mouth, the obliviousness countering the vulnerability. In the twilight years of Hollywood's golden era, she gave us the most authentically American blonde bombshell since Jean Harlow. Marilyn was many things to many moviegoers, but above all, she was a child of the fifties.

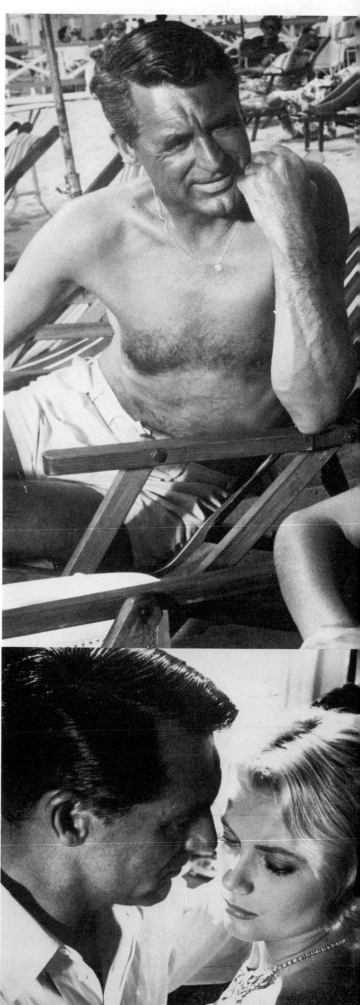

Jessie Royce Landis, Grace Kelly, John Williams

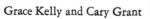

Grace Kelly and Cary Grant

138

On The Riviera: Cary Grant, Grace Kelly

To Catch a Thief

Paramount (1955)

Produced and directed by Alfred Hitchcock; screenplay by John M. Hayes, based on a novel by David Dodge.

CAST: *John Robie* (Cary Grant); *Frances Stevens* (Grace Kelly); *Mrs. Stevens* (Jessie Royce Landis); *H. H. Hughson* (John Williams); *Bertani* (Charles Vanel); *Danielle* (Brigitte Auber); *Foussard* (Jean Martinelli); *Germaine* (Georgette Anys); *Claude* (Roland Lesaffre); *Mercier* (Jean Hebey); *Lepic* (René Blancard); *Big Man in Kitchen* (Wee Willie Davis)

While Marilyn Monroe offered an idealized image of an all-American sex symbol, Grace Kelly was the princess next door: an uncanny combination of small-town virtues and regal demeanor. Underneath that prim, proper, ladylike iceberg of a surface we always suspected there beat the heart of a female animal, waiting for the right man to come along and perform the necessary melting operation. In 1956 she left her Hollywood career at its height, announcing her forthcoming marriage to Prince Rainier of Monaco. The events of the coronation were followed closely by an ador-

ing American public, who knew something the rest of the world did not: the marriage only made her title as "Princess Grace" official, for she had been America's own princess all along. Her most perfect incarnation of that role was in Alfred Hitchcock's masterly exercise in the suspense thriller vein, *To Catch a Thief.*

A slight but sophisticated and sexy film, it combined romance, mystery and comedy to perfection, and stands as the consummate example of what fifties viewers considered titillating and chic, including handsome on-location shooting along the French Riviera, and sharp dialogue filled with sexual double entendres.

John Robie (Cary Grant), a former cat-burglar, lives in luxury in his seaside mountaintop villa. When Cannes is struck by a rash of robberies done in his distinctive style, Robie is immediately suspect. Since he has no alibi his only answer is to catch the thief himself. Arriving in Monte Carlo, he searches for a suspect but finds time to romance Frances Stevens (Grace Kelly), a beautiful, rich young American midwesterner traveling in the company of her fun-loving nouveau riche mother (Jesse Royce Landis), whose diamonds are inevitably the thief's next target.

The culprit, it turns out, is a pert little French girl, Danielle (Brigitte Auber), the daugher of one of Robie's friends from the Resistance days. But before the climactic moment when Robie unmasks her, at night, on top of the elegant hotel as a masked ball goes on beneath them and spotlights pierce the darkness, Hitchcock seizes the opportu-

nity to take the viewer on a guided tour of the casinos, hotels, even the gorgeous seascapes of the surrounding Côte d'Azur.

Grace Kelly proved the perfect foil for Cary Grant who continued, throughout the fifties, to prove he was still the cinema's finest light-comedy performer. In one early sequence, Grant escorts Kelly on their first date to all the plush places, but she seems singularly unimpressed with him. Much to his consternation she speaks barely a word all evening long. But as the evening draws to a close and he begrudgingly walks her to her door, she turns at the last possible moment, kisses him ravenously, then closes the door behind her without so much as a "good night." Grant turns to face the camera, looks out at us in perplexed (but not unpleasant) surprise, and staggers away.

If the beauty of that sequence is its wordlessness, the dialogue bristles when, shortly thereafter, they drive to a breathtaking spot for a picnic. "Would you like a leg?" she asks, handing him basket of fried chicken. "I think I'd prefer a breast, actually," he sighs, after some consideration. But it is director Hitchcock who provides the movie's most stunning metaphor, when he cuts from their passionate embrace in her darkened hotel room to the blazing fireworks display outside, back and forth again and again until the explosions in the sky become representational of their lovemaking. Later films would depict the sex act more graphically, but they would never do so more effectively.

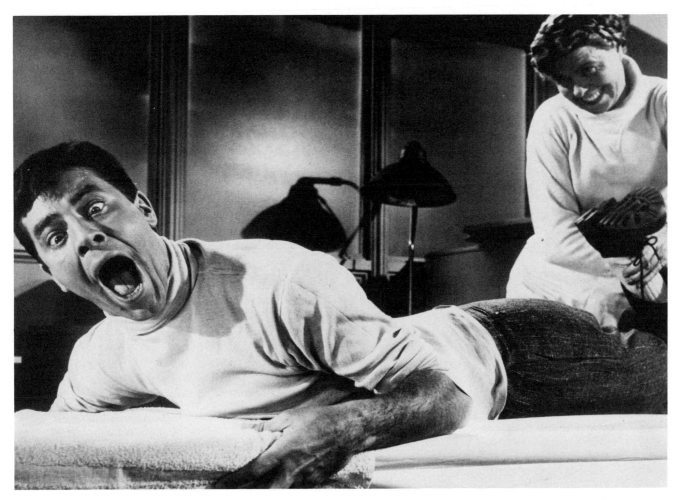

Jerry Lewis assumes a typical pose

Artists and Models

Paramount (1955)

Produced by Hal Wallis; directed by Frank Tashlin; screenplay by Mr. Tashlin, Hal Kanter and Herbert Baker; adaptation by Don McGuire, based on a play by Michael Davidson and Norman Lessing; music by Harry Warren; lyrics by Jack Brooks.

CAST: *Rick Todd* (Dean Martin); *Eugene Fullstack* (Jerry Lewis); *Bessie Sparrowbush* (Shirley MacLaine); *Abigail Parker* (Dorothy Malone); *Mr. Murdock* (Eddie Mayehoff); *Sonia* (Eva Gabor); *Anita* (Anita Ekberg); *Richard Stilton* (George (Foghorn) Winslow); *Ivan* (Jack Elam); *Secret Service Chief Samuels* (Herbert Rudley); *Secret Service Agent Rogers* (Richard Shannon); *Secret Service Agent Peters* (Richard Webb)

Dean Martin and Jerry Lewis succeeded in building themselves a large, loyal audience and an equally strong critical reputation on the cabaret circuit. They were thus well-known long before they appeared in their first film, *My Friend Irma*, a 1949 vehicle based on Marie Wilson's popular radio show. Though Dean and Jerry only received "featured player" billing, there was little doubt their presence made the programmer a box-office smash; just one year later, Martin and Lewis were receiving top billing in features tailored especially to their talents.

But despite generous budgets, most of their pictures were extremely disappointing. A notable exception is *Artists and Models,* the duo's first for director Frank Tashlin who, before entering the movie industry, had found employment as

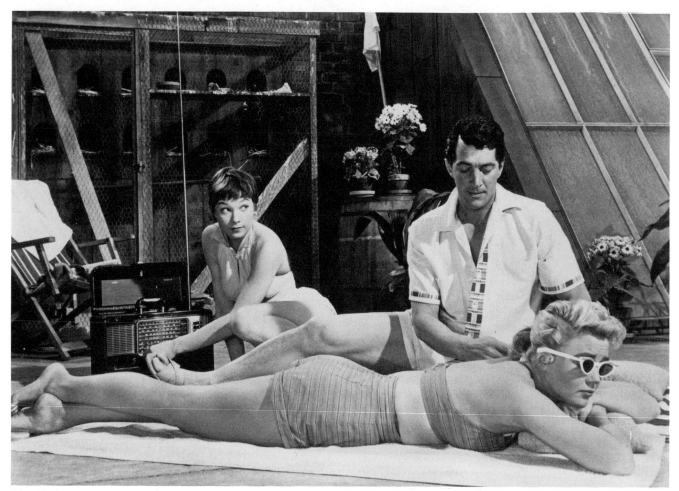

Elfin Shirley MacLaine attracted attention as the pixie-ish girl who grew jealous of Dean Martin's attentions toward Dorothy Malone

a professional cartoonist. He possessed a unique gift for endowing his films with the visual sense of a comic strip, a stylistic touch strikingly proper for the zany antics of Martin and Lewis—and exactly right for the subject matter of this film.

For though the scandal over violent comic books may be all but forgotten today, in the mid-fifties it was an explosive subject—as mothers and teachers loudly crusaded against the more bloodthirsty magazines. This is the only major picture to deal with the situation: Dean plays Rick Todd, a frustrated artist willing to sell out and work for a comic book publisher (Eddie Mayehoff) if only he can come up with enough wild ideas. Enter Jerry as Eugene Fullstack, virtually obsessed with comic books and able to articulate fantastic stories—while fast asleep. Before long, they are partners; Dean's talents for drawing and Jerry's for dreaming add up to a successful violent comic book that

soon has them under attack from pressure groups.

Besides comic books, the film also deftly satirized another institution of the fifties: the live TV talk show, in a memorable sequence featuring Jerry as a member of a televised panel–debate over the effects of comics on kids.

Two of the decade's important female stars received good exposure: the elfin Shirley MacLaine, in an early rendition of the charmingly brash, headstrong career girl she was to make famous, and Anita Ekberg, a gargantuan living caricature of Scandinavian sexuality. But most of all it was a vehicle for the comedy team that came off like Abbott and Costello with class: the handsome, casual Dino and the hysterical, childish Jerry, two opposites who complemented one another to perfection. But it was a perfection soon to end —one year and two pictures later, they went their separate ways.

A child's nightmare: Sally Jane Bruce and Billy Chapin view their mother, Shelley Winters, and their future foster-father, Robert Mitchum

The Night of the Hunter

United Artists (1955)

Produced by Paul Gregory; directed by Charles Laughton; screenplay by James Agee, based on the novel by Davis Grubb.

CAST: *Preacher Harry Powell* (Robert Mitchum); *Willa Harper* (Shelley Winters); *Rachel* (Lillian Gish); *Icey* (Evelyn Varden); *Ben Harper* (Peter Graves); *John* (Billy Chapin); *Pearl* (Sally Jane Bruce); *Birdie* (James Gleason); *Walt* (Don Beddoe); *Ruby* (Gloria Castille); *Clary* (Mary Ellen Clemons); *Mary* (Cheryl Gallaway)

Once *The Night of the Hunter* was in the can, nobody knew what to do with it. The film combined the talents of a significant star, Robert Mitchum; an important new character actress, Shelley Winters; a screenplay by one of the cinema's most gifted writers, James Agee; and the first (and only) directorial attempt by an important actor, Charles Laughton. It was conceived of and executed as an "art" film, but the resulant picture was a perverse, eerie tale of sexual repression and psychological aberration. United Artists had no idea how to best exploit *Hunter*, and finally it

Rachel (Lillian Gish) and her brood

was released as a programmer on a double bill with a B western. Oddly enough, it had its greatest exposure at kiddie matinees—and gave more than one child of the fifties nightmares for years after.

Many films of the early fifties sentimentalized the thirties; *Hunter* put an end to that. The film begins with the image of a starlit sky, while fairy-tale music is heard on the sound track and the face of a kindly old lady (Lillian Gish) appears, telling moralistic stories to little children. Suddenly, the scene shifts to a realistic view of the rural South during the Great Depression. Some children playing hide-and-seek—photographed from an odd aerial view—discover the molested body of a woman in a cellar. Immediately thereafter we meet Preacher Harry Powell (Robert Mitchum), a mad evangelist who holds frequent conversations with God and believes he is under direct orders from heaven to marry and kill wealthy widows. While attending a girlie show, where he falls into a fit of disgust and desire, he is hauled off to jail by some police officers who have discovered his car is a stolen one.

Powell's cellmate turns out to be young Ben Harper (Peter Graves), a man condemned to die for killing a man while robbing a store. Learning that the money has never been recovered, Powell after his release journeys to the man's home town, courts, marries, and eventually murders the man's brainless widow (Shelley Winters), then learns that only the two children, John (Billy Chapin) and Pearl (Sally Jane Bruce), know where the money is hidden.

The film becomes a nightmare–odyssey from a child's point of view, as John and Pearl escape downriver on an old barge, pursued by the mysterious, dark-clad figure who illustrates his mad, inverted Bible tales to unsuspecting peo-

ple by wrestling his two hands one against the other, the right featuring the letters L-O-V-E tattooed on the fingers, the left featuring H-A-T-E. When the children are adopted by lonely old Rachel (Lillian Gish), who cares for lost orphans, the preacher engages in a long duel with her—for the lives, and the souls, of the little ones.

The film juxtaposes the most obvious studio shots with vividly realistic images; but instead of clashing, they mesh into a strikingly original vision. The style of filmmaking obviously owes much to D. W. Griffith, whose own great superstar—the magnificent Miss Gish—gives the film a central core of decency. When she reads from the Bible to the two lost children, they are at first frightened because of their association with Powell. In time, though, they realize that instead of fire and brimstone she offers gentleness and reassurance in her interpretation of the book.

There is also a strong denunciation of vigilante justice and witch-hunting mentality, when the town gossip (Evelyn Varden) and her alcoholic husband (Don Beddoe)—originally responsible for matching the widow Harper with Powell—are the first to scream for his lynching and whip the townspeople into a bloodthirsty mob.

One of the picture's most powerful moments comes when young John, watching Powell being dragged off after Rachel has cornered him in the barn, loses control, as the act appears exactly the same as when his father was taken away. He grabs his sister's little rag doll—the hiding place for the money—and beats his mother's killer over the head with it, calling him "Dad" and finally breaking the doll apart, allowing the money to blow away. The picture ends on an optimistic note as the children, safe in Rachel's house, enjoy their first Christmas in her protective custody.

expressionistic lighting and camera angles added
e film's nightmarish quality: Shelley Winters and
rt Mitchum

The making of a modern folk hero: Audie Murphy, Paul Langton and Bruce Cowling

To Hell and Back

Universal-International (1955)

Produced by Aaron Rosenberg; directed by Jesse Hibbs; screenplay by Gil Doud, from the autobiography by Audie Murphy.

CAST: *Audie Murphy* (Audie Murphy); *Johnson* (Marshall Thompson); *Brandon* (Charles Drake); *Lieutenant Manning* (Gregg Palmer); *Kerrigan* (Jack Kelly); *Valentino* (Paul Picerni); *Maria* (Susan Kohner); *Novak* (Richard Castle); *Sanchez* (Art Aragon); *Swope* (Felix Noriega); *Lieutenant Lee* (David Janssen); *Saunders* (Brett Halsey); *Captain Marks* (Bruce Cowling); *Colonel Howe* (Paul Langton); *Steiner* (Julian Upton); *Mrs. Murphy* (Mary Field); *Thompson* (Denver Pyle)

Attempts to turn celebrities from the worlds of sports, politics and other areas of national interest into movie stars invariably fail—not because the person may lack acting talent but because he or she does not prove an effective movie "type." An exception is Audie Murphy who, after emerging from World War II as the most decorated American soldier of all time, was whisked off to Hollywood where he proved a natural for films: the perfect embodiment of the quietly courageous American hero. Murphy was most comfortably cast in B westerns and reigned as their undisputed king

throughout the decade. One of his rare ventures into major features was *To Hell and Back*, a fictionalized film account of his own combat experiences.

The film begins with Murphy's boyhood on a destitute Texas farm where, after the death of his mother (Mary Field), he supports his younger brothers and sisters by doing chores for the neighbors after school. With the outbreak of war Audie attempts to enlist first in the marines and then in the navy, but is rejected by both. Finally he is accepted by the army, despite his diminutive size, and performs numerous acts of heroism—culminating in the single-handed destruction of an entire fleet of German tanks, for which he is awarded the Congressional Medal of Honor.

Believing that a non-actor like Murphy would need all the help he could get, the filmmakers hired all the bright up-and-coming male performers in Hollywood to play the members of his squad. Each tried to out-act the others, with the result that they all look more like hammy actors than soldiers. Only Murphy struck a completely believable note: there isn't a moment when the viewer doubts the total sincerity of his self-portrayal, and his clipped, unemotional delivery of the lines, touched with a slight Texas drawl, is the strongest thing in the picture.

Otherwise it is quite disappointing. Though the battle sequences were exuberantly and extravagantly staged, the characterizations were cliché-ridden, the performances wooden, and the dialogue trite. But Murphy's charming awkwardness gave unplanned tenderness even to a slight romantic interlude involving him with a pretty Italian girl (Susan Kohner), and a warmth and conviction clearly far in excess of anything in Gil Doud's routine script or Jesse Hibbs's competent but unexciting direction.

Other than Murphy's presence, the most striking element of the film is its almost sentimental approach to the war years. Both the opening and the closing of the film feature soldiers gallantly marching in parade, filmed in glorious color. Though the picture is filled with death and destruction, the overall effect is not unpleasant. The soldiers never look muddy and underfed like those in *The Steel Helmet*, but clean, fresh and ready to go. No one questions for a moment their reasons for risking their lives in the war against Hitler. The Korean conflict failed to create equally strong patriotic feelings, or to stir Americans at home to a sense of community. *To Hell and Back* made the days when good and evil were as clear as black and white seem suddenly attractive and stirred more than one child to ask his father: "What did *you* do in the war, Daddy?"

147

Henry Fonda as Mister Roberts: a pacifist who longs for war

William Powell and Jack Lemmon

James Cagney and Henry Fonda

Mister Roberts

Warner Bros. (1955)

An Orange Production, produced by Leland Hayward; directed by John Ford and Mervyn Le Roy; screenplay by Frank Nugent and Joshua Logan, based on the play by the late Thomas Heggen and Joshua Logan, from the novel by Mr. Heggen, as produced on stage by Leland Hayward.

CAST: *Lieutenant Roberts* (Henry Fonda); *The Captain* (James Cagney); *Doc* (William Powell); *Ensign Pulver* (Jack Lemmon); *Lieutenant Ann Girard* (Betsy Palmer); *Chief Petty Officer Dowdy* (Ward Bond); *Mannion* (Phil Carey); *Dolan* (Ken Curtis); *Reber* (Nick Adams); *Stefanowski* (Harry Carey, Jr.); *Lindstrom* (Fritz Ford); *Bookser* (Pat Wayne); *Insigna* (Robert Roark)

Mister Roberts was first popular as a book by Thomas Heggen and then successful as a Broadway play as staged by Joshua Logan, so it seemed natural enough when plans were announced to turn it into a movie. But the project was hampered by serious arguments from the start. First there was director John Ford's insistence that Henry Fonda recreate his Broadway role and his flat refusal to direct if Warner Brothers gave the part to their first choices, William Holden or Marlon Brando. Then followed Ford's famous feud with Fonda, which culminated when the director left after one week of shooting, after which Mervyn Le Roy filled in. Despite such troubles, when the picture was finally released the popular and critical reception were all anyone could have hoped for.

Lieutenant Roberts (Fonda) is the cargo officer on a navy supply vessel, *The Reluctant.* Constantly he mourns the fact that he is missing the entire war. There is plenty to keep him busy, though, for the captain (James Cagney) is a small-time dictator, a harmless Queeg whose petty policies make the men's lives a state of perpetually mild misery. Roberts is their champion: his most effective means of upsetting the captain is tearing the man's beloved palm tree out of its pot and throwing the dismembered branches overboard. Roberts is aided in his plots by Doc (William Powell), a restrained, aging medical officer, and Ensign Pulver (Jack Lemmon), a wisecracking oddball who almost never leaves his berth. Their antics include smuggling some navy nurses, led by Lieutenant Ann Girard (Betsy Palmer) onto the boat, and setting off a homemade firecracker in the ship's laundry, which causes the entire vessel to be bathed in soapsuds.

Always, Roberts must compromise his own desire to transfer to a battleship with his concern for the crew. In the last sequence, after he has finally left, the men learn via a telegram that Mr. Roberts has been killed in a freak accident. At that point the previously cowardly Pulver takes over Roberts' role, marches up the ladder to the captain's lookout, and throws his precious palm tree overboard. Though Lemmon received a Best-Supporting Actor Oscar

for his portrayal, he often overplays the part. It is Fonda's lean, intelligent, and regrettably underrated performance that gives power and resonance to the picture.

Even though it is the film for which most moviegoers remember him, Fonda has never been particularly happy with the results. Everything that was subtly comic in the play had to be broadened for the wide screen—one nurse was changed to a whole fleet of nurses—and the distortion did not sit well with him. It did not, however, bother the film's audiences one whit.

Despite the abundance of good fun the film offered, much of its popularity was inherent in its timing. Without ever actually showing the war, it did manage to represent a romantic vision of combat and, like *To Hell and Back*, offered a picture of a simpler, less-complicated lifestyle that had, with the war's end, necessarily ended too. Underneath the light comedy, there is something dark and frightening about the conception: Mr. Roberts' perpetual desire to be done with the apathy and the boredom he experiences ends in sudden oblivion rather than the conclusive action he had hoped for. With the missiles poised and ready, just such a quick and total destruction appeared more and more likely to be the means by which our own ennui would end. Though set during World War II, what *Mister Roberts* really captured was the tone of the country in the mid-fifties.

Dan Dailey, Cyd Charisse, and Gene Kelly

It's Always Fair Weather

Metro-Goldwyn-Mayer (1955)

Produced by Arthur Freed; directed by Gene Kelly and Stanley Donen; story and screenplay by Betty Comden and Adolph Green.

CAST: *Ted Riley* (Gene Kelly); *Doug Hallerton* (Dan Dailey); *Jackie Leighton* (Cyd Charisse); *Madeline Bradville* (Dolores Gray); *Angie Valentine* (Michael Kidd); *Tim* (David Burns); *Charles Z. Culloran* (Jay C. Flippen); *Rocky Lazar* (Hal March); *Kid Mariacchi* (Steve Mitchell); *Mr. Fielding* (Paul Moxie)

The combined talents of librettists Betty Comden and Adolph Green, producer Arthur Freed, director Stanley Donen and choreographer–star Gene Kelly had all come together to make *Singin' in the Rain* a triumphant expression of early-fifties nostalgia for the thirties. Three years later the entire team reunited to create the definitive statement of mid-fifties disillusionment with the present. *It's Always Fair Weather* (the title, along with everything else in the film, is bitingly sarcastic) may just be the most cynical musical-entertainment move ever made, and one of the last

A celebration of optimism: Michael Kidd, Gene Kelly and Dan Dailey

great original movie musicals, a breed of films that all but disappeared by the decade's end.

The opening image is of Ted Riley (Gene Kelly), Doug Hallerton (Dan Dailey) and Angie Valentine (Michael Kidd) returning from World War II like a modern Spirit of '76—flags waving, drums beating, smiles of victory plastered across their faces. Thrilled to have the "last war ever" behind them and a future filled with nothing but peace, prosperity, and sweet promises ahead, they toast each other in a New York bar before going their separate ways. Virtually dancing in the streets at the thought of all the exciting promises their futures hold in store, they vow to meet in that same place exactly ten years hence. Then, a montage of newspaper headlines—depicting Eisenhower's election, the Cold War setting in, the Korean conflict raging, experiments with the Bomb—indicates the years slipping away far too quickly, as the world takes on a less than pleasant tone. And suddenly, it is 1955.

Each man returns to the bar, positive the others will not show. Each has failed to realize his dream. Ted, desirous of becoming a big-time entrepreneur, is a two-bit fight promoter. Doug, the would-be serious artist, has sold out for the big money of Madison Avenue's newly developed "creative advertising," and has turned into a stuffed-shirt junior executive. Angie, who wanted to become a gourmet chef, tolerates his life as a diner operator by referring to his place as "a cuisine." Worst of all, the men immediately realize that the sense of community they experienced during the crisis of World War II has dissolved. The one-time buddies now see that they have nothing in common—except some sentiment for the old, lost warmth.

But at that point the film abruptly changes its direction to focus on the important new medium which has come to dominate American life. One of Doug's business associates introduces Ted to Jackie Leighton (Cyd Charisse) and he pursues the pretty girl. At first, she isn't interested—but when Ted mentions his sour reunion with Doug and Angie, she takes note of him. For Jackie is a junior executive for a metropolitan TV station and is always faced with the task of finding original material for the late-night live talk show called *Throb of Manhattan*, presided over by an egomaniacal singing star/host, Madeline (Dolores Gray). On one section of the show, Madeline always condescendingly toasts a few of "the little people who make New York such a wonderful town," and Jackie plots to manipulate the three guys onto the set so their reunion can fill up the time spot that she is responsible for. Jackie doesn't do this maliciously but is oblivious to the feelings of those involved. However, when Ted, Doug and Angie are suddenly in front of the television cameras—their truly tragic reunion turned into a phony, sentimental "human interest featurette" that's sandwiched between home-viewer giveaways, audience participation gimmicks, and grotesque singing commercials—she experiences a sudden realization of the corruptness of her work.

It's Always Fair Weather allowed its audience to laugh at the apathy that had quietly but completely overcome us during the first half of the decade. In so doing, it helped us take a major step toward understanding, and eventually overcoming, our ennui.

Spencer Tracy and Ernest Borgnine

Bad Day at Black Rock

Metro-Goldwyn-Mayer (1955)

Produced by Dore Schary; directed by John Sturges; screenplay by Millard Kaufman, adapted by Don McGuire, from a story by Howard Breslin.

CAST: *John J. Macreedy* (Spencer Tracy); *Reno Smith* (Robert Ryan); *Liz Wirth* (Anne Francis); *Tim Horn* (Dean Jagger); *Doc Velie* (Walter Brennan); *Pete Wirth* (John Ericson); *Coley Trimble* (Ernest Borgnine); *Hector David* (Lee Marvin); *Mr. Hastings* (Russell Collins); *Sam* (Walter Sande)

By mid-decade, America was steeped enough in apathy that in films as diverse as *Mister Roberts, To Hell and Back,* and *It's Always Fair Weather,* we could wistfully recall the war years as "the good old days." But *Bad Day at Black Rock* took a decidedly different approach, suggesting that what for the last few years had been eating away at our country had its roots in the repressed, collective guilt left over from half-forgotten deeds of a decade ago.

The story begins as one-armed John J. Macreedy (Spencer Tracy) steps off a train at a lonely California desert

153

Spencer Tracy and Robert Ryan

Spencer Tracy and Walter Brennan

Spencer Tracy and Anne Francis

power-crazed, racist demagogue Reno and "patriotically" killed the oriental farmer at the height of World War II.

Macreedy, it turns out, is a wartime buddy of the Japanese farmer's son, who died saving Macreedy's life in combat. His stopover in Black Rock was only an attempt to pay his respects to the boy's father, and pass along a posthumous medal for heroism. But as the situation draws to a climax, the various townspeople are forced to choose sides. Pete Wirth (John Ericson), the young hotel clerk and old Doc Velie (Walter Brennan) try to help Macreedy find a means of escape, while Liz (Anne Francis), Pete's pretty young sister, aids Reno in his plot to kill the stranger.

After leading Macreedy into ambush on the desert by night, Liz is intentionally killed by Reno. But, before he can close in and finish off Macreedy, the one-armed man creates a makeshift Molotov cocktail out of some things he finds in the car, and uses it to incapacitate Reno. Finally, Macreedy's visit becomes a form of mass catharsis for the citizens of Black Rock, as those who find the courage to admit their involvement in the brutal, racist act of the past are freed from their gnawing sense of guilt.

Tracy's easygoing but unyielding presence—a man stranded in a hostile environment where nobody wants to get involved—helped elevate this picture into a modernized equivalent of *High Noon*. And, as in that earlier picture, the essential power comes from the richness of characterization (a wide spectrum of interesting and well-developed minor figures) that comes across in what is a remarkably compact picture (less than ninety minutes in length); but the film is certainly far more optimistic in its final fade-out, as the people face the truth and display an essential courage instead of allowing the loner to be killed. Fast-paced and involving as pure suspense melodrama, it also intelligently conveyed the crucial (though somewhat unconscious) problems of the time, proving that serious message-movies could also provide first-rate entertainment. Reno is clearly a Joseph McCarthy figure, manipulating the people to brutal acts they would not have believed themselves capable of, in the name of patriotism; the destruction of the Japanese farmer (even his land has been scarred), and the collective guilt of everyone's involvement in his fate, expressed the lingering memories of the bombing of Hiroshima.

One of the most effective moments occurs when the one-armed Macreedy is goaded into a fight with Coley, the fat bully, in the café. He uses a strange form of judo to defend himself and, momentarily, becomes an avenging spirit for the dead Japanese. The entire population of this ugly, isolated, self-contained town provide one of the most extreme cinematic renderings of the "lonely crowd" syndrome of the fifties.

town. A half-dozen inhabitants go into an actual state of shock at the sight of a stranger (it is the first time the Streamliner has stopped at their shabby crossroads in four years) and then turn hostile when he begins asking questions about a Japanese farmer who lived nearby some time back. Two of the locals, Coley (Ernest Borgnine) and Hector (Lee Marvin) try to goad Macreedy into a fight; the ineffectual sheriff (Dean Jagger) is stricken by the realization of what is going to happen but is afraid to do anything about it; the town boss, Reno (Robert Ryan), openly hints that the Macreedy man will never leave the area alive. Eventually the stunned Macreedy realizes that they suspect he's either a cop or a private detective, searching for the murderer of the Japanese. It is an act which all the townspeople are collectively guilty of—having followed the orders of the

The Killers: Stephen McNally, Lee Marvin, and J. Carrol Naish

Violent Saturday

20th Century-Fox (1955)

Produced by Buddy Adler; directed by Richard Fleischer; screenplay by Sydney Boehm, from a novel by William L. Heath.

CAST: *Shelley Martin* (Victor Mature); *Boyd Fairchild* (Richard Egan); *Harper* (Stephen McNally); *Linda* (Virginia Leith); *Harry Reeves* (Tommy Noonan); *Dill* (Lee Marvin); *Emily* (Margaret Hayes); *Chapman* (J. Carrol Naish); *Elsie* (Sylvia Sidney); *Stadt* (Ernest Borgnine) *Mrs. Stadt* (Ann Morrison); *David Stadt* (Kevin Corcoran); *Anna Stadt* (Donna Corcoran); *Mary Stadt* (Noreen Corcoran); *Slick* (Boyd Morgan); *Bank Teller* (Ellene Bowers); *Bartender* (Robert Osterloh); *Amish Farmer* (John Alderson)

In many respects *Violent Saturday* presented the definitive study of America during the decade. On the surface it was a slickly packaged, cinematically compact little crime picture. But the story picked up many elements from *High Noon* and predated many others of *Peyton Place*. Every detail, from the clearly representational characters to the very geography of the town, helped make *Violent Saturday* a perfect reflection of fifties mentality.

Three bank robbers (Lee Marvin, J. Carrol Naish, and Stephen McNally) journey to a small Arizona mining town where they plan to pull off a robbery. Their style is, significantly, "modern"—they have plotted out their course of action with the clinical care of a scientific team. As the trio checks into the hotel and plans for the heist they will enact

ashamed because, unlike the other kids' dads, Shelley did not see active service during the war.

Other townspeople, seemingly sedate enough, are also torn by deep problems. Elsie (Sylvia Sidney), the beloved old librarian, is in despair because the bank is about to foreclose on her house, and she steals a purse that a well-to-do lady leaves in the book rack. But when Elsie tries to dispose of the evidence that night, she runs into the bland bank clerk, Harry Reeves (Tommy Noonan), who quickly realizes what she's doing. She just as quickly notices that he is actually a peeping Tom out to watch a pretty nurse, Linda (Virginia Leith) undressing in her room. Elsie threatens to disclose his secret if he says anything about her.

At the town's country club on Friday night, the robbers casually enjoy a drink while Boyd picks up Linda. But though the girl finds him attractive, she brings him back to his home and puts him to bed. When Emily staggers in from her adulterous escapades, Linda tells her that she'd better work hard at keeping her husband or she may lose him. After Linda leaves, Boyd and Emily quarrel. In the morning they decide to try and save their marriage by going away for an extended vacation, and Emily heads for the bank to pick up some travellers' checks. She is in line next to Elsie, who is paying off her mortgage with the stolen money, when the robbery takes place. Elsie grows hysterical when the three men try to take her money away; bank clerk Harry reaches for a gun and the robbers shoot him; Emily is killed by a stray bullet.

The escaping robbers jump into Shelley's car and force him at gunpoint to drive to the isolated farm of a pacifist Amish man (Ernest Borgnine) and his family. The robbers tie up Shelley and the family in the barn, but they manage to break loose. Shelley kills the robber guarding him and then uses the man's shotgun to fight the others. At first the farmer refuses to help him, but when one of his children is hit by a stray bullet, he seizes a pitchfork and saves the wounded Shelley from the last of the robbers.

Shelley's ordeal serves as a substitute for the war he missed; his son finally accepts his executive father as a "real" man. The Amish farmer, attempting to live near but apart from the mainstream, is a second cousin to Grace Kelly in *High Noon*; he must cast off his isolationism and accept violence as a necessary means of exorcising evil. Boyd is deeply upset over the death of his wife, but the presence of the understanding Linda suggests a possible future for him.

Above all, the town itself—with its executive–engineers and bored housewives, its modern industrial economic base and growing sense of guilt over the war experience of a full ten years earlier, its seemingly normal but inwardly neurotic people and pocket of would-be dropouts—is an archetypal distillation of the various American types and trends of the time.

Saturday at noon, the film's focus turns toward the townspeople who lethargically go about their everyday lives but who will shortly be seriously affected by the upcoming incident.

Boyd Fairchild (Richard Egan) owns the mine that is the town's source of income. His constant work at the office has caused his wife Emily (Margaret Hayes) to grow bored with her affluent life; she spends her days either playing golf or making love with the town's available men. The knowledge of this, coupled with an inability to do anything about it, has driven Boyd to the brink of alcoholism, and he envies his hardworking executive-engineer, Shelley Martin (Victor Mature), who "always knows where his wife is." But Shelley has problems of his own; his young son is

Mickey Rooney, William Holden and Earl Holliman

Grace Kelly and William Holden

The Bridges at Toko Ri

Paramount (1955)

A Perlberg–Seaton Production, produced by William Perlberg and George Seaton; directed by Mark Robson; screenplay by Valentine Davies, based on the novel by James A. Michener.

CAST: *Lieutenant Harry Brubaker (USNR)* (William Holden); *Nancy Brubaker* (Grace Kelly); *Rear Admiral George Tarrant* (Fredric March); *Mike Forney* (Mickey Rooney); *Beer Barrel* (Robert Strauss); *Commander Wayne Lee* (Charles McGraw); *Kimiko* (Keiko Awaji); *Nestor Gamidge* (Earl Holliman); *Lieutenant Olds* (Richard Shannon); *Captain Evans* (Willis B. Bouchey); *Kathy Brubaker* (Nadene Ashdown); *Susie* (Cheryl Lynn Callaway); *Asst. CIC Officer* (James Jerkins); *Pilot* (Marshall V. Beebe); *MP Major* (Charles Tannen); *Japanese Father* (Teru Shimada)

Because the Korean conflict was a confused, clouded and complex situation, people wanted to forget rather than be reminded of it. Understandably, then, very few films resembling the propagandistic pictures of the early forties were made during the fifties. *Bridges at Toko Ri* was the most important studio film to deal with the conflict but avoided the major issues involved, dealing instead in an almost documentary fashion with the way in which the modern navy works in conjunction with the other armed forces. Interlaced with this was a psychological study of a man called back to active duty who believes he has already done enough for his country.

Lieutenant Harry Brubaker (William Holden) resents the intrusion of this new war on his life with his wife Nancy (Grace Kelly) and kids, but doggedly goes about his duty as a bomber pilot. Between missions he enjoys the

good-natured drinking company of a couple of likable helicopter rescue team members, Mike Forney (Mickey Rooney) and Nestor Gamidge (Earl Holliman), as well as earning the respect of his flight commander, Wayne Lee (Charles McGraw), and Rear Admiral George Tarrant (Fredric March), both of whom very much want to see Brubaker survive and return to the life he left. But during a crucial mission on a series of enemy bridges, Brubaker's plane is downed and, despite the efforts of his entire squadron and helicopter relief units, he is finally killed by enemy soldiers.

The film's intensity derives from the exceptionally realistic photography of naval operations, something author James Michener had been careful to describe in minute, knowing detail in his popular best seller, and which was here recorded with a kind of detached objectivity by the camera. It gave the film the visual style of a government-made training picture and, in fact, *Toko Ri* was made with full cooperation of the U.S. Navy. This provided the perfect backdrop for the depiction of Brubaker, who became a representational figure for all the servicemen of the Korean conflict, torn between a basic sense of patriotism and the nagging feeling that this war was a forgotten, thankless, unglorious affair. William Holden's face provided a perfect image of perpetual doubt, while Grace Kelly expressed in her one brief but significant scene an idealized conception of the kind of woman the Brubakers of the era longed to return home to.

Mike (Mickey Rooney) clutches the body of his pal Nestor (Earl Holliman) after the youth is killed in combat

159

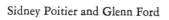
Sidney Poitier and Glenn Ford

Sidney Poitier, Vic Morrow, Paul Mazursky, Rafael Campos, Dan Terranova and Jameel Farah give the eye to Margaret Hayes

Blackboard Jungle

Metro-Goldwyn-Mayer (1955)

Produced by Pandro S. Berman; directed by Richard Brooks; screenplay by Mr. Brooks, based on the novel by Evan Hunter.

CAST: *Richard Dadier* (Glenn Ford); *Anne Dadier* (Anne Francis); *Jim Murdock* (Louis Calhern); *Lois Judby Hammond* (Margaret Hayes); *Mr. Warneke* (John Hoyt); *Joshua Y. Edwards* (Richard Kiley); *Mr. Halloran* (Emile Meyer); *Dr. Bradley* (Warner Anderson); *Professor A. R. Kraal* (Basil Ruysdael); *Gregory W. Miller* (Sidney Poitier); *Artie West* (Vic Morrow); *Belazi* (Dan Terranova); *Pete V. Morales* (Rafael Campos); *Emmanuel Stoker* (Paul Mazursky); *Detective* (Horace McMahon); *Santini* (Jameel Farah); *De Lica* (Danny Dennis)

The distinctive sounds of the new, youth-oriented musical groups were at first ignored by the general public. However, the high-pitched sound was an integral part of a new, frightening environment. So when Hollywood decided to film Evan Hunter's gutsy study of current youth's lifestyles, they were wise to realize that a traditional musical score would be inappropriate. Subsequently, *Blackboard Jungle* became the first major film to use rock 'n' roll as background music.

The story unfolds from the point of view of Richard Dadier (Glenn Ford), a dedicated young teacher who accepts a job in a major urban high school only to learn, on the first day of classes, that his students are totally uninterested in studying English and Social Studies. They answer

Artie (Vic Morrow) confronts Mr. Dadier (Glenn Ford) in the classroom

his questions rudely and sarcastically, communicating among themselves in jive talk and referring to him as "Daddy-O," a line of their lingo that sounds very much like his name. Jim Murdock (Louis Calhern), a fellow teacher who has grown cynical and indifferent from watching the changes in teenage styles during the last few years, hints to Dadier that he'd better understand the students are nothing more than animals, perfectly willing to commit acts of violence against the teachers. At first Dadier resists such a notion, but gradually comes to see it is not farfetched when an attractive young instructor, Lois Hammond (Margaret Hayes), is almost raped by some of the boys.

The film clearly indicates that the gangs are not to be taken as symbolic of all American teenagers, when Dadier visits another school and finds the students well mannered and eager to learn. But he turns down the opportunity to transfer there, deciding that this would be an admission of his own failure to deal with a modern phenomenon that has to be handled by somebody. Dadier concentrates on breaking through to Greg Miller (Sidney Poitier), a gifted Negro teenager with strong leadership abilities. But Dad-

ier's dedication is sorely tried when he learns one of the boys has been making threatening phone calls to his wife Anne (Anne Francis), forcing her to the edge of a nervous breakdown. Finally a classroom confrontation erupts between Dadier and Artie West (Vic Morrow), the ringleader of the troublemakers. Disarming the hoodlum of his switchblade, the teacher earns the respect of the class through his physical prowess.

Critics were quick to point out Sidney Poitier's outstanding performance—his impressive ability to project great human dignity beneath a brooding, uncertain exterior—and helped launch him on the road to stardom. Yet most reviewers were unkind to Vic Morrow, complaining that he merely imitated Brando in *The Wild One*. What they failed to take into account was that, in addition to reflecting many of the mannerisms and styles of the new breed, Brando had unwittingly provided the street punks with an ideal model which they copied scrupulously. Morrow's "Brando-isms" were a necessary part of his portrayal of a typical hoodlum, and also brought up the difficult but unavoidable question: do movies imitate life, or does life imitate the movies?

162

Natalie Wood and James Dean

Rebel Without a Cause
Warner Bros. (1955)

Produced by David Weisbart; directed by Nicholas Ray; screenplay by Stewart Stern, from an adaptation by Irving Shulman and a story by Mr. Ray.

CAST: *Jim* (James Dean); *Judy* (Natalie Wood); *Jim's Father* (Jim Backus); *Jim's Mother* (Ann Doran); *Judy's Mother* (Rochelle Hudson); *Judy's Father* (William Hopper); *Plato* (Sal Mineo); *Buzz* (Corey Allen); *Goon* (Dennis Hopper); *Ray* (Edward Platt); *Mil* (Steffi Sidney); *Maid* (Marietta Canty); *Lecturer* (Ian Wolfe); *Crunch* (Frank Mazzola)

There was no way anyone could have guessed *Rebel* would be anything more than a "misunderstood youth" exploitation programmer. In fact, when Nicholas Ray first presented his original story idea at Warner Bros., a number of junior executives insisted that it would make a marvelous co-staring vehicle for two highly touted new stars, Tab Hunter and Jayne Mansfield. But Ray refused to make the picture with anyone but James Dean and Natalie Wood—both considered untried and unlikely names for a theatre marquee —in the leading roles. He had watched Dean closely in his friend Elia Kazan's movie *East of Eden*, and felt convinced

The Staircase Confrontation: Ann Doran and James Dean

Dennis Hopper (far left) and hoodlum friends terrorize Sal Mineo

Sal Mineo and James Dean

164

given everything that money can buy—would have any reason to rebel in such a wild manner. Jim's parents (Jim Backus and Ann Doran) have just moved into new neighborhood from some unstated place following Jim's recent growing reputation there as a troublemaker. What they fail to grasp is that their own inability to provide him with strong moral examples and a stable home environment sends Jim out at night.

The following morning, as Jim departs for his first day at a new school, his parents plead with him to make "some *nice* friends" this time. He spots Judy leaving her home and offers her a ride, but she refuses as a group of her friends come riding up wildly, almost spilling out of their convertible. Her boyfriend Buzz (Corey Allen) is the leader of the school's toughest crowd and, during the day, the two boys are forced by circumstances into a rumble with a switchblade knife. Jim is befriended only by the lost, lonely Plato, who sees in the strong-willed fellow an ideal pal. But Jim is forced to prove his courage by meeting Buzz that night for a "chickie race" in which they will drive stolen cars over the end of a cliff, with the one who jumps out first being the loser.

When Buzz is trapped in his car and killed, all the kids panic and run away. Judy is drawn to Jim almost in the manner of a primitive woman naturally belonging to her mate's conqueror. Pursued both by the police and the other hoodlums, Jim, Judy and Plato hide in an abandoned mansion on a hill overlooking the city. They momentarily form a makeshift family unit in which Jim and Judy care for the frightened Plato. But when they find themselves unable to prevent the boy's death at the hands of a trigger-happy police sniper, Jim and Judy come away from the experience considerably more empathetic about their own parents' inadequacies.

The film's central scene occurs in a darkened planetarium where the teenagers view, as part of their science class, a representation of the earth's eventual destruction, while the casual voice of a scientist explains that our world "is not missed in the universe." Essentially, the decade's breakthroughs in science robbed from young people our traditional beliefs in man's importance and immortality—without providing any substitute to fill the vacuum. The film's title is ironic, for in the picture, as in real life, their disorderly rebellion grows from precisely this problem. The corresponding scene is the chickie race on the cliff, which symbolically depicts their chaotic but headlong rush toward an oblivion which, in a frightening way, is highly attractive to these impressionable young people trapped in a world without meaning.

that the young man's burning intensity perfectly expressed the desperate torment of the nation's youth, while Natalie Wood's combination of light-hearted mockery and inner vulnerability would provide a perfect complement. Ray was quite right and, thanks to the perfect casting, coupled with the director's own impressive imagination, *Rebel* emerged as the most perceptive and significant film to deal with the lives of adolescents at mid-decade.

Rebel obeys an almost classical unity of time and place, beginning one night and ending on the dawn of the following day. In the opening sequence Jim (James Dean) is picked up by the police and questioned at the precinct house by the youth officer, Ray (Edward Platt), as are two other teenagers, Judy (Natalie Wood) and Plato (Sal Mineo). At first they appear very much like the juvenile delinquents in *Blackboard Jungle*, but that is not the case: as compared to the deprived slum kids in that film, these are all well-to-do children of parents who live in the upper-middle-class suburbs of Los Angeles. And as their folks are called down to the police station to pick up their children, they cannot understand why their kids—having been

Director Nicholas Ray found the perfect visual metaphors for his story. As Jim enters the school for the first time he is seen stepping on the official crest, symbolizing the unintentional nature of his conflict with tradition. When his parents argue on the staircase of his house, he is between them; at those moments when his father asserts control the camera records the scene realistically but at those when Jim's mother is in authority, the visual image is distorted—suggesting Jim's mental state and his need for a strong father figure. At one point Jim finds his father (who is wearing an apron) picking up some food he has just dropped, "before your mother sees it," and the youth attempts to convince the man to leave it lying there. "If only Dad had the guts to knock Mom cold once!" he sighs to himself later.

For Dean, *Rebel* signified cult worship and immortality. Brando had disavowed similar attention for his role of Johnny in *The Wild One*, insisting vehemently he was not in any way like the character he'd portrayed. Dean, on the other hand, relished the identification of his own personality with the inarticulate, deeply troubled figures he embodied—so much so that in this, his most clearly personal picture, he and his character share the same first name.

Betsy Blair and Ernest Borgnine

Marty

United Artists (1955)

A Harold Hecht–Burt Lancaster Presentation, produced by Harold Hecht; directed by Delbert Mann; screenplay and story by Paddy Chayefsky.

CAST: *Marty* (Ernest Borgnine); *Clara* (Betsy Blair); *Mrs. Pilletti* (Esther Minciotti); *Catherine* (Augusta Ciolli); *Angie* (Joe Mantell); *Virginia* (Karen Steele); *Thomas* (Jerry Paris); *Ralph* (Frank Sutton); *The Kid* (Walter Kelley); *Joe* (Robin Morse)

"What do you wanna do tonight, Marty?"

"I don't know, Angie. What do *you* wanna do?"

That simple exchange of dialogue quickly became one of the most quoted of the decade, and established a new school of motion pictures dealing with the ordinary problems of simple people. They came to be called "clothesline dramas," an industry term for stories centering around what one

Esther Minciotti and Ernest Borgnine

Marty (Ernest Borgnine) and Angie (Joe Mantell) try to pick up some girls

housewife says to another while hanging up the afternoon wash. Such films also provided a new way for the motion picture industry to adjust to television. Instead of criticizing the new threat or instigating gimmicks like 3-D and Cinerama, producers discovered that television could provide as important a source of material as popular novels and Broadway plays had traditionally furnished. The live television playhouses served as a testing ground for new writers like Reginald Rose and Rod Serling: film people could pick and choose among the hundreds of plays presented in any one season, buying the rights to the very best ones for future projects. *Marty* was one of the first, and by far the most commercially and artistically successful, of all such TV-to-film adaptations.

Originally presented on the highly respected "Playhouse 90," Paddy Chayefsky's drama did undergo some serious revisions en route to the big screen. Most notably, the Jewish butcher portrayed on TV by Rod Steiger was turned into an

Italian, for no better reason than that Italian Americans constitute a significantly larger minority group (and thus a possibly larger paying audience) than Jewish Americans. Despite such purely commercial concessions, no one could deny the picture's simple, sincere power.

Like *Rebel Without a Cause, Marty* obeys a classical sense of the unities of time and place in telling a love story about two lonely people. But whereas *Rebel* offered a pair of attractive, romantic youngsters, *Marty* focused on a fat man (Ernest Borgnine) who meets a homely woman (Betsy Blair) but must overcome the well-meaning advice of his family and friends who believe he deserves better. The story climaxes with his eventual rejection of their sentimental notions about him, and his courageous self-realization that the woman his pals call a "dog" and whom his mother (Esther Minciotti) rejects for not being Italian, is the best thing that's ever happened to him. In the final sequence he wrenches free of their influence and calls her for a second date; jubilant about his personal victory, the inarticulate man walks out onto the street and expresses his happiness by slamming a "STOP" sign with his fist.

Significantly, the woman's loneliness is depicted by a shot of her listlessly watching "The Ed Sullivan Show" on television—filmmakers could not resist a subtle potshot at the competition. But most of Chayefsky's perceptive observations of what life is really like for ordinary people were retained, including a warmly comic sequence in which Marty and his buddies discuss their favoirte "intellectual" writer, Mickey Spillane. As they fondly recall their favorite blood-and-guts passages, which sound absurd from the descriptions, one of the guys continually asserts: "Boy, he sure c'n *write!*" The New York locations gave the film a corresponding visual authenticity.

By mid-decade, styles in film had become polarized. The medium-budget productions all but died out, giving way to wide-screen stereophonic-sound spectaculars on the one hand, and small-screen black-and-white ninety minute kitchen-sink dramas on the other. *Marty* epitomized this trend. Yet is was one of those films that "almost didn't get made": some producers at United Artists were positive nobody would go see a movie about an overweight and balding Bronx butcher. The picture's unexpected commercial success caused all the major studios to carefully scrutinize the high-quality TV anthologies, and dozens of other adaptations followed. But none enjoyed the success of *Marty*. Too often, oversized budgets drowned the essentially small stories in production values and actually detracted from the human interest drama that had been so effective on the smaller home screen.

Liberace, Dorothy Malone

Sincerely Yours

Warner Bros. (1955)

An International Artists Ltd. Production, produced by Henry Blanke; directed by Gordon Douglas; screenplay by Irving Wallace.

CAST: *Anthony Warren* (Liberace); *Marion Moore* (Joanne Dru); *Linda Curtis* (Dorothy Malone); *Howard Ferguson* (Alex Nicol); *Sam Dunne* (William Demarest); *Sarah Cosgrove* (Lori Nelson); *Mrs. McGinley* (Lurene Tuttle); *Alvie Hunt* (Richard Eyer); *Grandfather Hunt* (James Bell); *J. R. Aldrich* (Herbert Heyes); *Dr. Eubank* (Edward Platt); *Dick Cosgrove* (Guy Williams); *Mr. Rojeck* (Ian Wolfe); *Zwolinski* (Otto Waldis); *Mrs. Cosgrove* (Barbara Brown)

Marty demonstrated one way in which movies could adjust to television. But in addition to immortalizing the best of the live TV originals, moviemakers also experimented with starring the most popular television personalities in feature films. For the most part such attempts failed. When TV's most beloved husband-and-wife team, Lucille Ball and Desi Arnaz, were co-starred in *The Long, Long Trailer*, the film surprised its makers by dying at the box office. Movie producers learned very quickly that the qualities which made a show business personality popular on the small screen might make that figure quite unfit for the very different demands of larger-than-life film stardom. Also, audiences were less than willing to pay to see someone they could view at home at no charge.

Liberace, Dorothy Malone

One of the most fascinating attempts to create a movie star out of a pop-culture phenomenon was the casting of Liberace in *Sincerely Yours*. Liberace first tried out his act in nightclubs, where audiences were bowled over by the elaborateness of his "mood music" style. Sitting at a grand piano in his sequined tuxedo and surrounded by candelabras, knocking out popular polkas and classics by Chopin with equal enthusiasm, smiling toothily as his dimples cracked in his cheeks and then dispensing in a babyish voice some sentimental dribble about his brother George, Liberace predated what came to be called "Camp"—and, perhaps, inspired it. Television, hungry for time-killers, was quick to tap him for a show that was highly popular—though no one knew for certain whether viewers tuned in because they were ardent music lovers or simply had to see Liberace to believe him.

Warner Bros. decided to give him a try at film stardom, but while the picture was a moneymaker Liberace's motion picture career turned out to be a virtual one-shot. He played Anthony Warren, a successful concert pianist whose life is happy until he suddenly loses his hearing. For a brief while he becomes an embittered man. His faithful and adoring secretary Marion (Joanne Dru) and his beautiful fiancée Linda (Dorothy Malone) try to keep his mind off his plight. In a bizarre combination of Hitchcock's recent hit *Rear Window* and the classic drama *The Man Who Played God*, Anthony confines himself to his elegant Manhattan penthouse apartment; realizing that as his hearing has diminished his sense of sight has heightened, he begins scrupulously studying the world on the street below through a telescope. Eventually Anthony masters an ability to read the lips of the people below him and chastises himself for his self-pity when he sees that the great masses of people have problems far worse than his.

His zest for living is revived when he decides to come down from his ivory tower and help those in need. When he views a poor old Irish lady (Lurene Tuttle) whose daughter (Lori Nelson) has married into society and is now ashamed of her own mother, he arranges for the elderly woman to appear at the "in" event of the social season, a gala charity ball, wearing a marvelous gown; she shows up everyone and is befriended by the daughter's stuffy in-laws. A crippled child (Richard Eyer) who dreams of being an athlete is given an operation—and a football helmet. But Anthony's most self-sacrificing act comes when, through his telescope, he lip-reads a conversation between his fiancée and a strange man and learns that she has fallen in love with the fellow but is too good at heart to leave Anthony when he needs her more than ever. After Anthony sets Linda free, two miracles occur: first, he discovers that Marion is really the right woman for him, and second, his hearing returns.

Liberace was given ample opportunity to play a wide selection of beloved songs. But his personality, while quite astonishing, was hardly suited to movies. After *Sincerely Yours*, he returned to nightclubs and television, where he continued his highly successful career.

Kevin McCarthy and Dana Wynter

Invasion of the Body Snatchers

Allied Artists (1956)

Produced by Walter Wanger; directed by Don Siegel; screenplay by Daniel Mainwaring, based on a *Collier's* Magazine story by Jack Finney.

CAST: *Dr. Miles Binnel* (Kevin McCarthy); *Becky Driscoll* (Dana Wynter); *Dr. Dan Kauffman* (Larry Gates); *Jack* (King Donovan); *Theodora* (Carolyn Jones); *Sally* (Jean Willes); *Nick* (Ralph Dumke); *Wilma* (Virginia Christine); *Uncle Ira* (Tom Fadden); *Mr. Driscoll* (Kenneth Patterson); *Psychiatrist* (Whit Bissell); *Gas Man* (Sam Peckinpah); *Doctor* (Richard Deacon)

When Allied Artists released *Invasion of the Body Snatchers*, they had no idea that it was anything but a second-rate programmer. But the film's impact was phenomenal: for the remainder of the fifties, all anyone had to do to give people the chills was to mention the word "pod."

Dr. Miles Binnell (Kevin McCarthy) returns to Santa Mira, his small home town in Southern California, following a medical society convention in a nearby city. He is shocked to find his usually quiet office overflowing with would-be patients, all hysterically claiming that members of their family are not really the people they look like, but im-

Searching the cellar for "pods": Larry Gates, Tom Fadden, King Donovan, Kevin McCarthy

An American Nightmare: the small town becomes a police state

172

posters. Though fascinated with what he takes to be a mild case of mass hysteria, Miles is distracted by lovely Becky Driscoll (Dana Wynter), an old flame who has just returned to town following an unpleasant divorce. He is shocked, though, when the hysteria stops as quickly as it started: the people who were so upset only the day before come to reassure him that they were just being silly.

Miles soon comes to believe that the claims he had laughed at are serious when his friends Jack (King Donovan) and Theodora (Carolyn Jones) discover an amorphous corpse in their cellar. He has them call the police, but the body disappears and the officers refuse to take them seriously. Miles wonders if the seemingly pleasant town is in the grip of some terrible force. When Becky analyzes her uncle's actions since her return, she admits he has been acting strangely too. Finally they find in their respective cellars huge pods which are creating exact duplicates of them, to take over completely while they sleep.

When Miles and Becky try to flee, they find that the smiling faces they encounter are part of a vast conspiracy to keep them from escaping: the gas station attendants insist the pumps are dry, the police explain that roads are washed out, telephone operators apologize that all lines to Washington are tied up. Hiding in Miles' office and fighting to keep from falling asleep, the two observe the townspeople obeying their police leader like a herd of sheep. The town psychiatrist (Larry Gates) arrives and explains that resistance is foolish since possession is painless. In the pod society there are no emotions, and while that means no love, it also rules out hate, war, and crimes of passion—a beautiful world without discord. But Miles and Becky are repulsed by the idea of allowing their love to end.

They flee and hide in a cave above the city, but when Becky falls asleep for a moment and Miles tries to kiss her awake, it is like kissing a corpse; he knows she is one of them. They pursue him to the highway, where he tries to hop a truck heading for the outside world. But Miles falls to the pavement when he sees the contents: pods being transported to other towns. Standing in the highway and screaming at passing motorists, who laugh at what they think is an obnoxious drunk, he frantically turns to the audience and screams: "They're coming . . . and *you're* next!"

When Allied Artists executives screened the film, they found it so terrifying that they insisted director Don Siegel add an explanatory prologue and epilogue, closing with the implication that the pods will be stopped. The additions so compromise the movie that, often when it is shown on television today, these scenes are removed.

Susan Strasberg and Kim Novak

Cliff Robertson and William Holden

William Holden and Verna Felton

Picnic

Columbia (1956)

Produced by Fred Kohlmar; directed by Joshua Logan; screenplay by Daniel Taradash, based on the play by William Inge.

CAST: *Hal Carter* (William Holden); *Rosemary Sydney* (Rosalind Russell); *Madge Owens* (Kim Novak); *Flo Owens* (Betty Field); *Millie Owens* (Susan Strasberg); *Alan Benson* (Cliff Robertson); *Howard Bevans* (Arthur O'Connell); *Mrs. Helen Potts* (Verna Felton); *Linda Sue Breckenridge* (Reta Shaw); *Bomber* (Nick Adams); *Mr. Benson* (Raymond Bailey); *Christine Schoenwalder* (Elizabeth W. Wilson); *Juanita Badger* (Phyllis Newman); *Policeman* (Don C. Harvey); *Policeman* (Steve Benton)

Films of the thirties and forties romanticized life in small-town America; films of the fifties criticized it, hinting that behind the charming façade of ordinary small-town inhabitants there existed empty, unsatisfied people. William Inge dramatized that dissatisfaction in his Broadway play *Picnic*, and won a Pulitzer Prize for his efforts. By mid-decade, Hollywood had reached a level of maturity that allowed moviemakers to deal with the subject in a non-compromising manner.

The story unfolds in a quiet Kansas town preparing for its annual Labor Day picnic. Into that milieu wanders Hal Carter (William Holden), a stranger who hops off a freight train and searches out Alan Benson (Cliff Robertson), son

Betty Field and Kim Novak

Kim Novak and William Holden

Rosalind Russell and Arthur O'Connell

of the town's wealthiest man and a friend of Carter's from college. Benson insists Carter join the festivities and meet his fiancée, Madge Owens (Kim Novak), a poor but beautiful girl. But the moment the two come into contact, they fall in love.

Picnic is filled with fascinating emotional battles both between and inside of its characters. In addition to the growing resentment between the young men, there is the hatred of Madge's mother Flo (Betty Field) for this footloose fellow who would carry off her well-placed daughter—a situation aggravated by Flo's memory of her own passionate love for a handsome, shiftless husband who deserted her. Madge's younger sister Millie (Susan Strasberg), just on the outskirts of adolescence, represses her frustration at not being beautiful by playing to the hilt her role as the town's lovable tomboy—at first enjoying having Hal for her "date" and then boiling over with anger when, like everyone else, he is intoxicated by her sister.

But Kim Novak made Madge the most intensely interesting character in the film, a sweet girl bored with being told she's beautiful and, at the same time, a morosely romantic character. Madge clutches to her half-dreams that the "right" man will come along, while accepting the prospect of marriage to the likable rich boy who can offer her everything except a fulfillment to her notion that life should hold something more than financial security. Complementing her, Holden brought his screen image as a sardonic loner to his role, turning Hal into the fifties concept of a dropout from society—and a symbolic alternative to middle-class morality.

Hal's presence not only wreaks havoc with the Owens and Benson families, but also people only peripherally related to the central conflict. Rosemary (Rosalind Russell), the lovably wisecracking unmarried schoolteacher explodes, in Carter's company, into an hysterical old maid shrieking to her businessman beau (Arthur O'Connell) for a ring. When director Joshua Logan lit up the sky with frantic fireworks, he employed the CinemaScope screen to create a visual symbol impossible in the original stage version: the frantic display of colors provides a mute metaphor for Carter's effect on the entire town—clearly symbolic, in its quality of averageness, of Middle America.

Logan subscribed to the popular new trend of shooting entirely on location, and brought his cast and crew to Halsted, Kansas; as a result, his wide screen is constantly filled with panoramic images of life in the heartlands that struck audiences as clearly authentic, while the screenplay by Daniel Taradash (who had proved his talents as an adapter

William Holden and Kim Novak

of film properties from other sources with *From Here to Eternity*) retained the play's poetic qualities but adjusted them to the more realistic medium of film. The total effect was to strip away all remaining sentimental illusions that audiences might still harbor about small-town life, by at last bringing into the open all the deep-rooted doubts and interpersonal conflicts of "normal" American people.

Gregory Peck and Jennifer Jones

The Man in the Gray Flannel Suit

20th Century-Fox (1956)

Produced by Darryl F. Zanuck; directed by Nunnally Johnson; screenplay by Mr. Johnson, from the novel by Sloan Wilson.

CAST: *Tom Rather* (Gregory Peck); *Betsy* (Jennifer Jones); *Hopkins* (Fredric March); *Maria* (Marisa Pavan); *Judge Bernstein* (Lee J. Cobb); *Mrs. Hopkins* (Ann Harding); *Caesar Cardella* (Keenan Wynn); *Hawthorne* (Gene Lockhart); *Susan Hopkins* (Gigi Perreau); *Janie* (Portland Mason); *Walker* (Arthur O'Connell); *Bill Ogden* (Henry Daniell); *Mrs. Manter* (Connie Gilchrist); *Edward Schultz* (Joseph Sweeny); *Barbara* (Sandy Descher); *Pete* (Mickey Maga); *Mahoney* (Kenneth Tobey); *Florence* (Ruth Clifford); *Miriam* (Geraldine Wall)

The in-fightings of junior executives received ample screen treatment in *Executive Suite, Woman's World* and a half-dozen lesser imitations; producer Darryl F. Zanuck seized on the notion of taking this melodramatic figure and giving him epic dimension. He based his two-and-a-half-hour super-production on Sloan Wilson's best-selling novel which featured, as its cover illustration, the silhouette of a handsomely tailored man in a Brooks Brothers suit—a symbol of every fellow who had moved into a vice-presidency within some corporate structure since the war. For the film version, that suit was perfectly filled by Gregory Peck, whose personal intensity and unsentimental warmth made the character of Tom Rather a singular and believable individual, yet also a clearly representational image of the modern man of the fifties.

Tom Rather lives in the newly fashionable suburbs of Westport, Connecticut, and commutes by train each day to his executive job in New York City. His position within a major industry is respectable but not entirely satisfying. Tom has a highly ambitious relationship with his boss, Mr. Hopkins (Fredric March), and, to try and further himself, takes on an extra job as ghost-writer for the president of a major television and radio network. But he finds that he has spread himself too thin; he cannot cope with all the petty corruptions he encounters everyday at work or the constant problems that arise after he reaches home—where his wife Betsy (Jennifer Jones) and children expect him to be alert to every little trauma of their own.

Tom Rather's world at first appears an admirable one, but quickly we realize that he lives a life of quiet desperation. An endless series of assaults on his psyche turn his outwardly comfortable lifestyle into a split level trap. And while his daily routine becomes ever more nightmarish—constantly wearing away at his energies while denying him any opportunity to fulfill his potentials—he must also face a haunting memory from a decade earlier.

The war years, though seemingly the long-buried past, return to trouble modern suburban man as clearly as they do the rural rubes of *Bad Day at Black Rock*. Traveling to work on the train, the leather jacket of a fellow seated in front of Tom forces him to recall an incident in which, by accident, he caused the death of his best friend during a combat mission. But the experience of the war destroyed his innocence in more ways than one, for it also initiated a gnawing sense of guilt—long repressed but gradually, inevitably working its way out into the open—that Tom can never quite escape from. Pressures from all sides force him to at last reveal to Betsy the fact that he fathered a child during a brief wartime romance with a lovely Italian girl (Marisa Pavan).

Gregory Peck's simple yet eloquent performance elevated what could easily have become another variation of an already stereotyped figure into a man of tragic dimensions; his Tom Rather is a fundamentally decent person trapped between present and past, caught up in the destructive comforts of suburbia and defeated in his creative desires by the dangerous lure of the new affluence. Sloan Wilson's story provided what was clearly an insider's view of the people inhabiting the newly created commuter world, stretching between the skyscraper landscape of Manhattan and the suburban sprawl of Connecticut, while Nunnally Johnson's direction turned the wide screen into a movie-mirror, allowing the audience to see, in perspective, their world.

Lee J. Cobb, Jennifer Jones and Gregory Peck

Gregory Peck and Jennifer Jones

Jeffrey Hunter, John Wayne, Harry Carey, Jr. and Monument Valley

The Searchers

Warner Bros. (1956)

Produced by Merian C. Cooper for C. V. Whitney Pictures; directed by John Ford; screenplay by Frank S. Nugent, based upon the novel by Alan LeMay.

CAST: *Ethann Edwards* (John Wayne); *Martin Pawley* (Jeffrey Hunter); *Laurie Jorgensen* (Vera Miles); *Captain Reverend Sam Clayton* (Ward Bond); *Debbie Edwards* (Natalie Wood); *Lars Jorgensen* (John Qualen); *Mrs. Jorgensen* (Olive Carey); *Chief Scar* (Henry Brandon); *Charlie McCorry* (Ken Curtis); *Brad Jorgensen* (Harry Carey, Jr.); *Emilio Figueroa* (Antonio Moreno); *Mose Harper* (Hank Worden); *Debbie (as a child)* (Lana Wood); *Lieutenant Greenhill* (Pat Wayne); *Look* (Beulah Archuletta); *Aaron* (Walter Coy).

The concern with civil rights led to numerous motion pictures dealing directly with the problem of racism. But it also made itself felt in more subtle ways, invading areas as unlikely as the western. John Ford, one of the most traditional practitioners in that genre, bypassed most of the new styles in "adult" and Freudian westerns, continuing instead to make the conventional cowboy pictures he had brought back into fashion with *Stagecoach* in 1937. But even Ford was influenced, however unconsciously, by the new styles and themes that were entering the American mainstream. In many respects, *The Searchers* (his best film of the decade and, in the judgment of some Ford scholars, his best film) is a traditional John Ford western. It is filled with Texas Rangers, the United States Cavalry, courageous homesteaders and marauding Indians—not to forget the entire John Ford stock company of players. However, in just as many other ways, it is a western that could have been produced only in the fifties—containing bizarre, often unspeakable relationships between people and a clear attempt to deal with the problem of racism in America.

The Searchers also provided John Wayne with his most demanding role since Howard Hawks' *Red River* in 1948, and Wayne gives the kind of complex performance he delivers when, on rare occasions, his considerable talents as a dramatic and comic player are taxed. As Ethan Edwards, he portrays a westernized Wandering Dutchman who returns to the Texas homestead of his brother Aaron (Walter Coy) two years after the end of the Civil War. He gives no explanation as to his whereabouts during the intervening period, but his saddlebags are filled with gold. Ethan takes an immediate resentment to young Martin Pawley (Jeffrey Hunter), a suspected half-breed who now lives with the family on an equal basis. But when the Texas Rangers under the command of Captain Reverend Clayton (Ward Bond) ride up and ask for help in searching out some reservation-jumping Indians, Ethan and Martin volunteer to go along so that Aaron can stay and protect the family. While they are gone, however, Chief Scar (Henry Brandon) and his warriors return, killing all but the child Debbie (Lana Wood), whom they carry off.

From that point on, Ford follows the five year search of the uneasy allies as they relentlessly track the tribe across the American West, trying to recover Debbie. Occasionally, they return home to the Edwards' neighbors, Lars Jorgenson (John Qualen) and his wife (Olive Carey). But though Martin is in love with their daughter Laurie (Vera Miles), he refuses to let Ethan set out alone on the trek for fear that the racist Ethan may not, after all, want to save little Debbie.

And he is right. When they eventually find the girl (now played by Natalie Wood) Ethan wants to shoot her since she has been sleeping with an Indian and is, to him, "one of them." He is stopped only by the intervention of Martin, and the frightened Debbie runs away. Ironically, the search finally ends at home, where Ethan and Martin have returned in exhaustion: the cycle is completed as Captain Clayton rides up to report Scar's presence in the area. A raid on the Indian village allows Ethan to come into contact with Debbie once more. Face to face with his blood kin, he realizes that "Indian" or not, she is still his—and, in a marvelous gesture, sweeps her up into his arms with the words: "Let's go *home*."

The story is a morality play in which the rugged Ameri-

Jeffrey Hunter and Natalie Wood

can individualist Ethan—and, subsequently, America itself —works himself free of racism, which ultimately centers around a fear of miscegenation. But this fear, as well as Ethan's dedication to Debbie, is given an extra dimension by the playing of the early scenes: the unstated tenderness between Ethan and his brother's wife, culminating in the short, powerful sequence in which they exchange wordless glances of love in front of the embarrassed Captain Clayton, suggests they have previously been lovers. And since Debbie is dark like Ethan instead of fair-haired, as her father and sister are, there is a strong hint that she is actually Ethan's daughter—a concept which justifies the otherwise unwarranted steadfastness of his search.

Nothing of the sort is ever clearly stated in the film but is inherent in its mood and manner. The Freudian undertones are there, a sense that the typical American family is not what it seems, on the surface, to be. Present also is a scene in which the U.S. Cavalry, glorified in such classic 1940s Ford westerns as *Rio Grande* and *She Wore a Yellow Ribbon*, massacre without motivation an entire village of Indian women and children—an act which even Ethan cannot comprehend. But subtler forms of racism are also explored, as the "liberal" hero Martin proves to be more prejudiced than he realizes: when he inadvertently marries an Indian woman, Look (Beulah Archuletta), he feels degraded, and treats her terribly.

In the film's striking ending, Ethan carries Debbie inside the pioneer household, steps to one side as the others enter, and then turns away. Framed through the open doorway, he wanders back into the wilderness—aware that his outdated ideas will not fit into the new, "integrated" America which he, ironically enough, has helped to bring about.

Shakespeare in outer space: Jack Kelly, Warren Stevens, Leslie Nielsen, Walter Pidgeon and Robby the Robot

Walter Pidgeon, Leslie Nielson and Anne Francis

Forbidden Planet

Metro-Goldwyn-Mayer (1956)

Produced by Nicholas Nayfack; directed by Fred McLeod Wilcox; screenplay by Cyril Hume, based on a story by Irving Block and Allen Adler.

CAST: *Dr. Morbius* (Walter Pidgeon); *Altaira Morbius* (Anne Francis); *Lieutenant "Doc" Ostrow* (Warren Stevens); *Lieutenant Farman* (Jack Kelly); *Chief Quinn* (Richard Anderson); *Cook* (Earl Holliman); *Bosun* (George Wallace); *Grey* (Bob Dix); *Youngerford* (Jimmy Thompson); *Strong* (James Drury); *Randall* (Harry Harvey, Jr.); *Lindstrom* (Roger McGee); *Moran* (Peter Miller); *Nichols* (Morgan Jones); *Silvers* (Richard Grant); *Commander Adams* (Leslie Nielsen).

Critics who entered the theatre expecting another routine outer space adventure were shocked to discover that this film bore an eerie resemblance to Shakespeare's *The Tempest.* In that classic fantasy–romance, a number of people traveling on a sea voyage are swept by a storm onto a magical island where they encounter Prospero, a charming old enchanter; Miranda, his unkissed daughter; Ariel, their faithful sprite–servant; and Caliban, a dangerously uncontrollable primitive force. *Forbidden Planet* concerns a team of astronauts forced down on the unexplored planet Altaira Four, where they meet Dr. Morbius (Walter Pidgeon), survivor of an expedition which crash-landed twenty years ear-

Anne Francis and Robby the Robot: Beauty and The Beast, circa 1956

lier; his delightful daughter Altaira (Anne Francis); their mechanical friend Robby the Robot; and an invisible Id monster which mars the otherwise dream-world atmosphere by roaming at night, killing whomever it encounters.

Produced on a budget far in excess of most science-fiction films, with a more reputable cast and obvious loving care from all concerned, *Forbidden Planet* at once stood out as a classic of its genre—and despite dialogue which dated badly (and quickly) has retained that status over the years. The jungle of the planet's surface—complete with two moons hanging in a sea-green sky, complemented by baby-pink sand dunes—along with the subterranean powerhouses of the Krells (long since destroyed inhabitants of Altaira) were convincing and believable—in a fairy tale kind of way.

But Robby the Robot continually stole the show. The charmingly couth computer-man spoke 200 languages and proved equally adroit at performing vast feats of strength or just mixing the universe's most marvelous dacquiri martinis.

Complete with special attachments that lit up whenever he answered questions through his grill-plate mouth, Robby quickly became a great favorite with children—and there was, eventually, a Robby the Robot line of toys.

On the serious side, *Forbidden Planet* continued the decade's notable trend of casting a questioning eye toward the well-meaning but potentially dangerous figure of the scientist. The story line departs from Shakespeare's when we discover the Id monster is actually the kindly Dr. Morbius' evil unconscious, released when he is asleep. Following the development of the A-bomb, Americans had entered the new decade with a previously implausible popular hero: the scientist suddenly stood alongside the cowboy and the athlete as national idol. But with the speedy realization that the Bomb's inventors were not necessarily in control, a backlash set in—already noticeable in films as diverse (and unlikely) as *The Crimson Pirate* and *Rebel Without a Cause*. In *Forbidden Planet*'s climax, such fears reached their summit.

Edmond O'Brien, Paul Newman, Walter Pidgeon and Wendell Corey

The Rack

Metro-Goldwyn-Mayer (1956)

Produced by Arthur M. Loew; directed by Arnold Laven; screenplay by Stewart Stern, based on the television play by Rod Serling.

CAST: *Captain Edward W. Hall, Jr.* (Paul Newman); *Major Sam Moulton* (Wendell Corey); *Colonel Edward W. Hall, Sr.* (Walter Pidgeon); *Lieutenant Colonel Frank Wasnick* (Edmond O'Brien); *Aggie Hall* (Anne Francis); *Captain John R. Miller* (Lee Marvin); *Caroline* (Cloris Leachman), *Colonel Ira Hansen* (Robert Burton); *Law Officer* (Robert Simon); *Court President* (Trevor Bardette); *Sergeant Otto Pahnke* (Adam Williams); *Millard Chilson Cassidy* (James Best); *Colonel Dudley Smith* (Fay Roope); *Major Byron Phillips* (Barry Atwater)

The plight of American soldiers accused of having collaborated with the enemy during the recent Korean combat received sincere but awkward treatment in *The Rack.* A disproportionately large number of servicemen were found guilty of such actions during this conflict, as compared to the number who did so during World War II, and the question of why this was so haunted us even as the war itself receded into history.

Based on a well-received TV play by Rod Serling, *The Rack* was notable as an attempt at using films to respond to the public's concern over an immediate issue. But it was presented too soon after the fact to offer any kind of perception on the problem, posing an uncomfortably familiar question without supplying an acceptable answer.

The Trial: Paul Newman, Edmond O'Brien and Wendell Corey

Captain Edward W. Hall, Jr. (Paul Newman) returns from his ordeal in Korea only to find himself the defendant in a military trial. Making the unpleasant situation worse are the facts that his father, Colonel Edward Hall, Sr. (Walter Pidgeon), is a highly respected career soldier, while his younger brother was killed in action. Prosecuting lawyer Major Sam Moulton (Wendell Corey) is unhappy with his role, but goes through the motions of assembling a case against the young man; defense lawyer Lieutenant Colonel Frank Wasnick (Edmond O'Brien) attempts to convince the officers of the jury that Hall was psychologically "put on a rack" every bit as monstrous—though physically invisible—as any used to torture people during the Middle Ages.

For the most part, the film is a strong example of courtroom melodrama. Its oddness rests in the resolution. Throughout the picture, the audience is educated about mental torture. The defense attorney never denies Hall's collaboration, but convinces the jury (and the audience) that brainwashing is the most torturous form of ordeal ever devised, and therefore Hall's cracking under the strain was understandable. However, in the film's final five minutes, Hall—without any apparent motivation—suddenly shouts out that, on final consideration, he now feels he should have been able to stand up under it, leaving the astounded court with no choice but to find him guilty by his own admission.

The effect of Hall's unlikely outburst and the inevitable decision of the jury is to make mincemeat out of everything the film has been illustrating for almost two hours. When Hall is found guilty he looks not so much like a martyr as a fool, for the viewer doesn't believe his last statement—that he hadn't really been pushed to the limit. Perhaps some elements of the recent McCarthy-inspired house-cleaning were responsible for *The Rack* turning, in a matter of minutes, from a plea for the public's understanding of the new tools of emotional and psychological torture into a pious, patriotic statement.

The film's chief value was in providing newcomer Paul Newman with his most challenging role thus far. After his film debut in *The Silver Chalice* (1954), a ludicrous costume epic, Newman was so disenchanted that he abandoned movies for over two years, doing stage work instead. He returned to films as the Brando-ish hero of the gritty fight melodrama, *Somebody Up There Likes Me*. But it was in *The Rack* that he solidified his own screen image: a clean-cut outsider, and an interesting cross between the junior executive types on the one hand and the bohemian dropouts on the other.

Robert Newton, Shirley MacLaine, Cantinflas and David Niven

Around the World in 80 Days

United Artists (1956)

Produced by Michael Todd; directed by Michael Anderson; screenplay by S. J. Perelman, based on a Jules Verne novel.

CAST: *Phineas Fogg* (David Niven); *Passepartout* (Cantinflas); *Mr. Fix* (Robert Newton); *Princess Aouda* (Shirley MacLaine); *Members of the Reform Club* (Robert Morley, Trevor Howard, Finlay Currie, Basil Sydney, Ronald Squires) and Charles Boyer, Joe E. Brown, Martine Carol, John Carradine, Charles Coburn, Ronald Colman, Melville Cooper, Nöel Coward, Reginald Denny, Andy Devine, Marlene Dietrich, Luis Miguel Dominguin, Fernandel, Sir John Gielgud, Hermione Gingold, José Greco, Sir Cedric Hardwicke, Glynis Johns, Buster Keaton, Evelyn Keyes, Beatrice Lillie, Peter Lorre, Edmund Lowe, Victor McLaglen, Tim McCoy, A. E. Matthews, Mike Mazurki, John Mills, Alan Mowbray, Edward R. Murrow, Jack Oakie, George Raft, Gilbert Roland, Cesar Romero, Frank Sinatra, Red Skelton, Harcourt Williams

Mike Todd established for himself a considerable reputation as an entertainer–entrepreneur, and was one of the most fascinating figures of the fifties. It was only inevitable that he would extend his lavish style to motion pictures. Borrowing much from the techniques pioneered by the Cinerama people, he put them to a more functional use in the context of his own Todd-AO system, which capitalized on the oversized screen's effectiveness at documenting and recording the larger wonders of the world, natural and manmade. But Todd succeeded in making them part of an engaging story, at once funny and exciting. *Around the World in 80 Days* maintained a precarious balance between the two, emerging as a gargantuan film extravaganza that existed somewhere in the middle ground between art and entertainment.

S. J. Perelman's tongue-in-cheek adaptation of Jules Verne's classic adventure yarn fit Todd's purposes well, relating the intrigues of one Phineas Fogg (David Niven)

The spectacular balloon ride across a European countryside and occasional cities

who in 1872 enters into a wager with his fellows at the British Reform Club that he can traverse the globe in 80 days. Accompanied by his loyal valet, Passepartout (Cantinflas), he leaves by balloon and later travels by ship, railroad and elephant, picking up along the way Aouda (Shirley MacLaine), a beautiful Indian princess in danger and Mr. Fix (Robert Newton), a gruff, bulldog-ish detective who threatens to ruin Fogg's schedule.

During the course of the journey, Mike Todd threw in everything from Marlene Dietrich and Frank Sinatra as saloon entertainers in the American West to José Greco and his troupe of flamenco performers dancing in a Spanish café. He even created a new term, "the cameo performance," to describe such walk-ons. The film combined crass and class in equal portions; if it didn't further anyone's definition of cinematic art, at least it contained much that

was truly artful—including the masterful photography and musical accompaniment as the travelling balloon glides across Europe's picturesque countrysides. Most of the action sequences, including a rampaging Indian elephant and an American Indian attack on a frontier train, were played simultaneously for suspense and for laughs, with Niven keeping a British stiff upper lip and Cantinflas cavorting like a Chicano Chaplin.

Above all, the film was high quality showmanship. After winning the love of Elizabeth Taylor, the most elegant beauty of the decade, Todd was killed abruptly in an airplane crash. In what turned out to be his only film, Todd had suggested that he might become for the fifties what Cecil B. De Mille had been before him—the cinematic showman who understood better than anyone else what the audiences of his time wanted from their entertainment.

Dathan (Edward G. Robinson) and the worshippers of The Golden Calf

The Ten Commandments

Paramount (1956)

Produced and directed by Cecil B. De Mille; screenplay by Aeneas MacKenzie, Jesse L. Lasky, Jr., Jack Gariss and Frederic M. Frank.

CAST: *Moses* (Charlton Heston); *Nefretiri* (Anne Baxter); *Rameses* (Yul Brynner); *Sephora* (Yvonne De Carlo); *Sethi* (Sir Cedric Hardwicke); *Lilia* (Debra Paget); *Dathan* (Edward G. Robinson); *Joshua* (John Derek); *Bithiah* (Nina Foch); *Memnet* (Judith Anderson); *Aaron* (John Carradine); *Baka* (Vincent Price); *Yochabel* (Martha Scott); *Miriam* (Olive Deering); *Jannes* (Douglass Dumbrille); *Pentaur* (Henry Wilcoxon); *Amminadab* (H. B. Warner)

In *Sunset Boulevard*, Norma Desmond pays a visit to the Paramount studio where her old friend Cecil B. De Mille is shooting a picture. And while time has left the once-glamorous star behind, the veteran director is still working. Yet the fifties were to spell an end not only to De Mille's career, but to the kind of film he perfected as well. With *The Ten Commandments*, a remake of his own earlier silent classic, the producer–director created his costliest, longest and, ultimately, last biblical epic. Combining high purpose with a sizable quantity of pure hokum, expressing strict fundamentalist moralizing through a whimsically Hollywood-ish depiction of the ancient world, De Mille turned out a film that was old-fashioned even for its time; it was

The erection of a pyramid, Cecil B. De Mille style

The Red Sea closes in on the Egyptian armies

Charlton Heston as Moses

Martha Scott, Charlton Heston and Nina Foch

so completely a Dream Factory creation that even the scenes shot on outdoor locations often managed to look as though they were done in a studio. *The Ten Commandments* was a huge dinosaur of a movie that roared and spouted and delighted audiences (but not critics) everywhere it played.

De Mille is to the modern cinema what England's Sir Walter Scott and America's James Fenimore Cooper are to the novel: his plots are complex, his ideas simplistic, and his feeling for details of background and local color patently phony but nonetheless delightful. The story line of his ultimate extravaganza was, as in all previous ones, a hybrid of scripture and soap opera. The audience first meets Moses (Charlton Heston) as a strapping young Eygptian buck, riding his chariot wildly about the pyramids and competing with the equally robust Rameses (Yul Brynner) for the love of a captivating princess, Nefretiri (Anne Baxter). Their mindlessly youthful preoccupations end abruptly, however, when the Pharoah (Sir Cedric Hardwicke) learns that Moses is not an Egyptian at all, but the son of a Hebrew slave, rescued by his own daughter from the bull-

rushes years earlier.

De Mille concentrates so intensely on the romantic triangle that it was easy for audiences to momentarily forget they were seeing a film based on the book of Exodus. At this point, however, the film returns to the biblical origins. Moses wanders into the wilderness, where he confronts the God of the Hebrews, meets and then marries the Midianite shepherdess Sephora (Yvonne De Carlo) and is befriended by both Aaron (John Carradine) and Joshua (John Derek), the Hebrew leaders.

In the earlier portions of the picture, De Mille kept his love of spectacle restrained to panoramic shots of slaves erecting pyramids and the splendors of the Egyptian palaces. In the final third, he let loose his ultimate concoction of special effects and epic spectacle. First come the vividly visualized plagues on Egypt, then the exodus of thousands of extras from the elaborately conceived city. That everyone who saw the film knew what was coming next added rather than detracted from the pleasure, allowing us to anticipate how De Mille would put it on screen. The Red Sea swirls wildly as Moses raises his staff to the sky and black clouds roll in overhead, then the water crushes down on the Egyptian chariots as they attempt to pursue. When Moses receives the tablets on Sinai, they are carved into the stone by a flying ball of fire; when he returns and finds his people worshipping the golden calf, he curses those who have reverted to paganism and they are swallowed up by the earth.

Despite its box-office success, the film was widely attacked for its blatant sentimentality, in comparison to recent, more psychological religious epics such as *The Robe*. Noticeably, De Mille's film did not fare well at the Oscar ceremonies or with the New York film critics when they drew up their lists. Slicker, more "modern" biblical tales would appear shortly, ranging from the ridiculous jewel-in-the-naval antics of Gina Lollobrigida in *Solomon and Sheba* to the impressive, intelligent handling of De Mille's own star, Charlton Heston, in *Ben Hur*.

Elizabeth Taylor and Rock Hudson

Rock Hudson in action

Marriage on the rocks: Elizabeth Taylor and Rock Hudson

Giant

Warner Bros. (1956)

Produced by George Stevens and Henry Ginsberg; directed by Mr. Stevens; screenplay by Fred Guiol and Ivan Moffat, based on the novel by Edna Ferber.

CAST: *Leslie Benedict* (Elizabeth Taylor); *Bick Benedict* (Rock Hudson); *Jett Rink* (James Dean); *Luz Benedict the Second* (Carroll Baker); *Vashti Snythe* (Jane Withers); *Uncle Bawley* (Chill Wills); *Luz Benedict* (Mercedes McCambridge); *Angel Obregon the Third* (Sal Mineo); *Jordan Benedict the Third* (Dennis Hopper); *Dr. Horace Lynnton* (Paul Fix); *Bob Dace* (Earl Holliman); *Pinky Snythe* (Robert Nichols); *Old Polo* (Alexander Scourby); *Judy Benedict* (Fran Bennett); *Whiteside* (Charles Watts); *Juana* (Elsa Cardenas); *Bale Clinch* (Monte Hall); *Adarene Clinch* (Mary Ann Edwards); *Angel Obregon the First* (Victor Millan); *Sarge* (Mickey Simpson)

Giant served as the last installment of George Stevens' epic trilogy on American history, as seen through the eyes of the simple people who unknowingly created it. The films were all related from the perspective of the fifties, and each dealt with some significant aspect of transition: in *Shane*, the changeover from the open ranges of the cattle barons to the fenced-in plots of the homesteaders; in *A Place in the Sun*, the difficult shift to urban living. *Giant* dealt on a mammoth scale with what was, finally, the most important shift of all—the replacement of cattle as the source of wealth to the "new money" of oil, and the complex effect it had on the lives of the people involved.

As in Edna Ferber's novel, the situation was viewed by a virtual outsider: the beautiful, spoiled Virginia blueblood Leslie (Elizabeth Taylor) who falls unexpectedly, uncontrollably in love with the rich, handsome young owner of

James Dean and Elizabeth Taylor

the immense Reata ranch, Bick Benedict (Rock Hudson). She marries him, and moves to Texas at once. The romance is quickly blunted when she must adjust to the dusty, dehumanizing terrain, as well as the attitude Bick shares with the other cattle barons: when serious talk begins, women should disappear. Leslie's conflict with her husband's tough, unyielding sister Luz (Mercedes McCambridge) leads to the older woman's death while riding an unbroken horse, and in her will Luz leaves a small pocket of land to Jett Rink (James Dean), a surly ranch hand with an immense crush on Leslie and an even greater hatred for Bick. When the cattle barons try to buy his few acres he refuses to sell, steadfastly drills for oil and, eventually, finds it.

The film lives up to its title through an immense, complicated, sometimes soap opera-style story line, which follows the principals through several decades in their lives. Just as epic is the panoramic visual style: a vast, breathtaking rendering of the Texas landscape which would have been impossible without the developments in wide-screen technique of the early fifties, and which further proved the fact that instead of a mere gimmick, the wide screen could become an integral part of the story and style of certain kinds of motion pictures. Rock Hudson graduated from leads in B movies to win an Oscar nomination for the important role of

a hardheaded but always likable masculine character; Elizabeth Taylor demonstrated that, in addition to being the screen's most beautiful female, she could also handle the difficult role of a woman who goes through numerous transitions—from a pampered child through a period as a disturbed mother to an intelligent, mature lady. James Dean also proved that besides the misunderstood young rebel he'd incarnated in *East of Eden* and *Rebel Without a Cause*, he could also portray a complex, fascinating, but finally unsympathetic character. In the last third of the film he plays Jett as an obnoxiously rich, aging man, desperately trying to make love to Bick's attractive young daughter (Carroll Baker) and incurring the wrath of Bick's sensitive but strong-willed son (Dennis Hopper). It was a sad footnote that the film was released after Dean's death, and he was one of the rare actors to receive a posthumous Academy Award nomination for Best Actor.

Giant is a less perfect film than either *A Place in the Sun* or *Shane*, mainly because it is so mammoth that the various plots, themes and characters often ramble in different directions. It stands, though, as one of the immense undertakings of the decade, an attempt to handle mature, modern melodrama that is both socially commentative and stylistically innovative.

Giulietta Masina and Anthony Quinn

La Strada

Trans-Lux Films (1956)

Produced by Dino De Laurentiis and Carlo Ponti; directed by Federico Fellini; story and screenplay by Federico Fellini and Tulliio Pinelli; dialogue by Signor Pinelli.

CAST: *Zampano* (Anthony Quinn); *Gelsomina* (Giulietta Masina); *Matto the Fool* (Richard Basehart); *Colombaini* (Aldo Silvani)

The art-house audience was virtually a creation of the fifties. Previously, European imports were occasional and uncommon, mostly confined to clear-cut classics like *The Blue Angel, M* and *Potemkin.* But with exposure to international cultures that Americans experienced during World War II, a taste for the continental was cultivated. Immediately following the war European films—both good and bad

Matto The Fool (Richard Basehart) and Gelsomina (Giulietta Masina) don clown make-up in a distinctively Fellini-ish scene

—were imported at an ever-increasing rate. They were successful because they offered a relatively small but highly loyal audience something they couldn't get either on television or from the Hollywood product. The influence on American moviemakers was clear in pictures as diverse as the independently produced *Little Fugitive* and the blockbuster *On the Waterfront.* Movies from France, India, Japan and England all enjoyed popularity, but perhaps most typical of the art-house were the Italian neorealist works, with their artless, shot-in-the-street look and peasant heroes.

The masterpieces included Roberto Rossellini's *Paisan* and *Open City*, along with Vittorio De Sica's *The Bicycle Thief* and *Shoe-Shine*. But most memorable of all was Federico Fellini's *La Strada.* American actors Anthony Quinn and Richard Basehart, so often stuck in secondary roles as Indians and gangsters, displayed previously unseen talents when cast opposite Fellini's wife, Giulietta Masina, a tiny powerhouse of dramatic intensity and comic charm.

The title literally translates as "The Road," a concept Fellini employed as a metaphor for life in Italy during those difficult days following the war. Zampano (Quinn), a huge, inarticulate strong-man travels from city to country village, earning a modest living performing his one trick: tying himself in chains and breaking them by expanding his chest. He is brute male power incarnate. Yet he is human, and in need of companionship virtually buys a mentally deficient child-woman, Gelsomina (Giulietta Masina) from her mother, whisking her off in his motorcycle-trailer to fulfill his basic needs for someone to cook, copulate with and, on occasion, talk to. In her simplicity, she represents Fellini's concept of the essential greatness in

woman: a limitless capacity for loyalty to the man who has taken her as his own, no matter how unpleasant a creature he may be.

Quite symbolically, they are happy when playing the fairs in the countryside. But once they move close to Rome—the big city with its complexities and potential for corruption —their primitive idyll is shattered. A circus performer called Matto the Fool (Basehart) teases the stupid brute of a man and tries to lure his woman away. Though he offers her gentler treatment, she cannot conceive of betraying Zampano. But when fate plays a trick on them all and they meet later at a crossroads, the ox-like Zampano kills Matto. Gelsomina cannot silence her weeping at the cruel deed, and as the sound of her whining drives Zampano to madness, he finally deserts her—attempting to leave his conscience behind. But when he learns, months later, that she died alone on the road, the seemingly impregnable wall of strength is seized with tears—realizing that in destroying her, he destroyed his own soul, and with it, his only tie with humanity.

Anthony Quinn returned to Hollywood to find more demanding roles waiting for him and, after two decades as a character actor, stardom in the late fifties. But Mr. Fellini remained in his own country, where he continued to work. Unlike his contemporary De Sica, who answered Hollywood's call to come and make pictures (none of which turned out well), Fellini sensed that the big budgets of American movies could only interfere with his highly artistic intentions. With each successive picture, Fellini left the Italian neorealist style further behind, growing ever more personal until, at last, his films emerged as the totally unique work of a major artist.

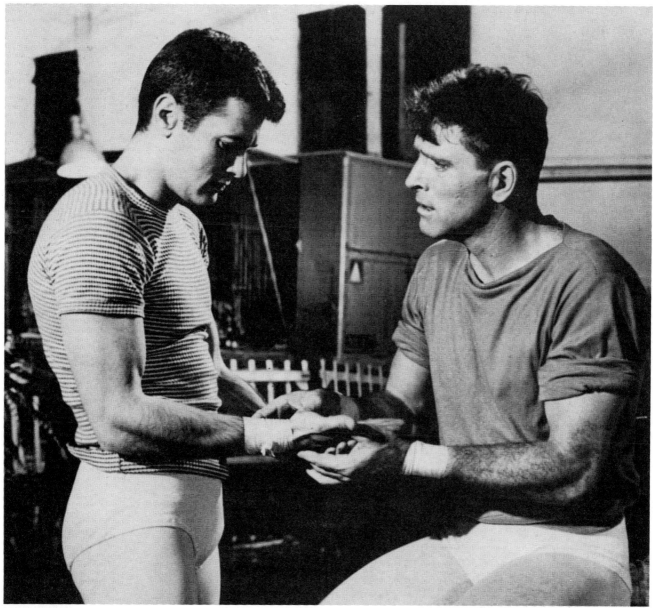

Burt Lancaster and Tony Curtis

Trapeze

United Artists (1956)

A Susan Productions, Inc. picture, presented by Hecht–Lancaster; directed by Sir Carol Reed; screenplay by James R. Webb, adaptation by Liam O'Brien.

CAST: *Mike Ribble* (Burt Lancaster); *Tino Orsini* (Tony Curtis); *Lola* (Gina Lollobrigida); *Rosa* (Katy Jurado); *Bouglione* (Thomas Gomez); *Max the Dwarf* (Johnny Puleo); *John Ringling North* (Minor Watson); *Chikki* (Gerard Landry); *Otto* (J. P. Kerrien); *Snake Man* (Sidney James)

The critics were not very kind to *Trapeze,* but audiences loved it. For despite the wooden acting, sentimental story, maudlin dialogue and surprisingly flat direction of the highly respected Sir Carol Reed, the film contained the perfect combination of elements that spelled box-office chemistry. In a CinemaScope screen filled with the most garish of color, set against a circus background and authentic European locales, it told the story of young Tino Orsini (Tony Curtis) who joins the travelling circus of Bouglione (Thomas Gomez) in order to befriend Mike Ribble (Burt

Tony Curtis, Burt Lancaster and Gina Lollobrigida

Lancaster). Mike is one of the world's great aerialists, though his career was cut short by a crippled leg suffered when his "catcher" failed to grab him in time as he finished a triple somersault—the most dangerous of all mid-air tricks; it is exactly that feat Orsini wants to learn. At first Mike refuses to teach the lad something so dangerous, but eventually he gives in—hoping to live out his own unfulfilled potential through the younger man.

But while they are rehearsing their act for introduction at the renowned Cirque d'Hiver in Paris, Lola (Gina Lollobrigida), a devastatingly seductive woman, joins the troupe. She is immediately attracted to the sullen Mike, but when he shows little interest, she flirts with the more impressionable Tino. Lola plays the men one against the other, eventually turning their brotherly love and professional respect into near hatred. She worms her way into the act and diverts the spectators' eyes from the men's skillful routines by wearing the skimpiest and tightest of costumes. The smoldering emotions finally reach their height at the moment Tino is to perform the triple somersault for the first time—without a net, and with Mike as his catcher.

Essentially, *Trapeze* is a celebration of how wonderful a masculine relationship can be—until a woman comes along and spoils it. For Burt Lancaster, *Trapeze* meant the chance to do a circus picture at last. He had worked as a roustabout and acrobat before making his way into motion pictures,

and had been on the lookout for a story dealing with that milieu ever since he and Harold Hecht had formed their company. *The Crimson Pirate* had established him as an entertainer while *From Here to Eternity* proved his worth as an actor; *Trapeze* was clearly an attempt to combine the two elements of his talents.

Tony Curtis rose through the ranks from bit player to juvenile lead, but starred in so many regrettable B pictures that it seemed unlikely he would ever rise above the Robert Wagner–Tab Hunter level of matinee idol and movie-magazine cover boy. Curtis later explained that, realizing this, he set out to "educate" his audiences by seeking out second-leads in more respectable films starring Lancaster or Kirk Douglas. The gamble paid off, and more discriminating audiences gradually learned to accept Curtis' presence in major films.

Gina Lollobrigida was one of the many European sex sirens who found American audiences suddenly enthusiastic for ladies from the Continent. With an astoundingly perfect figure, large in the bosom and narrow around the waist, she provided quite an eyeful, and specialized in a new kind of role—somewhere between a nice, simple girl and a dangerous shady lady. *Trapeze* was by far her flashiest vehicle. The circus costumes offered her marvelous opportunities to show off her figure, while the cliché-ridden script was perfectly suited to her uncertain delivery of English.

Caroll Baker and Eli Wallach

Baby Doll

Warner Bros. (1956)

A Newton Production; directed by Elia Kazan; story and screenplay by Tennessee Williams.

CAST: *Archie* (Karl Malden); *Baby Doll* (Carroll Baker); *Silva Vaccaro* (Eli Wallach); *Aunt Rose Comfort* (Mildred Dunnock); *Rock* (Lonny Chapman); *Town Marshall* (Eades Hogue); *Deputy* (Noah Williamson)

The struggle that major filmmakers encountered when attempting to leave the studio dream worlds behind and attack adult subject matter, which might be old hat to Broadway audiences but was still shocking for the middle-American moviegoing public, reached a point of impasse with *Baby Doll*. The film had high credentials, being the joint product of Tennessee Williams and Elia Kazan, respectively America's leading playwright and film director. At the same time, their story dealt graphically enough with sexual infidelity for the film to earn a resoundingly loud condemnation from the Roman Catholic Church, which set off a controversial nationwide debate on the question of motion picture censorship and the value of the Production Code. The Legion of Decency insisted: "It dwells almost without variation or relief upon carnal suggestiveness." And *Life* Magazine summarized the situation when it flatly called *Baby Doll* "the most fiercely controversial film of the decade."

Part of the problem was due to the milieu that *Baby Doll* so scrupulously studied. In their previous joint undertaking, *A Streetcar Named Desire*, Kazan had shaken the Production Code by transferring Williams' electrifying play to the screen with few changes. Yet in that case, the frankness of the sexual relationship was treated within the framework of poetic grandeur and tragic inevitability. *Streetcar* told the highly symbolic story of the old South, in the person of Vivien Leigh's Blanche Du Bois, finally succumbing to the level of the poor white trash (perfectly represented by Marlon Brando's Stanley Kowalski). The meaning behind their confrontation, and the sense of importance it conveyed, won for *Streetcar* the wholehearted endorsement and protective concern of the critical establishment.

Not so *Baby Doll*. Bosley Crowther of the *New York Times* complained that the film's people were without

A new style in sex symbols: Karl Malden and Carroll Baker

Caroll Baker and Eli Wallach

"character, content or consequence," while *Time* Magazine scoffed that this was "just possibly the dirtiest American picture ever legally exhibited." For the first time, Williams concerned himself solely with the Stanley Kowalski ilk, and the total absence of the old aristocracy he usually portrayed with such grace made this piece seem more like one of Erskine Caldwell's tawdry potboilers than the product of the man who wrote *The Glass Menagerie*. In accordance with the script, Kazan altered his visual style. Usually his images immediately convey to viewers the notion that we are in the presence of something important—as in his ability to make the lowlife of the docks a metaphor for modern life in *On the Waterfront*. But for *Baby Doll* he created a tone that, while most appropriate to the material, nonetheless added to the overall feeling that the picture was an effective but ultimately meaningless study.

The effect was rather like watching a freak show. Archie Lee Meighan (Karl Malden) an aging rube, lives in the backwoods of Mississippi, where he runs a cotton gin and fears the competition of a tricky young Sicilian, Silva Vaccarro (Eli Wallach), enough to sneak onto the man's property and set fire to his gin. But Vaccarro suspects, and to learn if Archie is indeed responsible, he spends a long, seductive day with the man's virgin wife—an underage but overdeveloped child-woman called Baby Doll (Carroll Baker) whom Archie married under the sacred oath that he would not sleep with her until she reached twenty.

Though the mere mention of the film can still spark controversy, it is extremely mild in comparison to films that followed within a year or two; whether or not Silva actually seduces Baby Doll is never made explicit. The extreme condemnations from the church had the effect of making everyone in the country want to see the "shocker" that would otherwise most likely have passed by without notice. Ironically, Carroll Baker's depiction of the near-idiot created, quite unintentionally, a new style in sex symbols. Baby doll pajamas, cut in exactly the style that she wore in the film, became the biggest sellers since Davy Crockett caps.

Mildred Natwick and Debbie Reynolds

Tammy and the Bachelor

Universal (1957)

Produced by Ross Hunter; directed by Joseph Pevney; screenplay by Oscar Brodney, based on a novel by Cid Ricketts Sumner.

CAST: *Tammy* (Debbie Reynolds); *Peter Brent* (Leslie Nielsen); *Grandpa* (Walter Brennan); *Barbara* (Mala Powers); *Professor Brent* (Sidney Blackmer); *Aunt Renie* (Mildred Natwick); *Mrs. Brent* (Fay Wray); *Alfred Bissle* (Philip Ober); *Ernie* (Craig Hill); *Osia* (Louise Beavers); *Tina* (April Kent)

Debbie Reynolds proved herself as an actress and singer numerous times following her screen debut in *June Bride* in 1948—in pleasant musicals like *Hit the Deck,* light comedies such as *The Tender Trap,* and powerful dramas including *The Catered Affair.* But while she firmly established herself within the industry and became the darling of the movie magazines (which built her marriage to the boyish pop singer Eddie Fisher into the romance of the decade, and then exploited its demise to the hilt) she never became a top box-office star until the role of "Tammy" came along.

Urban sophisticate Leslie Nielsen falls for the sincere charms of backwoods girl Debbie Reynolds

The picture was conceived by Universal as a routine programmer to appeal almost exclusively to unsophisticated teenage girls. Agreeing to do it was a big step down for Debbie from her status parts in major M-G-M and Warner Brothers films. But the picture enjoyed an unforeseen success—thanks in part to its catchy title song, which also provided Miss Reynolds with her biggest hit record—and Debbie Reynolds was elevated to real stardom.

While the story was hardly one destined to satisfy intellectuals, it did provide a modern fairy tale that simply couldn't fail with the mass audience. Peter Brent (Leslie Nielsen), a well-to-do son of a plantation owner, crashes his private plane while flying over the backwater Mississippi bayous, and is rescued by an unlikely pair of hermits —the charming young Tammy (Debbie Reynolds), a fresh, lovely creature who knows almost nothing about the great world outside her domain, and her crotchety old Grandpa (Walter Brennan). The two nurse Peter back to health; before returning home, he suggests that if Grandpa should ever become incapacitated, he'd be delighted to have Tammy spend some time with him. Shortly thereafter the local authorities haul Grandpa off to jail for a few months for operating a hidden gin-mill. Tammy, remembering Peter's offer, sets off for the Brentwood Estates.

She encounters an acute case of fifties apathy. Instead of enjoying their wealth the family lives without motivation or sense of direction. Professor Brent (Sidney Blackmer) has, out of disgust with the world situation, withdrawn into his library where his only pleasures come from classical books. Mrs. Brent (Fay Wray) scurries about her house neurotically. But it is Peter who clearly establishes the source of all their problems when, at one point, he tells Tammy that he's been "just drifting since the war."

But Tammy, with her blissful ignorance and exuberant optimism, manages to cure them all by getting their minds off the problems of the world and helping them to rediscover life's most simple and innocent pleasures. She even wins Peter away from a spoiled, classy society girl (Mala Powers) and revitalizes him through the power of her positive personality.

Fifties audiences had no difficulty empathizing with the Brents, and wistfully enjoyed the prospect of a Tammy figure shaking them out of their Cold War-atomic threat doldrums. Essentially, Tammy was a romantic conception that could only make sense during this decade. The picture's success caused Universal to prod Debbie to appear in an immediate sequel, but she wasn't interested. Instead, she used her sudden surge in popularity as leverage for the better roles she deserved.

Robinson Crusoe of the Atomic Age: Grant Williams arms himself with a needle

The Incredible Shrinking Man
Universal (1957)

Produced by Albert Zugsmith; directed by Jack Arnold; screenplay by Richard Matheson, from his novel.

CAST: *Scott Carey* (Grant Williams); *Louise Carey* (Randy Stuart); *Clarice* (April Kent); *Charlie Carey* (Paul Langton); *Dr. Thomas Silver* (Raymond Bailey); *Midget* (Billy Curtis)

In the opening sequence of *The Incredible Shrinking Man*, middle-class businessman Scott Carey (Grant Williams) and his attractive wife Louise (Randy Stuart) are spending a quiet, sunny afternoon relaxing on their small cabin cruiser. In a voice-over narration, Carey explains to us that this average day was the beginning of his unending nightmare. We watch as he jokingly nags his wife into going below to

A struggle for survival: Grant Williams vs. the spider

fetch him a cold beer; while she's gone a strange, thick cloud passes over him and then disappears. Within a few days, Carey realizes that he's shrinking. His doctor, Thomas Silver (Raymond Bailey), supposes that the cloud must have contained some sort of atomic waste from a nuclear experiment, which is now causing Carey to diminish in size by an inch a week.

Though a team of crack scientists manage to provide an antidote that will cease his shrinkage, Carey has already diminished to half his normal size—and there is no foreseeable means to return him to normal. In desperation, he wanders away from home. Taking refuge in a circus, he finds himself falling in love with a young, attractive midget (April Kent). But Carey misses his injection of the antidote and begins shrinking again; by the time he is rescued, he must be kept in a doll house for protection. While his wife is shopping, the family cat attacks him; in escaping he is forced into the cellar. When Louise returns and finds the doll house destroyed, she assumes that Scott has been killed by the cat. On his own, Scott is armed only with a discarded sewing needle, fighting to the death against the spiders and insects that inhabit the cellar.

Unlike most of the atomic-inspired films, which suggested the imminent destruction of mankind as the result of experimentation with the Bomb, *The Incredible Shrinking Man* dealt with the problem on the level of a single indi-

vidual. The ordinariness of his personality and the random manner in which the cloud happens to come into contact with him—purely by chance—illustrated more frightfully even than the giant ants of *Them!* that the average American was completely vulnerable, at all moments, to the atomic powers science had unleashed. Carey's total alienation is perfectly communicated in a powerful scene in which, shortly after his shrinking has begun, his wife attempts to assure him of her steadfastness by insisting: "As long as that ring is on your finger, I'll be here . . ."; at that moment, the ring slips off his slightly shrunken finger and falls onto the floor.

The film was also impressive in its use of an open ending. While most science fiction films conclude either with the salvation or the destruction of such a victim, this picture closed with Carey's disappearance from sight, accompanied by his sudden realization that the limitation of man's vision is meaningless. He need not fear dissolving into nothingness, since he will now enter the realm of the microscopic and, after that, the submicroscopic. "To God, there is no zero!" he cries out, as in a point-of-view shot we see the receding heavens suddenly replaced by an approaching molecular structure. In addition to expressing our atomic paranoia on an acutely human level, *The Incredible Shrinking Man* also made the concept of infinity perfectly understandable to the popular moviegoing audience.

Darren McGavin and Jerry Lewis as Damon and Pythias

The Delicate Delinquent

Paramount (1957)

Produced by Jerry Lewis; written and directed by Don McGuire

CAST: *Sidney Pythias* (Jerry Lewis); *Mike Damon* (Darren McGavin); *Martha* (Martha Hyer); *Monk* (Robert Ivers); *Captain Riley* (Horace McMahon); *Artie* (Richard Bakalyan); *Harry* (Joseph Corey); *Patricia* (Mary Webster); *Mr. Herman* (Milton Frome); *Mr. Crow* (Jefferson Searles)

The rumors of a breakup between Dean Martin and Jerry Lewis began almost as soon as they achieved superstardom as the decade's top comedy team. To dispel that notion, the duo went so far as to tack an extra ending onto one of their biggest-budgeted projects, *Pardners* (1956), in which they assured the public they deeply loved and respected each other. But before their next film, *Hollywood or Bust*, was even in release the two men had obtained a "professional divorce" on the grounds of irreconcilable differences—

Darren McGavin, Jerry Lewis and Martha Hyer

which meant, according to numerous sources, that each feared the other was the key to the team's success. Martin went directly into a routine romantic comedy, *Ten Thousand Bedrooms,* which flopped at the box office and momentarily threatened to end his movie career. Lewis was more immediately successful on his own: his first independent venture, *The Delicate Delinquent,* was a solid hit. The script had orginally been tailored for Martin and Lewis to do together, but Jerry's part was beefed up and the Dean Martin role, considerably trimmed down and minus the songs, was handed to a fine actor, Darren McGavin.

The picture satirized all the new films dealing with juvenile delinquency. It was a clever choice for Jerry, since many of the great silent comics such as Buster Keaton had enjoyed great success when spoofing currently popular film trends. The opening sequence effectively demonstrated how the latest cinema styles and clichés can be humorously deflated. Late at night in a dimly lit, deserted alley, two warring teenage gangs meet wordlessly for a rumble. They appear out of nowhere, like phantoms, and move toward each other in an almost choreographed rhythm to the tune of a rock-jazz sound track. Each hoodlum wears a Brando-ish black leather jacket, sports a Presley-style ducktail haircut, or carries his body in the anguished posture of the late James Dean. Their preparations for a fight are as stylized as if they were Arthurian knights entering a joust. The three members of one gang draw their weapons out slowly, one by one: a knife, a metal pipe, a stretch of chain. In answer to the challenge the others whisk out, in perfect unison, switchblade knives. The tempo of the music increases as they close the remaining distance between them. As the excitement and intensity reach a climax, the suspense is suddenly shattered as a door flies open, Jerry appears to empty some garbage cans, and screams hysterically at the sight of the duel.

Unfortunately, not much in the film measures up to that opening. Sidney Pythias (Jerry) is a shy janitor in a big city apartment house, where he lives in constant dread of the juvenile delinquents infesting his neighborhood. The night of the rumble he is mistakenly hauled into the police precinct with them. The kindly Captain Riley (Horace McMahon) decides to give the boy a second chance, and tells patrolman Mike Damon (Darren McGavin) to take him under his wing, in hopes that the young man will shape up enough to eventually make the police academy. The frightened lad sums up his courage and, in the end, saves Mike and his girlfriend Martha (Martha Hyer) from a teenage gang.

Much of the film's awkwardness comes from a problematic script: *The Delicate Delinquent* meanders back and forth between a comic spoof of street gangs and a serious indictment of them. The two don't jell (at least not in this context) as the film alternates between a didactic attack on the hoodlum lifestyle (at which times it grows talky and boring) and a perceptive satire of their manners (or, more correctly, the current Hollywood conception of them). If nothing else, the venture proved that Lewis could draw audiences on his own, and very shortly he would be both writing and directing his films.

The Condemned: Timothy Carey, Ralph Meeker and Joseph Turkel

Paths of Glory

United Artists (1957)

Produced by James B. Harris, presented by Bryna Productions; directed by Stanley Kubrick; screenplay by Mr. Kubrick, Calder Willingham and Jim Thompson, based on the novel by Humphrey Cobb.

CAST: *Colonel Dax* (Kirk Douglas); *Corporal Paris* (Ralph Meeker); *General Broulard* (Adolphe Menjou); *General Mireau* (George Macready); *Lieutenant Roget* (Wayne Morris); *Major Saint-Auban* (Richard Anderson); *Private Arnaud* (Joseph Turkel); *Private Ferol* (Timothy Carey); *Colonel Judge* (Peter Capell); *German Girl* (Susanne Christian); *Sergeant Boulanger* (Bert Freed); *Priest* (Emile Meyer); *Private Meyer* (Jerry Hausner); *Shell-shocked Soldier* (Frederic Bell); *Captain Nichols* (Harold Benedict); *Captain Rousseau* (John Stein)

As one of the foremost stars to move into producing his own projects, Kirk Douglas exerted a significant influence on the American cinema by balancing each of his entertainment vehicles with a film comparable to the European art pictures. His most memorable venture into this realm was *Paths of Glory*, a box-office disaster on initial release but a film that grew in stature and reputation with each passing year, until it finally reached the status of classic. Douglas first bought the rights to a highly controversial novel by Humphrey Cobb and then hired a little-known but gifted young director, Stanley Kubrick, to translate it into a film. The resultant picture was a shocker for its time: as Colonel Dax, Douglas portrayed a French combat officer who, during World War I, is ordered by his Machiavellian commandment, Broulard (Adolphe Menjou), to take an impos-

Kirk Douglas as Colonel Dax

sible enemy situation, "The Ant Hill." When the attack understandably fails, the generals decide to salvage their own reputations at any cost, and the blame is unfairly placed on the foot soldiers. A shortage of men rules out punishing the entire company; instead, three men are chosen by lot, tried in a military court, and executed for the supposed cowardice of the regiment.

The picture does not employ the incident solely for an anti-war statement, but also as a means to attack the nature of class systems, and the ways in which men at the top of an executive ladder will cover themselves at any cost, feeling no guilt but actually believing themselves to be morally correct in doing so. Acting as the defense attorney for the three men, Douglas' Dax has ample opportunity to perform as the author's spokesman. But *Paths of Glory* was not just another of the many liberal message movies which proli-

ferated during the decade; if that had been the case, it would have been far more acceptable to audiences. The film refused to turn the three soldiers (Wayne Morris, Joseph Turkel and Timothy Carey) into martyr symbols or place the blame on a clear-cut villain. Instead it presented, in an upsettingly objective vision, the entire situation with all its moral ramifications and social implications. Stanley Kubrick's powerful visual style gave this sordid (and true) story a sense of great significance, filled with memorable sequences. Especially unforgettable was the final wordless episode in which a lonely, frightened young German girl sings one of her country's songs in a café filled with French soldiers; at first hostile, they quiet down and listen to the universal beauty of her peasant voice, realizing at last that she is not their enemy.

Lana Turner is shocked by the new attitudes toward sex that her daughter and fellow teenagers demonstrate

Peyton Place

20th Century-Fox (1957)

Produced by Jerry Wald; directed by Mark Robson; screenplay by John Michael Hayes, from the novel by Grace Metalious.

CAST: *Constance MacKenzie* (Lana Turner); *Selena Cross* (Hope Lange); *Dr. Michael Rossi* (Lee Philips); *Dr. Swain* (Lloyd Nolan); *Lucas Cross* (Arthur Kennedy); *Norman Page* (Russ Tamblyn); *Allison* (Diane Varsi); *Betty Anderson* (Terry Moore); *Rodney Harrington* (Barry Coe); *Nellie Cross* (Betty Field); *Ted Carter* (David Nelson); *Mrs. Thornton* (Mildred Dunnock); *Harrington* (Leon Ames); *Prosecutor* (Lorne Greene); *Seth Bushwell* (Robert H. Harris); *Margie* (Tami Conner); *Charles Partridge* (Staats Cotsworth); *Mrs. Page* (Erin O'Brien-Moore)

Grace Metalious' novel was the most scandalous best seller of the decade, a sometime seamy, sometimes perceptive analysis of the various sociological problems and psychological secrets hiding under the handsome exterior of Middle America. Thanks to such films as the ground breaking *From Here to Eternity*, filmmakers had by 1957 reached the point of maturity where it was possible for Hollywood to handle such explosive material as rape and illegitimacy in outspoken terms. As produced by Jerry Wald, the film version emerged as a hybrid between a glossy soap opera and an uncompromising study of modern lifestyles.

The central character, Constance MacKenzie, was played by Lana Turner, who only a few years before had desperately tried to retain her youthful image by playing in tepid womens' pictures and inane costume epics. Attempting a more mature role, she proved a strong enough actress to re-

211

The Generation Gap: communication breaks off between Diane Varsi and Lana Turner

Hope Lange, Russ Tamblyn, David Nelson, Diane Varsi and Lloyd Nolan

Lana Turner and Lee Philips

ceive an Academy Award nomination for her portrayal of an emotionally headstrong, highly attractive middle-aged woman whose short-sightedness in handling her maturing daughter grows out of long-repressed guilt over what her own vulnerability has cost.

The story takes place in the 1940s, but is really an analysis of how the urban-suburban community of the fifties came into being. Most of all, it is a study of small-town America in transition, made clear in the opening sequence in which the beloved old teacher, Mrs. Thornton (Mildred Dunnock), is passed over for the position of school principal when the board decides to award the job to an outsider, Dr. Michael Rossi (Lee Philips), a bright young man, who will bring fresh ideas into the area. He is quickly attracted to the widow MacKenzie, and surprised when she does not respond to him. But he criticizes Constance's stern behavior with her daughter Allison (Diane Varsi) when the teenager is reprimanded for turning her birthday celebration into a petting party.

As Rossi and Constance continue their uneasy relationship, Allison and her classmates adjust to their upcoming graduation from school. Rodney Harrington (Barry Coe) marries a sexy co-ed, Betty (Terry Moore), against his fathers' wishes; Norman Page (Russ Tamblyn) tries to escape the control of his mother through his platonic friendship with Allison; Selena Cross (Hope Lange) is raped by her vicious father-in-law, Lucas (Arthur Kennedy), and later accidentally kills him. Everyone's lives are temporarily disjointed by the advent of World War II, but Allison has already broken with her mother and moved to New York, where she tries to put her feelings about the small town down on paper. It is at the trial of Selena Cross that she and her mother are finally reunited, and she learns of her mother's acceptance of Dr. Rossi's marriage proposal, following Constance's admission that the reason for her overprotectiveness was that she never married, and that Allison had been born out of wedlock.

At its most mundane, *Peyton Place* is merely the greatest tearjerker of all time. Its power lies in its cataloging the small details of how people and places change. The feeling for the town itself, searching for a new identity as much as its inhabitants, was greatly aided by the location shooting in Camden, Maine. At one point near the film's end, the once close friends Allison and Norman meet on a train headed for their hometown, and almost don't recognize each other —so totally have they changed in the few years that have elapsed sinced they were friends. In addition to adapting the decade's most gossiped-about novel into a respectable film property, the makers of *Peyton Place* also succeeded in commenting on the creation of our current lifestyles.

Lloyd Nolan and Arthur Kennedy

No Down Payment

20th Century-Fox (1957)

Produced by Jerry Wald; directed by Martin Ritt; screenplay by Philip Yordan, based on the novel by John McPartland.

CAST: *Leola Boone* (Joanne Woodward); *Isabelle Flagg* (Sheree North); *Jerry Flagg* (Tony Randall); *David Martin* (Jeffrey Hunter); *Troy Boone* (Cameron Mitchell); *Jean Martin* (Patricia Owens); *Betty Kreitzer* (Barbara Rush); *Herman Kreitzer* (Pat Hingle); *Markham* (Robert Harris); *Iko* (Aki Aleong); *Mr. Burton* (Jim Hayward); *Sandra Kreitzer* (Mimi Gibson); *Harmon Kreitzer* (Donald Towers); *Michael Flagg* (Charles Herbert)

The title of the film offered a perfect indication of its concerns. *No Down Payment* was the first film to deal on a grand scale with the sharp social issues raised by the development of the new suburbia subculture. As brought to the screen by the young but already highly respected director Martin Ritt (one of the many people to prove himself through live television work) it dealt with the various types of people who made up the new conformity inhabiting that creation of the fifties, "the housing development." The changes in our society—economic, political and social—produced during the decade a new American middle class that lived almost exclusively on the installment plan and could

Patricia Owens, Tony Randall and Cameron Mitchell

Alcoholism as an escape from an unsatisfying lifestyle: Tony Randall, Sheree North

Joanne Woodward as the alienated housewife who begins drinking the moment her husband leaves for work

Cameron Mitchell and Joanne Woodward

afford to move into a cut-rate version of the American Dream only if they could do so on a "no down payment" basis. John McPartland's novel had attempted to illustrate that syndrome and the problems it raised by focusing on four fairly typical couples, each the perfect prototype of some element of the new lifestyle. Twentieth Century-Fox bought it as a vehicle for eight of the younger players in its stock company. What emerged was a collection of four separate but interlocking stories, each presenting a particular problem and all, taken together, delivering a strong critical statement.

The fictitious name of "Sunrise Hills" was given to this typical suburban community, in which each neat little prefabricated house looks like the next, even to the point of identical barbeque grills in every backyard. David Martin (Jeffrey Hunter), an ex-GI, has taken the advice of the many magazine advertisements which after the war urged vets to go into electronic engineering, since it would be "the wave of the future"; but his own future is threatened when his attractive wife Jean (Patricia Owens) is sexually assaulted by a drunken neighbor. Jerry Flagg (Tony Randall) tries to make his way in the world as a used-car salesman, but the pressures of putting on a show as the happy-go-lucky wisecracking nice guy eventually lead to visions of grandeur and a case of alcoholism that his wife, Isabelle

(Sheree North), can neither comprehend nor tolerate—forcing her to consider divorce as the only solution.

Troy Boone (Cameron Mitchell) was decorated during the war, but finds things have gone downhill since those glorious days; he has moved to California from rural Tennessee, but has only managed to find work as manager of a gas station. Desperately, he searches for a means of achieving a position of power, status, and proximity to the violence he enjoyed a taste of in combat—as the city's new police chief. His wife Leola (Joanne Woodward) only wants to bring children into the world, an urge her crude, insensitive spouse cannot understand. Herman Kreitzer (Pat Hingle), a likeably pleasant manager of a hardware store, would like to help his hard-working Japanese assistant move into the development—an idea which startles his wife Betty (Barbara Rush), who is determined to keep minorities out at all costs.

Though the film's resolutions are predictably melodramatic, the attempt to deal with personal, human problems which also carry considerable social import, within the framework of an "entertainment picture," was in itself an achievement. The film assayed almost every major problem of the emerging middle class—from alcoholism to the subtler forms of racism.

Fred Astaire

Funny Face

Paramount (1957)

Produced by Roger Edens; directed by Stanley Donen; written by Leonard Gershe; music and lyrics by George and Ira Gershwin and also by Mr. Edens and Mr. Gershe.

CAST: *Jo* (Audrey Hepburn); *Dick Avery* (Fred Astaire); *Maggie Prescott* (Kay Thompson); *Professor Emile Flostre* (Michel Auclair); *Paul Duval* (Robert Fleming); *Marion* (Dovima); *Babs* (Virginia Gibson); *Special Dancers* (Suzy Parker, Sunny Harnett); *Laura* (Sue England); *Lettie* (Ruta Lee); *Hairdresser* (Jean Del Val); *Dovitch* (Alex Gerry); *Armande* (Iphigenie Castiglioni)

A 1920s musical comedy by George and Ira Gershwin seemed less than a likely vehicle to inspire one of the most telling musicals of the fifties. But as modernized by Leonard Gershe and directed by Stanley Donen, *Funny Face* emerged not only as a charmingly chic Cinderella story but a pointed satire as well.

Two of the most popular aberrations of the decade were the trend toward pink clothing, widely considered the ultimate attempt of high fashion magazines to create the most garish of fads for their too-loyal, fashion-conscious readers, and the Beat Generation, the fifties answer to the Lost Gen-

eration of a quarter century earlier, expressing their rejection of the American Dream of financial success by dropping out of the mainstream into a bohemian world of bulky sweaters, Zen Buddhist poetry, and pot smoking. Though each caught the public's fancy they were, inexplicably enough, largely overlooked by moviemakers until *Funny Face* came along, and allowed us the opportunity to laugh at them both.

The early part of the film flits back and forth between these two cultures as they coexist in New York City's supposedly antithetical worlds of Madison Avenue and Greenwich Village. Dick Avery (Fred Astaire) is the renowned photographer of a *Vogue*-ish magazine whose editor has, on a whim, decided to instruct her female readers that a most unpleasant shade of pink will be the "in" color for the following season. Searching for a fresh young face to turn into

218

Fred Astaire and Audrey Hepburn

the new cover girl, Avery happens upon Jo (Audrey Hepburn), a slender, innocent young book-store clerk in Greenwich Village. He proceeds to pull a Pygmalion and turn her into an immediately recognizable fashion personality—falling madly in love with her in the process.

Director Donen staged the dance numbers in his stylized, madcap manner, making especially good use of the downbeat cellar clubs (filled with thick smoke, cool jazz, and poets sporting goatees) and the ultrasophisticated offices of the uptown magazine (where super-slim models langorously pose against antiseptic white walls). By poking equal amounts of fun at the high seriousness of the beatniks' existentialism and the sophisticated superficiality of modern fashion publishing and advertising, *Funny Face* saved itself from becoming too one-sided: it didn't attack either of the lifestyles, but humorously pointed out the ridiculous excesses of each. In addition, it provided Audrey Hepburn with one of her best roles as the slim pixie, at once worldly yet childishly refreshing, which she perfected in films throughout the fifties, while giving Fred Astaire his most delightful vehicle of the decade.

Jo Van Fleet and Kirk Douglas

Gunfight at the OK Corral

Paramount (1957)

Produced by Hal Wallis; directed by John Sturges; screenplay by Leon Uris, suggested by an article by George Scullin.

CAST: *Wyatt Earp* (Burt Lancaster); *Doc Holliday* (Kirk Douglas); *Laura Denbow* (Rhonda Fleming); *Kate Fisher* (Jo Van Fleet); *Ringo* (John Ireland); *Ike Clanton* (Lyle Bettger); *Cotton Wilson* (Frank Faylen); *Charles Bassett* (Earl Holliman); *Shanghai Pierce* (Ted De Corsia); *Billy Clanton* (Dennis Hopper); *John P. Clum* (Whit Bissell); *John Shanssey* (George Mathews); *Virgil Earp* (John Hudson); *Morgan Earp* (DeForest Kelley); *James Earp* (Martin Milner); *Bat Masterson* (Kenneth Tobey); *Ed Bailey* (Lee Van Cleef); *Betty Earp* (Joan Camden); *Mrs. Clanton* (Olive Carey)

One of the most popular recurring motifs in American movies has always been the distinctively masculine relationship, in which two larger-than-life figures—exceptionally different in personality but equally matched in potentials—are thrown together as friendly enemies. Each respects the other's courage and convictions but continuously finds himself, through the whims of circumstance, in the position of fighting against the only other "real" man around as often as he is able to fight alongside him. The silent classic *What Price Glory* (1927) gave us Victor McLaglen and Edmund Lowe as a pair of brawling marines; *Boom Town* (1946) offered what many moviegoers consider the greatest team of all, Spencer Tracy and Clark Gable, as the simple earthy fellow and his roguish companion. In the fifties, the team was Burt Lancaster and Kirk Douglas, and their most satisfying vehicle was *Gunfight at the O.K. Corral*.

Doc (Kirk Douglas) is challenged by Johnny Ringo (John Ireland)

Leon Uris based his screenplay, which was more historically accurate than most films about Wyatt Earp and Doc Holliday, on numerous bits of biographical material, western mythology and newspaper records of the day. The story picks up with the first uneasy meeting of young Marshal Earp (Lancaster), a dedicated, moralistic lawman and the heavy-drinking, doomed-by-consumption devil-may-care gambler Doc Holliday (Douglas) in Fort Griffin, Texas. Earp, on the trail of some outlaws, saves Holliday from a trap by his enemies; Doc insists on returning the favor some time later in Dodge City, when the marshal finds himself short on deputies.

Each man is involved with a woman: Earp with the classy lady gambler Laura Denbow (Rhonda Fleming) and Holliday with the lowly saloon girl Kate Fisher (Jo Van Fleet), but the two men find themselves drawn to each other in an unlikely commitment that few can understand —least of all Earp's fellow lawmen and Doc's drinking companions. When Earp's brothers beg him to journey to Tombstone and help fight the notorious Clanton gang, his friend does not let him down and together they defeat the outlaw elements—even though both women walk out on the men as a result of their continued friendship and constant gunplay.

The film was a highly popular and strong western in all respects. But it just missed reaching the status of western classic, perhaps because it strove too consciously to be one. The film's style was carefully calculated to cash in on the two most popular trends of the decade: the wide-screen epic and the downbeat adult western. On the one hand there are endless panoramic vistas, an obviously lavish budget, and cameo appearances by a whole gamut of legendary gunmen (Kenneth Tobey as Bat Masterson, John Ireland as Johnny Ringo, Dennis Hopper as Billy the Kid); on the other, there are familiar devices borrowed none too subtly from *High Noon*, including an opening image of three outlaws approaching a town and a closing shot of the lawman dropping his badge in the dust, with a continuous theme song dubbed in by Frankie Laine, whose recording of *High Noon* had earned him a gold record. But the colorful CinemaScope extravaganza and the serious social western were fundamentally antithetical film forms, and though the packaging was often impressive, *Gunfight* was devoid of the inspiration that made *My Darling Clementine* (1946), John Ford's "little" film about the same events, a far greater motion picture in the long run.

Jose Ferrer and Ed Wynn

The Great Man
Universal-International (1957)

Produced by Aaron Rosenberg; directed by José Ferrer; screenplay by Al Morgan and Mr. Ferrer, from the novel by Mr. Morgan.

CAST: *Joe Harris* (José Ferrer); *Philip Carleton* (Dean Jagger); *Sid Moore* (Keenan Wynn); *Carol Larson* (Julie London); *Ginny* (Joanne Gilbert); *Paul Beaseley* (Ed Wynn); *Nick Cellantano* (Jim Backus); *Eddie Brand* (Russ Morgan); *Dr. O'Connor* (Edward C. Platt); *Mike Jackson* (Robert Foulk); *Harry Connors* (Lyle Talbot); *Charley Carruthers* (Vinton Hayworth); *Mrs. Rieber* (Henny Backus); *Mary Browne* (Janie Alexander); *Receptionist* (Vicki Dugan); *Mailboy* (Robert Schwartz)

Madison Avenue's massive power over the TV and radio networks—and thus, indirectly, over the mentality of the American people—was one of the most significant sources of movie material during the decade. One of the more effective and uncompromising exposés was *The Great Man.*

The multi-talented Jose Ferrer directed, co-authored and starred as Joe Harris, a top-notch investigative reporter assigned by his broadcasting network to compile a mammoth tribute to the title figure: a recently deceased, world-famous TV and radio personality. Not unlike the reporter in *Citizen Kane*, Harris, accompanied by his pretty assistant Ginny (Joanne Gilbert) interviews each of the various people who in some way knew "the great man" intimately, including:

Paul Beaseley (Ed Wynn), a bigoted small-town broad-caster who gave the superstar his first job; Sid Moore (Keenan Wynn), his ex-manager; Philip Carleton (Dean Jagger), president of a network; and Carol Lawson (Julie London), the deceased man's long-time mistress.

What becomes increasingly apparent to Harris is that the great man was, in fact, a louse; each person encountered was ruthlessly used and then discarded in the course of this ego-maniac's career. But when the reporter confronts his superiors with the findings, they insist he go on with the homage as scheduled. The show's sponsors are dedicated to the continued selling of this man's image to the public. Though quite aware that the facts directly contradict the legend, they consider the special program a final step in the "packaging" of his personality as a commodity for mass consumption.

Harris' reward for acting as host, perpetuating the hoax, and corrupting himself beyond redemption will be to emerge from the program as the logical successor to the deceased—the *new* "great man." His last-second decision, though unlikely, made for a stunning dramatic climax: Harris goes on the air "live," throws away the script, and informs his audience that he's going to tell them the truth. During the next hour Harris relates precisely what he learned, knowing full well that his producers and sponsors, though unable to stop him, will certainly make sure he never works again.

The Great Man stands as a significant cinematic warning against the public's developing too great a reliance on the immense new popularity and power of the broadcasting media—with their loyalty to sponsors and tendency, through "creative advertising" techniques, to perpetrate an image they themselves do not believe in.

Jose Ferrer and Keenan Wynn

A Face in the Crowd

Warner Bros. (1957)

Produced and directed by Elia Kazan for Newtown Productions; story and screenplay by Budd Schulberg.

CAST: *Lonesome Rhodes* (Andy Griffith); *Marcia Jeffries* (Patricia Neal); *Joey Kiely* (Anthony Franciosa); *Mel Miller* (Walter Matthau); *Betty Lou Fleckum* (Lee Remick); *Colonel Hollister* (Percy Waram); *Beanie* (Rod Brasfield); *Mr. Luffler* (Charles Irving); *J. B. Jeffries* (Howard Smith); *Macey* (Paul McGrath); *First Mrs. Rhodes* (Kay Medford); *Jim Collier* (Alexander Kirland); *Senator Fuller* (Marshall Nielan); *Sheriff Hosmer* (Big Jeff Bess); *Abe Steiner* (Henry Sharp)

The same year that witnessed José Ferrer's tour-de-force attack on the dangerously unlimited powers of the new media in *The Great Man*, saw another, and in many ways complementary, exposé in *A Face in the Crowd*. A joint production of writer Budd Schulberg and director Elia Kazan (a team that had clearly demonstrated its effectiveness with *On the Waterfront*), the film starred Andy Griffith, making his movie debut as "Lonesome Rhodes"—a country entertainer skyrocketed to dizzying (and previously impossible) heights of popularity and influence via the protean powers of modern broadcasting.

Whereas *The Great Man* had presented a behind-the-

The media-created monster: Andy Griffith as "Lonesome Rhodes" visits crippled children so that the incident can be televised

Television technicians try to restrain Patricia Neal from turning up the volume on "Lonesome Rhodes" and letting the public hear his real attitudes

Andy Griffith and Patricia Neal

scenes view of attempts to perpetrate a major star's image as a marketable commodity even beyond his death, *A Face in the Crowd* studied the means by which such a popular living legend is created. Marcia Jeffries (Patricia Neal), an executive-cum-talent-scout for a minor Arkansas TV station, must develop some sort of format to fill the daytime hours. By chance, she happens upon Rhodes: a charismatically cornball character who entertains his farmer friends with songs and gags around the cracker barrel. Marcia persuades her producers to give Rhodes a try as the local television personality; he turns out to be a bigger hit than anyone imagined possible, and is quickly picked up by a larger, state-wide station.

Rhodes and Marcia (who becomes his loyal friend and secret lover) climb the ladder to big-time success faster than either could have guessed. Ironically enough, a complex and sophisticated national television network becomes the means for spreading Rhodes' simpleminded songs and redneck chatter to the American people. The advertising executives delight in his power as an audience draw, but laugh at "the big hick" behind his back. What they fail to grasp is that their creation is far cleverer than they, and will soon emerge as a modern Frankenstein's monster. For Rhodes, despite his nightly enactment of an "Aw, shucks!" self-effacing regular guy (hence, the film's title), is actually an ambitious, cynical man who enjoys the taste of raw power and craves more.

It's just a matter of time before he's using his show to drop political hints to his faithful followers. First, Rhodes does small favors for pressure groups, then allies himself with an important presidential aspirant—offering to trade his influence over the public for equal influence with the man after he's elected. In a climax clearly related to that of *The Great Man*, Marcia, unable to stand what Rhodes has become, switches on the superstar's microphone from the control room unbeknownst to him, and the entire nation hears swaggering, contemptuous comments about their being his toys, his possessions. In a matter of seconds, the machinery of the media destroys its own creation faster than it had synthesized him.

Like *The Great Man*, *A Face in the Crowd* suggests that the man-made broadcasting networks had become a powerful, perhaps uncontrollable, entity with a life-force of its own. Its only vulnerability was that a sincere, uncorrupted human being like Marcia or Sam Harris could momentarily seize advantage of the "live" nature of its programming to let the public in on the truth behind the image. Very quickly thereafter videotape was perfected; shows were recorded well in advance of broadcast—and even that possibility was lost.

The two by-the-book commanders (Sessue Hayakawa and Alec Guinness)

The Bridge on the River Kwai

Geoffrey Horne, Jack Hawkins, and William Holden

The Bridge on the River Kwai

Columbia (1957)

Produced by Sam Spiegel for Horizon Pictures; directed by David Lean; screenplay by Pierre Boulle, based on his novel.

CAST: *Shears* (William Holden); *Colonel Nicholson* (Alec Guinness); *Major Warden* (Jack Hawkins); *Colonel Saito* (Sessue Hayakawa); *Major Clipton* (James Donald); *Lieutenant Joyce* (Geoffrey Horne); *Colonel Green* (Andre Morell); *Captain Reeves* (Peter Williams); *Major Hughes* (John Boxer); *Grogan* (Percy Herbert); *Baker* (Harold Goodwin); *Nurse* (Ann Sears); *Captain Kanematsu* (Henry Okawa); *Lieutenant Miura* (K. Katsumoto); *Yai* (M. R. B. Chakrabandhu)

The decade's desire for ever bigger screen entertainment too often led to bigness for its own sake, but in *Bridge on the River Kwai*, the new wide-screen process finally found its perfect function—telling a story that actually depended on the newly enlarged scope for its epic effect. Balancing psychological tension with grand-scale action, *Kwai* represented everything the spectacle-minded producers had been searching for. It was an immense success both critically and financially, reaching the status of all-time box-office champion and multi-Academy Award winner, including Best Actor (Alec Guinness) and Best Picture of the Year.

French novelist Pierre Boulle fashioned the script from his own novel, which had concentrated exclusively on the

Alec Guinness, William Holden and Jack Hawkins

tension between a British colonel and the Japanese commandant who holds him prisoner in the Ceylon jungles during World War II. To this Boulle added, at Hollywood's suggestion, a subplot about an American (William Holden) who escapes from the camp shortly after Colonel Nicholson (Alec Guinness) and his squadron are interned. For once the meddling of movie moguls did not harm an artistic novel, but helped to elevate a slim, minor triumph into an important international work of art.

As Shears frantically makes his way through the jungle to freedom, Nicholson flatly refuses Colonel Saito's (Sessue Hayakawa) orders to have his men do manual work on the construction of a Japanese railroad bridge. Nicholson undergoes the physical tortures of enclosure in a sun-baked box and near-starvation, but heroically holds out and, finally, has his way. Saito asks instead only that the British become "advisors," and since there is nothing in the book against that, Nicholson agrees—oblivious to the fact that his engineering capacities will aid the Japanese war cause far more than physical labor would have done. When a British commando, Major Warden (Jack Hawkins) is assigned to penetrate the jungle and blow up the near-completed bridge, he requests that the recently escaped Shears accompany him. Nicholson has put himself into the job wholeheartedly, committing himself to doing the best possible job as a self-respecting "professional." As the commandos begin planting charges it is Nicholson who discovers them, and reports his findings to Saito with the words: "Someone's trying to blow up my bridge!"

As Shears is killed while attempting to set off the explosives, Nicholson finally reaches the moral realization of what he's done, and blows up the bridge himself. "It's all madness," a British medic (James Donald) shouts wildly from a hill overlooking the scene, as the camera pulls back slowly to show us first the magnitude of the destruction and then, in turn, its relative minuteness in relationship to the encroaching, unending primordial jungle.

William Holden's cool, cynical presence communicated the fifties conception of the American soldier, committed to personal survival but willing to risk death to do his duty. Hayakawa and Hawkins were equally effective, but it was Guinness' film from start to finish. More than just a caricature of the career soldier, he made of Colonel Nicholson a subtly etched case study of the military mind, and the dangerous shortsightedness to which it was prone. "The Colonel Bogie March" became a hit record, foreshadowing the day when all major movies, and not just love stories, would have marketable theme songs. David Lean's sweeping direction juxtaposed the psychological with the epic, resulting in the first wide-screen film that was at once equally satisfying as movie art and movie entertainment.

Sweet Smell of Success

United Artists (1957)

A Hecht-Hill-Lancaster presentation, produced by James Hill, for a Norma-Curtleigh Production; directed by Alexander Mackendrick; screenplay by Clifford Odets and Ernest Lehman, from a novelette by Mr. Lehman.

CAST: *J. J. Hunsecker* (Burt Lancaster); *Sidney Falco* (Tony Curtis); *Susan Hunsecker* (Susan Harrison); *Steve Dallas* (Marty Milner); *Frank D'Angelo* (Sam Levene); *Rita* (Barbara Nichols); *Sally* (Jeff Donnell); *Robard* (Joseph Leon); *Mary* (Edith Atwater); *Harry Kello* (Emile Meyer); *Herbie Temple* (Joe Frisco); *Otis Elwell* (David White); *Leo Bartha* (Lawrence Dobkin); *Mrs. Bartha* (Lurene Tuttle); *Linda* (Autumn Russell); *Manny Davis* (Jay Adler); *Al Evans* (Lewis Charles); and the Chico Hamilton Quintet

In its golden quarter-century between the birth of sound and the end of World War II, Hollywood was known as the Dream Factory. That reputation was well earned for, despite an ever-present handful of serious films about social problems, the movie industry provided us—and the rest of the world as well—with an idealized vision of life, made all the more tantalizing by its seeming reality. But the quality of life in the fifties made such super-productions seem phoney and out of touch. The old heroes and heroines were replaced by characters with psychological problems, and new styles of filmmaking necessarily appeared to tell the tales in a manner that suited them.

High-minded writers, actors and directors who had shied away from the movie business out of a belief that it was impossible to make an "honest" film found the situation radi-

Tony Curtis and Burt Lancaster

Barbara Nichols and Tony Curtis

cally altered following the public acceptance of *From Here to Eternity* and *On the Waterfront*. Moviegoers displayed an unprecedented appetite for mature, uncompromising pictures and *Sweet Smell of Success* was the classic example. Shot entirely on location in New York City, it captured the look and feel of big-town life, from its seamiest spots to the poshest of night places, offering a convincing cross-section of the city's people and their lifestyles.

It also presented viewers with another variation of that decidedly fifties villain, the media-created monster. This time he was J. J. Hunsecker (Burt Lancaster), a widely read, nationally syndicated columnist who uses his power in the press to manipulate the thinking of the American public. His most important source of scoops is Sidney Falco (Tony Curtis), a self-effacing but inwardly ambitious youth eager to please "J. J." at all costs, hoping to eventually use Hunsecker's influence to achieve some level of success, power, and money for himself.

When J. J. learns that his younger sister Susan (Susan Harrison) is about to run off with and marry a small-time jazz musician, Steve Dallas (Marty Milner), Hunsecker responds by promising Falco his long-awaited passport to power if he will find a means to destroy the relationship. Though at first repulsed by the notion, the success-hungry Sidney eventually throws himself into the task with a vengeance—employing a "B" girl named Rita (Barbara Nichols) as part of his plan to destroy the young man's reputation.

The film's only weakness, and one pointed out by most of the critics, was the failure of Ernest Lehman's story to provide any clear motivation—other than just general cruelty—for Hunsecker's desire to see Dallas destroyed. If Hunsecker's rejection of even so pleasant a suitor was meant to suggest some Freudian protectiveness for his sister, it was the only thing in the film that failed to come off. This is, however, a minor detail, for James Wong Howe's strikingly downbeat black-and-white cinematography unforgettably captured the New York scene, while the Clifford Odets dialogue authentically delineated each of the various subcultures of Manhattan. Lancaster's laconic delivery of his lines made him a perfect choice for the icy Hunsecker, and at his suggestion Tony Curtis, his youthful co-star from *Trapeze*, was entrusted with the difficult role of the nervously energetic Falco. At just that point in time when his fellow teenage idols like Tab Hunter and Robert Wagner were on the wane, Curtis proved himself a serious actor ready for full stardom.

Boy on a Dolphin

20th Century-Fox (1957)

Produced by Samuel G. Engel; directed by Jean Negulesco; screenplay by Ivan Moffat and Dwight Taylor, from the novel by David Divine.

CAST: *Dr. James Calder* (Alan Ladd); *Phaedra* (Sophia Loren); *Victor Parmalee* (Clifton Webb); *Rhif* (Jorge Mistral); *Dr. Hawkins* (Laurence Naismith); *Government Man* (Alexis Minotis); *Niko* (Piero Giagnoni); *Bill B. Baldwin* (Charles Fawcett); *Miss Dill* (Gertrude Flynn); *Mrs. Baldwin* (Charlotte Terrabust); *Miss Baldwin* (Margaret Stahl); *Chief of Police* (Orestes Rallis); and The Penegrysis Greek Folk Dance and Songs Society

There was nothing in the script of *Boy on a Dolphin* to indicate it could prove the basis for anything but a routine romance-adventure programmer. But Twentieth Century-Fox turned it into one of 1957's major grossers, thanks to their understanding of the public's growing desire for two elements: on-location shooting at exotic European locales and breathtakingly endowed Italian women. They found the former in the coastlines of Greece, the latter in the lusty presence of Sophia Loren.

The story itself is little more than an underwater *Maltese Falcon*, but lacking the genuine wit and sense of self-satire that made the Humphrey Bogart-John Huston thriller a classic. Phaedra (Loren), a poor sponge diver, discovers the wreckage of a long-lost ship while swimming off the coast of the island of Hydra. Protruding from its bow is the valuable statue that gives the film its title. She is so taken with the phantom-like object that she almost loses her life in an accident while gazing at it. After surfacing, she tells her loudmouth boyfriend Rhif (Jorge Mistral) about it. He insists they must find a means of recovering the treasure and then sell it, escaping from their poverty forever. They enlist the aid of an American archaeologist, Dr. James Calder (Alan Ladd), who is excited enough about their find to want it for his museum. Phaedra is forced by the greedy Rhif to help deceive Calder and to take the statue away from him after its recovery.

An unscrupulous adventurer named Victor Parmalee (Clifton Webb) tempts Rhif with a great deal of money to bring him the priceless objet d'art. Phaedra finds herself in great inner conflict, her loyalty to her boyfriend suddenly dwarfed by her growing love and respect for the dedicated, handsome American. Her younger brother Niko (Piero Giagnoni) idolizes the man and, at the moment of decision, Phaedra throws in her lot with him.

Clifton Webb and director Jean Negulesco, previously teamed for the Italian-made *Three Coins in the Fountain,* were reunited for another on-location venture. No American filmmaking unit had ever employed the Greek coastlines before. But the promise of a glimpse of "the real thing" was the sort of incentive that lured viewers from the comforts of their television sets. As almost every major picture came to be shot on location, producers realized their projects were less costly than if shot in Hollywood with American extras at union scale. The various backgrounds for *Dolphin* included the Parthenon, the streets and byways of Athens, the ancient amphitheatre of Epidaurus, and the rocky landscape along the Aegean Sea. Seen in panoramic wide screen and color for the first time, the settings were lovely enough to help audiences ignore the triviality and predictability of the story.

But the real draw was the presence of Sophia Loren. The film had originally been planned as a vehicle for Alan Ladd, a nominal star at best. The advance publicity created much excitement about the latest Italian siren, claiming her physique was more magnificent than Gina Lollobrigida's. A huge shot of Sophia literally falling out of a paltry wet rag she wore while diving formed the basis of the film's publicity. Sophia incarnated the American male's idealization of the European peasant woman, earthy and experienced, and Alan Ladd served as the symbolic modern urban-intellectual who eventually wins her favors.

Laurence Naismith, Jorge Mistral and Sophia Loren

Brigitte Bardor, Jean Louis Trintignant and Christian Imarquand

And God Created Woman

A Kingsley International Release (1957)

Produced by Raoul J. Levy; directed by Roger Vadim; original screenplay by Mr. Vadim and Mr. Levy.

CAST: *Juliette* (Brigitte Bardot); *Eric* (Curt Jurgens); *Michel* (Jean-Louis Trintignant); *Antoine* (Christian Marquand); *Christian* (Georges Poujouly); *M. Vigier-Lefranc.* (Jean Tissier); *Mme. Morin* (Jane Marken); *Mme. Tardieu* (Marie Glory); *Lucienne* (Isabelle Corey); *Rene* (Jean Lefebvre); *Perri* (Philippe Grenier); *Mme. Vigier-Lefranc* (Jacqueline Ventura)

Though many a shapely blonde crossed the screen for our scrutiny throughout the decade, not one could really compete with Marilyn Monroe until a sensual little wisp of a woman named Brigitte Bardot appeared. Viewed in various stages of undress in a succession of inexpensively made European imports, she almost single-handedly changed the meaning of the term "art house" from an intellectual retreat for Fellini fans into a continental peep show.

Bardot starred in a half-dozen films before *And God Created Woman* and, in fact, was already something of a minor

sensation. But this picture, though not particularly good, was one of those accidental miracles of perfect timing that turn actors into stars, and stars into myths. Writer-director Roger Vadim, loudly touted as the Pygmalion responsible for Brigitte's Galatea, had filmed this seamy little saga on the French Riviera, in and around the picturesque port of St. Tropez. In it Juliette (Bardot), a young wastrel, receives the loving care of a solid middle-class family. She rewards their kindness by driving their two sons into states of repressed sexual arousal—much to her own bemusement. Eventually she marries Michel (Jean-Louis Trintignant), the younger, then gleefully seduces Antoine (Christian Marquand), the older—managing somehow to find time to strike up an affair with Eric (Curt Jurgens), a rich, lecherous yachtsman.

The film's fantastic power derives totally from the personality of its star. She shocked American audiences— women and men alike—not so much by the explicitness of her sexuality as by her casual attitude toward it. Always, she is seen in some "costume" as exotic as it is erotic: calypso slacks, tight-fitting sweaters, short-shorts, the most immodest bikini the world had yet seen—or just a revealingly draped sheet. Her unique appeal came from an ability to remain mysterious while unclothed (no mean feat!) and she was, in fact, at her best when entirely nude. The film's title, likening her to Eve, was an accidental stroke of genius. Half-aware, half-oblivious to the powers of her own sexuality over the Adams of the world, she represented primal woman incarnate: an uncanny combination of sophistication and innocence.

But Bardot's real significance rested in the fact that she was always as much a sociological symbol as a sexual one. *And God Created Woman* immortalized her legend in much the same way *Rebel Without a Cause* did James Dean's. No one thought for a moment that B. B. was *acting*: the film's great allure lay in the assumption that the irresponsible, irrepressible, irresistible sexual behavior was entirely her own. Dean's brooding masochistic self-destruction had come to symbolize early fifties anti-Establishment sentiment; Brigitte's gleefully contemptuous nose-thumbing at convention quickly emerged as its late-fifties counterpart.

Elvis Presley and Judy Tyler

Jailhouse Rock

Metro-Goldwyn-Mayer (1957)

Produced by Pandro S. Berman; directed by Richard Thorpe; screenplay by Guy Prosper, based on a Ned Young story.

CAST: *Vince Everett* (Elvis Presley); *Peggy* (Judy Tyler); *Hunk Houghton* (Mickey Shaughnessy); *Mr. Shores* (Vaughn Taylor); *Sherry Wilson* (Jennifer Holden)

Rock 'n' roll was around long before Elvis Presley appeared on the scene, but the new musical style failed to attract widespread attention until Elvis was introduced in 1956 on a TV show hosted by, ironically enough, those Big Band musicians, the Dorsey Brothers. Presley's wild gyrations thrilled teenagers and troubled their parents, who saw this young man as a hoodlum hero captivating their children.

Vince stares down a heckler

Vince (Elvis Presley) realizes he has killed a man in a barroom brawl

But Presley was undeniably the new singing star of the decade. He and his clever manager, Colonel Parker, sensed that television exposure could only diminish Elvis' rising star; if his fans wanted to see him, they would have to pay to see a movie. And, for a full ten years, they did just that.

Elvis was to be "introduced" in a supporting role in a B western, originally entitled *The Reno Brothers*. But during production his part was enlarged, additional singing sequences added, and the film eventually retitled *Love Me Tender*, in deference to his hit single. The movie was such a smash that Elvis received top billing in his next feature, *Loving You*. But it was too slow moving for his teenage audience, who also resented the romantic teaming of their hero with older woman Lizabeth Scott. His third film, *Jailhouse Rock*, perfected the "Presley vehicle." His role was ideally suited to him: a romanticized version of his own image.

As Vince Everett, Elvis is a good-natured country boy who ends up in the state penitentiary after a conviction for manslaughter. Presley's producers attempted to transfer some of the late James Dean's vulnerability to Elvis: Vince killed a man in defense of a barfly who was being bullied by the man. Elvis Presley's code of honor about women was to become a prime element in all his future pictures.

While serving his prison term, Vince becomes friendly with Hunk Houghton (Mickey Shaughnessy), who is impressed enough by his cellmate's warbling to build him up into the star of an elaborate prison show. After their release, Vince forms a recording company with pretty young Peggy (Judy Tyler), and eventually becomes a national success. They travel to Hollywood, where Peggy realizes her onetime shy companion is being turned into an egomaniac by his enormous power over the public via television performances. This theme had already formed the basis for a number of the decade's more important films, and here the motion picture industry's moralizing against the instant notoriety afforded by their bitter enemy television was turned into the subject of a teenage romance. But in *Jailhouse Rock* it was exploited rather than explored: Hunk shows up, gives the hero a good beating, and in a matter of minutes Vince is his old self, ready to settle down and marry Peggy.

Dozens of second-rate rock 'n' roll films soon followed, but only Presley enjoyed the distinction of having such movies tailored to his own personality. Though at first decidedly tacky, "the Presley film" quickly became an important money-making staple. And his thirty-odd films that followed stuck closely to the format first perfected in *Jailhouse Rock*.

Pat Boone

Bernardine

20th Century-Fox (1957)

Produced by Samuel G. Engel; directed by Henry Levin; screenplay by Theodore Reeves, based on Mary Chase's stage play.

CAST: *Beau* (Pat Boone); *Jean* (Terry Moore); *Mrs. Wilson* (Janet Gaynor); *Sanford Wilson* (Richard Sargent); *Fullerton Weldy* (Dean Jagger); *Lieutenant Beaumont* (James Drury); *Griner* (Ronnie Burns); *Mr. Beaumont* (Walter Abel); *Mrs. Beaumont* (Natalie Schafer); *Ruby* (Isabel Jewell)

Pat Boone was literally "created" by the recording industry to soothe the growing number of irate parents objecting to Elvis Presley. Boone offered a calmer pop idol no parent could possibly find fault with, as well as an alternative for young people who liked the new music but were not quite willing to emulate Presley's hoodlum look. Boone, an authentic descendant of America's most famous pioneer, wore his hair short, dressed like a college boy, and sang in a style somewhere between the declining "pop" music and rock 'n' roll. He hosted his own TV variety show for three years,

Pat Boone and Janet Gaynor

balancing this with a modestly successful movie career. He chose his roles rather than, like Presley, have his films tailored expressly for him, and they were understandably more diverse than Elvis'. The nearest thing to a Pat Boone "vehicle" was his first picture, *Bernardine*.

Based on a stage play by Mary Chase, the film mixed youthful music and melodrama with some perceptive observations about teenage life in the fifties. The story centers around a group of young boys on the verge of high school graduation. Usually they are found in the backroom of a hamburger joint, sipping cokes and talking about girls—but rarely dating them. Out of their common daydreams they create an ideal girl, name her Bernardine, and place long-distance phone calls to her in hopes that one of the operators they talk to will sound more exciting that the girls at school. Eventually the most unlikely fellow in their group, Sanford (Richard Sargent), does start dating a slightly older girl, Jean (Terry Moore). She has just moved into town and dates Sanford mainly because she hasn't met anybody more exciting—though she does object to his constant confusion of her name with Bernardine, and his dealing with her not as a flesh-and-blood reality but as an ideal come to life.

When Sanford realizes he must go into hibernation to cram for his final exams in order to graduate, his friend Beau (Pat Boone) comes up with a solution: he'll get his older brother (James Drury), home on leave from the service, to date Jean constantly and keep her away from the local wolves. But when the tests are behind them, Beau must break the news to his best friend that his brother is now engaged to Jean. Sanford responds by deserting his old gang and enlisting in the service. When he comes home the following year for Christmas vacation, considerably more mature, he learns that his foster father (Dean Jagger) has arranged a reunion with his former pals. At first, it is awkward for the boys, who no longer have anything in common with one another. But they are reunited when they sing the old "Bernardine" song, which at least momentarily brings back the memory of the ideal vision and the close sense of community they once shared.

All the boys experience parent problems of some sort. Beau is continually chastised for being less goal-oriented than his big brother, while Sanford is deeply disturbed by his mother's (Janet Gaynor) insistence on remarrying. The kids speak their own special jargon, which binds them together in a youth cult and simultaneously alienates them from their parents. But the film hit its most perceptive note by emphasizing the nature of the male community, almost to the exclusion of girls—excepting, of course, their unattainable ideal woman. There wasn't a teenage boy in the audience who hadn't experienced similar dissatisfaction with the available girls, or dreamed of a "Bernardine" of his own.

The Girl Can't Help It

20th Century-Fox (1957)

Produced and directed by Frank Tashlin; screenplay by Mr. Tashlin and Herbert Baker.

CAST: *Tom Miller* (Tom Ewell); *Jerri Jordan* (Jayne Mansfield); *Murdock* (Edmond O'Brien); *Mousie* (Henry Jones); *Wheeler* (John Emery); *Maid* (Juanita Moore); and Julie London, Ray Anthony, Barry Gordon, Fats Domino, The Platters, The Treniers, Little Richard and His Band, Gene Vincent and His Blue Caps, Eddie Fontaine, Abby Lincoln, The Chuckles, Johnny Olenn, Nino Tempo, Eddie Cochran

The only thing that could compete with rock 'n' roll as a box-office draw in 1957 was a beautiful dumb blonde. Marilyn Monroe proved so successful that numerous imitations, including Sheree North and Mamie Van Doren, were foisted on the public by virtually every studio. But by far, the most popular of all Monroe imitators was Jayne Mansfield. Essentially, she combined the Monroe mystique of the vapid bombshell with the gargantuan qualities of Anita Ekberg. Mansfield made her first major film appearance in *Illegal* (1955), a clear-cut copy of the classic crime drama *The Asphalt Jungle* which, in 1950, had introduced Mon-

Jayne Mansfield, Edmond O'Brien and Tom Ewell

Jayne Mansfield and Juanita Moore

An average American guy finds himself awestruck at Miss Mansfield's exceptional physique

roe; Mansfield's role as a showy gangster's moll was clearly modelled on Monroe's earlier portrayal. Jane was quickly elevated to a short-lived stardom, and one of her few really important vehicles was *The Girl Can't Help It*, a light comedy which attempted to tread a delicate balance between satirizing the newly popular rock 'n' roll and exploiting the phenomenon to the hilt.

Tom Ewell, in many ways the definitive comic hero of the fifties, played another variation of the modern urban man he had created in *The Seven Year Itch*. As Tom Miller, he is a heavy-drinking press agent. He is hired by an ex-gangster, Marty "Fats" Murdock (Edmund O'Brien), to make a singing star out of the tough guy's new girl-friend, Jerri Jordan (Jayne Mansfield). Murdock makes it clear to Tom that should he succeed, he will be handsomely rewarded but, if he yields to temptation and touches the irresistible Jerri, he will be "rubbed out." Trying to get to know the devastatingly endowed girl, Tom takes her out for a night on the town, where they watch many of the successful young rock 'n' rollers at work. Jerri notices that Tom is hitting the bottle and tries to learn why. He finally admits that he is carrying a torch for the lovely singer, Julie London, who jilted him.

Julie, in the meantime, is being schooled by Murdock in the new music styles; he convinces the classy pop singer that her finely tuned voice will only spell instant oblivion in the future. Tom, meanwhile, has discovered that Jerri has no voice whatsoever, but Murdock is positive that if she records a composition of his from prison days called "Rock Around the Rock Pile," it will be an instantaneous success.

Tom tries to sell the recording to "Legs" Wheeler (John Emery), the current king of the jukebox racket. But when Wheeler learns that it was written by his old enemy, their gangland feud is revived to see who will control the rock 'n' roll business. Murdock uses his gang's muscle to rip Wheeler's jukeboxes out of bars and taverns, replacing them with his own. Jerri's song is manipulated into a hit, thanks to their racketeer tactics and Jerri confesses to Tom that she loves him. Murdock, worried that he will be killed by Wheeler, is actually relieved when he learns that he has lost Jerri. When Wheeler's gang shows up at a rock 'n' roll jubilee to kill Murdock, Tom saves him by thrusting him out on the stage with the performers. He is so well received that Wheeler signs him to a long-term contract instead of killing him.

Girl was by far Miss Mansfield's most elegant vehicle: her eighteen wardrobe changes alone cost well over $35,000. And the amalgam of fourteen rock 'n' roll acts included (along with a number of people who quickly disappeared) such significant artists as Fats Domino, Little Richard and The Platters. The film's seventeen songs included a number of rhythm and blues classics such as "Ready Teddy," "Be Bop a Lula," and "Blue Suede Shoes." But the film received an extra boost of topicality by the fact that, at the time of its release, a payola scandal raged through the rock 'n' roll music business: the wild plot of *The Girl Can't Help It* turned out to be not all that far from the truth.

The expatriate returns: Charlie Chaplin as King Shahdov

A King in New York

Archway (England)

Produced, directed, written and scored by Charles Chaplin; photography by Georges Perinal.

CAST: *King Shahdov* (Charles Chaplin); *Madison Avenue Girl* (Dawn Addams); *The Queen* (Maxine Audley); *Rupert* (Michael Chaplin); Oliver Johnston, Jerry Desmond, Phil Brown, Harry Green, John McLaren, Alan Gifford, Shani Wallis, Joy Nichols, Joan Ingram, Sidney James

The greatest film artist of all time did not face his most difficult adjustment with the advent of sound in the late twenties, but with the arrival of the fifties. In 1940, Charles Chaplin savagely satirized Hitler before it became popular to do so, in *The Great Dictator*, and helped, through his comic artistry, make Americans realize that coexistence with such a person was unthinkable. But the uneasy peace that came out of World War II displeased him. Audiences could

Charles Chaplin and Dawn Adams

attitudes and liberal politics branded him as a man to be feared and hated. Many theatre owners refused to exhibit *Limelight*.

In *A King in New York* Chaplin portrayed Shahdov, the benevolent monarch of a small country called Estrovia. When the peasants revolt and threaten to destroy the aristocracy Shahdov must flee to the United States and, eventually, he comes into contact with all the elements of popular culture that have surfaced in America during the first half of the fifties. By studying the disbelieving foreigner's initial experiences with such phenomena as television, McCarthyism, rock 'n' roll, plastic surgery, Madison Avenue advertising techniques and corporate structure, Chaplin satirically attempted to shake his audiences into an awareness of the gross (and, far worse, dangerously inhuman) quality of the world we had allowed to develop during the decade.

Though Shahdov is penniless, many status seekers befriend him and become his benefactors because of his royal title. An attractive young junior executive (Dawn Addams) for an advertising agency offers to feature him in a number of her television commercials, in which he would exploit his title by hawking synthetic products. But when he nearly chokes to death while trying to swallow them on camera, the idea is quickly abandoned. Every little incident becomes a nightmare for Shahdov. When he tries to order a meal in a restaurant, the musical combo is so loud he cannot make himself understood; after friends insist he have his face lifted, Shahdov finds himself in terrible pain while watching a nightclub comic perform while necessarily restraining his laughter to keep from bursting the stitches.

But things quickly switch from amusingly annoying to downright terrifying when Shahdov befriends a small runaway boy. Rupert (Michael Chaplin) has become a fugitive because his parents have been called before the Committee on Un-American Activities, and the child can no longer stand the treatment he and his folks have received from their neighbors who have assumed that, since they are being investigated, they must be communists. Shahdov tries to calm the distraught child but no sooner does he do so than he is called before the Committee himself—a victim of guilt by association.

The near-hysterical lad names his parents' political associations to the Committee in hopes of helping his folks. They are cleared when it turns out their reason for refusing to give the names themselves was not guilt but a belief that their right of privacy was being invaded. Shahdov and his wife (Maxine Audley) take one last look at the America of the fifties and—clearly illustrating Chaplin's own point of view—make a hasty retreat to Europe.

not adjust to the dark mood Chaplin fell into, playing a mass murderer (although, intentionally at least, a sympathetic one!) in *Monsieur Verdoux* (1947). Verdoux's final words, after he has been apprehended and is about to be executed, struck many as Chaplin's own statement about our new society: "Haven't we *all* sent women and little children to their doom? And aren't we assembling powerful weapons of even greater destruction? As a murderer, I am an amateur. I shall see you *all*—very soon!"

Word spread like wildfire: Charlie Chaplin was a communist. He vehemently denied it, but no one listened. In a mellow mood he filmed *Limelight* (1952) in London as a farewell gesture to the America he had loved, and to his own youth—both of which, he felt, were lost forever. The film dealt with the relationship of an older artist to a younger one, capturing something of the transitional mood of society itself.

Despite some praise from the critics, *Limelight* had limited bookings. It was an era when the most unfounded suspicions were treated as fact, and Chaplin's individualistic

James Stewart with Kim Novak as Madeleine

Vertigo
Paramount (1958)

Produced and directed by Alfred Hitchcock; screenplay by Alec Coppel and Samuel Taylor, based on the novel by Pierre Boileau and Thomas Narcejac.

CAST: *John ("Scottie") Ferguson* (James Stewart); *Madeleine, Judy* (Kim Novak); *Midge* (Barbara Bel Geddes); *Galvin Elster* (Tom Helmore)

On the surface *Vertigo* was just a private-eye tale, an Alfred Hitchcock murder mystery that infuriated most moviegoers and movie critics of the time by revealing the "surprise" ending midway through. It was quickly written off as a perversely interesting failure, but over the years *Vertigo* amassed an underground reputation, until eventually it was revived as one of the director's best films.

Kim Novak as Judy, with James Stewart

James Stewart and Barbara Bel Geddes

In the nightmarish opening sequence we watch as detective "Scottie" Ferguson (James Stewart) contracts an extreme fear of heights when, in pursuit of a robber, he nearly falls from a tenement rooftop. Recuperating in the company of his dependable girlfriend Midge (Barbara Bel Geddes), he receives a phone call from an old friend, business magnate Galvin Elster (Tom Helmore). Elster soon explains to Scottie that he wants the detective to trail his beautiful, strange wife Madeleine (Kim Novak), who wanders San Francisco, convinced she has been possessed by the spirit of Carlotta Montez, a long-dead woman in a painting. Scottie takes the job but soon finds himself falling under the woman's mysterious spell. When she attempts to drown herself, Scottie rescues her and the love becomes mutual. Before he can tell her that he works for her husband, Madeleine is seized by a desire to climb to the top of an isolated tower. Scottie is unable to follow because of his vertigo, and she is killed in a fall.

Scottie takes the loss of Madeleine harder even than her husband, and experiences a nervous breakdown. He drifts aimlessly until he meets Judy, a crude shop-girl who bears a slight resemblance to the sophisticated Madeleine. Scottie attempts to mold her into his lost dream-girl by changing her hair style and mannerisms. But the audience is suddenly told what Scottie does not know: Judy *is* the woman he fell in love with. She was hired by Elster to impersonate his wife, who was murdered by Elster and dropped from the tower in what seemed to be the perfect crime. Scottie was the fall guy, backing up Elster's story to the police. The only snag is that Judy/Madeleine *did* fall in love with Scottie, and now frantically wants to keep him.

The remaining portion of the film follows her attempts to hide the truth from Scottie, as well as to find a way to make him love her for herself, not just as a replacement for the woman he believes dead. Gradually, though, Scottie realizes that he's been duped and forces her to return to the fated tower where, in the process of confessing, she becomes frightened and really does fall to her death. Looking down at her body, Scottie is at last cured of his vertigo.

Though Freud had stated the tenets of psychology a full forty years earlier, the fifties was the decade that seized on his concepts and made them a part of the popular culture. The mental crack-up ceased to be thought of as a rare, isolated experience for the mentally deficient and became a strong possibility for "normal" people, and in the history of motion pictures, nobody more completely embodied the image of normalcy onscreen than James Stewart.

Sidney Poitier and Tony Curtis

The Defiant Ones

United Artists (1958)

Produced and directed by Stanley Kramer; written by Nathan E. Douglas and Harold Jacob Smith.

CAST: *John (Joker)Jackson* (Tony Curtis); *Noah Cullen* (Sidney Poitier); *Sheriff Max Muller* (Theodore Bikel); *Captain Frank Gibbons* (Charles McGraw); *Big Sam* (Lon Chaney Jr.); *Solly* (King Donovan); *Mac* (Claude Akins); *Editor* (Lawrence Dobkin); *Lou Gans* (Whit Bissell); *Angus* (Carl Switzer); *The Kid* (Kevin Coughlin)

The "problem picture," that specialized breed of socially conscious film which saw its birth in the depression-ridden thirties, only to virtually disappear as the major studios began churning out propaganda films for the war cause, experienced a major renaissance in the fifties. This happened mainly because of the efforts of one man, producer-director Stanley Kramer, who reacted against the glamorous Hollywood "formula" picture and championed the cause of "message" melodramas. Kramer encouraged young, gifted New

York-based Method actors (including Marlon Brando) to appear in his films without fear of compromising themselves, and explored existing problems of the day in picture after picture—often with more sincerity than subtlety. Above all, he was dedicated to the cause of civil rights: his *Home of the Brave* (1949), an indictment of racism in the armed services, predated the major concern of the era and was widely considered a breakthrough picture in terms of attacking the problem head-on rather than merely paying lip service to it.

But his best-remembered civil rights story was *The Defiant Ones,* a hard-hitting illustration of the need for integration and, at the same time, a virtual tour de force for its two leads. John "Joker" Jackson (Tony Curtis) and Noah Cullen (Sidney Poitier), jailbirds in the deep South, are bound together by a stretch of iron chain but pitted against one another by mutual prejudice. Due to a freak accident, the two manage to escape into the backwaters and swamps. Their inability to break the chain and separate leads to bitter outbursts, interrupted only by the difficulties they encounter during their flight: hostile townspeople, a lynch mob, bloodhounds at the head of a posse, and a tender young widow (Cara Williams) in dire need of help. Step by step, incident by incident, the men grow to like, respect, and eventually love one another. The experience of struggling to survive gradually wears away their initial bigotry and allows them to discover and accept each other as human beings.

Sam Leavitt's striking black-and-white cinematography (which won an Oscar) vividly and starkly communicated a convincing on-the-spot realism; Kramer was more than any other American director of the decade influenced by the Italian neorealist films appearing in our art houses. Tony Curtis had already proved his substantial acting talent in *Sweet Smell of Success,* but *The Defiant Ones* proved he could handle the even more unsympathetic part of a racial bigot, mastering difficult dialect. More significant still, Sidney Poitier emerged as one of the most charismatic presences on the screen, and the first Negro actor to share top billing as a major film star.

In the masterfully played and shot final sequence, the two men run after a slow-moving freight train, their sure-fire means of escape. Poitier manages to crawl up onto one of the cars, but Curtis is unable to get a good grasp and follow him. The camera focuses, in powerful close-up, on two arms—one white, one black—locked together at last. Unable to save his buddy, Poitier falls back to the ground (and certain capture) with him. Through this simple incident Stanley Kramer managed to create a sense of the allegorical, and a realization in his audience that this remote little tale expressed a potent truth about the country's need for integration.

Professor Van Helsing (Peter Cushing) destroys a vampire

Count Dracula (Christopher Lee) carries off one of his victims, a lush vampire girl (Valerie Gaunt)

Horror of Dracula

Universal-International (1958)

Produced by Anthony Hinds, presented by Hammer Film Productions Ltd.; directed by Terence Fisher; screenplay by Jimmy Sangster, from the novel by Bram Stoker.

CAST: *Dr. Van Helsing* (Peter Cushing); *Count Dracula* (Christopher Lee); *Arthur Holmwood* (Michael Gough); *Mina Holmwood* (Melissa Stribling); *Lucy* (Carol Marsh); *Jonathan Harker* (John Van Eyssen); *Vampire Woman* (Valerie Gaunt); *Undertaker* (Miles Malleson); *Dr. Seward* (Charles Lloyd Pack); *Tania* (Janina Faye); *Gerda* (Olga Dickie); *Landlord* (George Woodbridge); *Inga* (Barbara Archer); *Frontier Official* (George Benson)

The conventional horror film, which had formerly enjoyed such glorious days, degenerated in quality through the late thirties and early forties. In the fifties such films disappeared almost entirely, due largely to the sudden interest in atomic monsters. But just as dinosaurs released by nuclear weapons were growing tiresome, a then-unknown British-based company called Hammer Films revived the classic figures of terror. Their first entry, *Horror of Dracula*, was a masterpiece of straightforward storytelling that many consider the finest horror film ever made.

The plot followed Bram Stoker's original novel considerably more closely than the earlier American version, begin-

nig with the journey of Englishman Jonathan Harker (John Van Eyssen) to Transylvania, where he is to be employed by the mysterious Count Dracula (Christopher Lee). Shortly after arriving he learns that Dracula is a vampire, a member of the undead who preys on hapless victims by sucking their blood. In attempting to kill the Count with a stake through the heart, he himself becomes a victim of the vampire. Dracula then travels to London in order to live off the blood of Harker's fiancé Lucy (Carol Marsh), only to encounter his eventual nemesis in the person of Dr. Van Helsing (Pater Cushing), a professor dedicated to seeking out and destroying such creatures.

Previously, horror films obeyed certain conventions almost religiously. They were shot in mood-drenched black-and-white studio settings that approximated a never-never land more than they did real European cities. But director Terence Fisher broke sharply with tradition, filming *Horror of Dracula* in realistic color at authentic locales. The Grand Guignol, high-camp dialogue was banished, and in its place were subdued, believable interchanges between characters: for the first time, the figures in a vampire movie acted and spoke like real people.

Anything that would strain credibility was omitted. Instead of a routine movie monster, Christopher Lee's Dracula emerged as an elegant European aristocrat whose infatuation with women was (another first) overtly played as a form of decadence. His fang bites are no longer so much the attack of an underworld creature as they are the seductive gestures of a sex deviant, a means of putting weak-willed women under his hypnotic spell and making them his slaves.

All his wives and intended victims are lush, fleshy women who, after falling prey to him, take on a pallor that suggests sexual degeneracy as much as vampirism. In the overpowering opening sequence, Harker is greeted at the entrance to Dracula's castle by a seductively beautiful but highly nervous woman (Valerie Gaunt) who begs Harker to take her away with him. Suddenly she embraces the surprised man, but as they kiss we see fangs protrude from her mouth as she loses control and bites wildly at his neck. We then are introduced to Christopher Lee's Count, who breaks in at that moment from some blood orgy of his own, tears the woman away from Harker, and carries her off.

Horror of Dracula simultaneously restored class and added sex to the horror film, starting a new cycle of them —with Hammer as the leading producer.

The beautiful vampire girl (Valerie Gaunt) turns into an old woman after Harker (John Van Eyssen) administers a stake through the heart

251

Sleazy Aunt Gwen tries to seduce her milk drinking young nephew: Mamie Van Doren and Russ Tamblyn

High School Confidential

Metro-Goldwyn-Mayer (1958)

Produced by Albert Zugsmith; directed by Jack Arnold; screenplay by Lewis Meltzer and Robert Blees, from a story by Mr. Blees.

CAST: *Tony Baker* (Russ Tamblyn); *Miss Williams* (Jan Sterling); *J. I. Coleridge* (John Drew Barrymore); *Joan Staples* (Diane Jergens); *Gwen Dulaine* (Mamie Van Doren); *Mr. A.* (Jackie Coogan); *Jerry Lee Lewis* (Himself); *Ray Anthony* (Himself); *Quinn* (Charles Chaplin, Jr.); *Jukey Judlow* (Burt Douglas); *Doris* (Jody Fair)

Albert Zugsmith, one of the all-time masters of the quickie exploitation flick, designed this often ludicrous, always lurid programmer to cash in on the new market for films dealing with the mores and manners of young people. From the moment that the picture began with Jerry Lee Lewis wailing out the song, "Rockin' at the High School Hop," while perched atop a beat-up station wagon, it moved at a frantic pace through an outrageous story that supposedly presented an inside glimpse of a "typical" high school. But the picture was so grotesque that, instead of merely being

written off as a disaster, it became almost everybody's all-time awful movie, and a cult classic whenever it played on the late-late show.

The initial plot development sounds suspiciously like *Rebel Without a Cause.* Tony Baker (Russ Tamblyn) is the new kid at a tough high school. Like James Dean he immediately picks up a sad sack sidekick (Charles Chaplin, Jr.) and takes on the school's toughest juvenile delinquent (John Drew Barrymore); but unlike the quiet, alienated Dean, this teenager is a jive-talking hep-cat. At the end of one day, he pretty much runs the entire show, receiving the attentions of amorous girls in knee socks and pigtails while dispensing orders to frightened hoodlums in black leather jackets.

At home his Aunt Gwen (Mamie Van Doren), a curvaceous blonde divorcée, continuously tries to drag the boy into her bed, but he dispels her attentions without ever blowing his cool. Instead he lavishes his time on the dedicated but ineffective teacher, Miss Williams (Jan Sterling), who must fight to repress her impulsive attraction toward the devil-may-care youth. Eventually it turns out that he is actually an FBI plant, out to get the goods on a big-time drug pusher, "Mr. A." (Jackie Coogan), who has begun circulating dope in the school.

The picture's cast was exemplary of the wild combinations that turned up in projects of this ilk. Russ Tamblyn's unconvincing imitation of a high school tough added an unintentional touch of humor, causing audiences to guffaw as he pushed around characters twice his size. There was also the presence of offspring of former movie greats Chaplin and Barrymore as well as the one-time child star Coogan, who spent the decade doing character parts in low-budget pictures. Rock 'n' rollers who never quite achieved Presley's prominence—like Lewis and Ray Anthony—made token appearances as themselves, doing a few numbers at the obligatory high school hop sequence and plugging their latest releases. Mamie Van Doren virtually made a career out of such films.

Despite its very obvious artistic limitations, the Zugsmith-style programmer did salvage the disappearing B-budget picture, indicating that there were still markets untouched by television that virtually begged for proper exploitation. Teenagers lapped up this fantasy about themselves. The realization that youth had a considerable amount of money to spend was a major breakthrough for Hollywood, and the financial success of *High School Confidential* helped prove that point.

The Rumble: Russ Tamblyn backs down some hoodlums with his switch blade knife

The World, the Flesh and The Devil

Metro-Goldwyn-Mayer (1959)

A Sol C. Siegel Production, produced by George Englund; directed by Ranald MacDougall; screenplay by Ferdinand Reyher, suggested by a story by Matthew Phipps Shiel.

CAST: *Ralph Burton* (Harry Belafonte); *Sarah Crandall* (Inger Stevens); *Benson Thacker* (Mel Ferrer)

The two recurring themes, the fear of an atomic war and the need for integration, had been hammered home to the point where another variation could offer little that was new. But by crossing the themes for the first time, Hollywood created a fascinating nightmare vision that was unique to the fifties.

Ralph Burton (Harry Belafonte) is an itinerant coal miner trapped beneath the earth as the result of a cave-in. Crouching in the darkness and waiting for rescue crews to reach him, he is shocked when the sounds of their work suddenly disappear. Slowly, he digs his way up to the surface. He finds no one there and, walking into a nearby town, fragments of a newspaper clue him in to what has happened: a vast atomic war has obliterrated mankind.

Desperately searching for other survivors, he heads toward New York City and finds the George Washington Bridge covered with thousands of deserted automobiles—but no people. Crossing over into Manhattan he is greeted by an empty city. Accepting his fate, Ralph sets himself up in a plush penthouse apartment, wanders the streets with a wagon seeking out sources of food, talking to department store mannequins he sets up everywhere. Gradually, though, he begins to suspect he is being watched by someone—or something.

Finally he traps his secret follower, discovering that it is a young woman, Sarah (Inger Stevens), who, like him, survived a holocaust by pure luck. Though equally lonely, she has not summed up the courage to show herself due to fears and prejudices of what a black man might do to a white woman. Resentful that bigotry could survive even an atomic war, he insists their relationship be only a mild form of friendship—something she quickly comes to resent. As Sarah learns to appreciate Ralph as an admirable human being, her old mental classifications quickly dissolve, until she begins to desire—then demand—a man-woman relationship. But he is unable to forget that, under ordinary circumstances, she wouldn't even associate with him.

At the moment he is about to give in and accept her overtures, another survivor suddenly appears. And though he is a less than likable character (Mel Ferrer), Ralph senses Sarah is quickly moving closer toward him—simply because he is white.

There are numerous plot loopholes, including the unlikely notion that a man trapped underground for a few days would be unaffected by radioactive fallout after he reached the earth's surface. But such elements were compensated for by the effective use of special effects. New York policemen cleared the streets during the early morning hours so the shooting could take place on actual locations rather than studio sets, giving the science-fantasy story a chilling realism. The black-and-white photography added a dreamlike quality, especially to the spectacular gun duel the two men finally engage in, chasing each other through de-

Harry Belafonte

Inger Stevens and Harry Belafonte

serted streets and firing wildly with automatic rifles across a nightmarish Manhattan skyline.

In the final scene they are reconciled and, in a denouement quite shocking for its time, decide to share Sarah—an idea she finds quite acceptable. The three walk away together, hand in hand, having at last excised their old prejudices completely, ready to start over again, turning the empty tenements into a post-nuclear Eden.

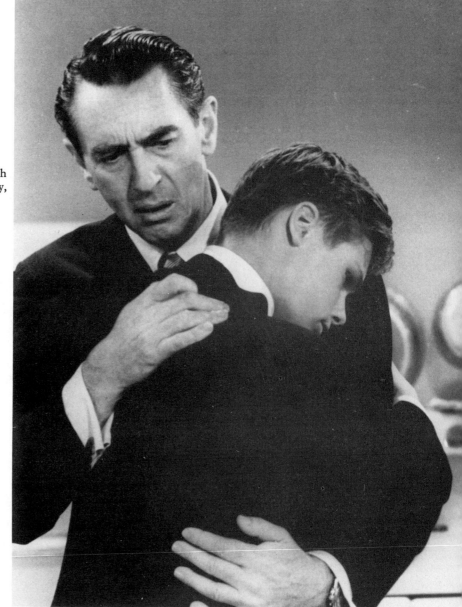

Bridging the Generation Gap through understanding: Macdonald Carey, Brandon De Wilde, Marsha Hunt

Blue Denim

20th Century-Fox (1959)

Produced by Charles Brackett; directed by Philip Dunne; screenplay by Edith Sommer and Philip Dunne, based on the play by James Leo Herlihy and William Noble.

CAST: *Janet Willard* (Carol Lynley); *Arthur Bartley* (Brandon de Wilde); *Major Malcolm Bartley* (MacDonald Carey); *Jessie Bartley* (Marsha Hunt); *Ernie* (Warren Berlinger); *Axel Sorenson* (Buck Class); *Lillian Bartley* (Nina Shipman); *Professor Willard* (Vaughn Taylor); *Cherie* (Roberta Shore); *Aunt Bidda* (Mary Young); *Vice President* (William Schallert); *Hobie* (Michael Gainey); *Marion* (Jenny Maxwell); *Woman in Car* (Junie Ellis)

The rash of films dealing with juvenile delinquency painted a picture of American youth in the fifties that, if preserved in a time capsule, could have future generations believing all teenagers wore black leather jackets, styled their hair in ducktails, and regularly beat up their parents and teachers. One of the rare films to point out that most teenagers were ordinary kids going through the normal but nonetheless difficult process of growing to maturity was *Blue Denim*. Based on a popular Broadway play. it offered a pretty tough premise to the moviegoing public: what does a nice ordinary boy do when he gets his nice ordinary girlfriend pregnant?

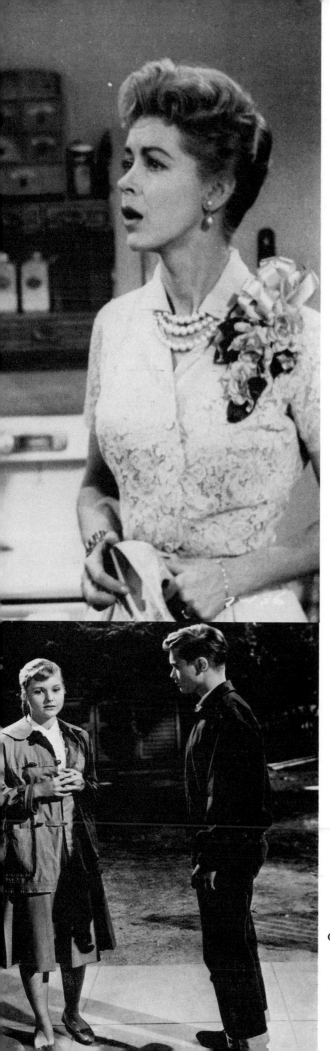

As the film begins, Arthur Bartley (Brandon de Wilde) is finding that adolescence isn't much fun. His parents don't understand him: Major Malcolm Bartley (MacDonald Carey) cuts too stern a father figure, demanding a false show of "masculinity" from the boy, while Jessie Bartley (Marsha Hunt) is too protective a mother. Between their drastically different approaches Arthur finds himself lost— not yet ready for the adult attitudes the one demands or able to tolerate any longer the childish treatment he receives from the other. He retreats into a world he creates in the cellar, where his wisecracking pal Ernie (Warren Berlinger) shares beer, poker games, and swearing sessions with him: the rites of manhood, fifties style.

But there is another rite. When Ernie isn't around, Arthur's attractive, uncertain girlfriend, Janet Willard (Carol Lynley) spends hours with him in the alternative world of the cellar. At first their experiments at lovemaking are primitive enough to be funny. But as the months go by, Janet learns that she's pregnant. In school she is a bundle of nerves, uncomfortable around girlfriends and teachers alike; at home, she is too frightened to tell her father (Vaughn Taylor), a distracted man, about her situation. Eventually Janet becomes desperate, and Arthur finds that he is the one she relies on. Knowing that to tell his parents would be disastrous, he and his friend Ernie manage to find an abortionist—and then frantically go about trying to raise the necessary but near-impossible $150 fee.

The frightened couple make a nightmarish trip to the appointed place, but at the last possible moment are unable to go through with it—frightened by the uncleanliness of the operating room and the ugliness of the act. Instead, they decide to confront their parents with the fact of her pregnancy and ask them for help in dealing with the situation.

In its resolution and indication of a happy ending, the film is a considerably compromised version of the much bleaker play. A good deal of the film is, in fact, unsuccessful: the characterizations are either too broad or too stereotyped, resulting in a general lack of believability. But in simply attempting to deal with such a delicate situation in non-exploitive terms, Twentieth Century-Fox pushed forward in freeing the industry from the old taboos of the Production Code. And in Carol Lynley, former model and child actress, they found a perfect heroine: vulnerable and spirited, haunting yet believable, she quickly became one of the most popular actresses with younger audiences.

Carol Lynley and Brandon De Wilde

An end to ennui: Kirk Douglas and Kim Novak

Strangers When We Meet

Columbia (1959)

A Bryna-Quine Production, produced and directed by Richard Quine; screenplay by Evan Hunter, based on his novel of the same name.

CAST: *Larry Coe* (Kirk Douglas); *Maggie Gault* (Kim Novak); *Roger Altar* (Ernie Kovacs); *Eve Coe* (Barbara Rush); *Felix Anders* (Walter Matthau); *Mrs. Wagner* (Virginia Bruce); *Stanley Baxter* (Kent Smith); *Betty Anders* (Helen Gallagher); *Ken Gault* (John Bryant); *Linda Harder* (Roberta Shore); *Marcia* (Nancy Kovack); *Honey Blonde* (Carol Douglas); *Dilabbia* (Ernest Sarracino); *David Coe* (Ray Ferrell); *Peter Coe* (Douglas Holmes); *Patrick Gault* (Timmy Molina); *Gerandi* (Paul Picerni)

In 1957 *No Down Payment* chronicled almost every ailment of modern suburbia—from alcoholism to racial discrimination—but it largely overlooked one element. "The love affair" between seemingly happily married people still waited patiently for filmmakers to broach the subject. Evan Hunter's novel *Strangers When We Meet* scrupulously studied just such an experience: an extramarital affair that was both unique enough to be interesting yet universal enough in its implications to appear highly representational. At the hands of producer-director Richard Quine, it became the first major motion picture to offer a serious analysis of this modern syndrome.

Larry Coe (Kirk Douglas) is a successful architect living in an upper-middle-class suburb of Los Angeles with his wife Eve (Barbara Rush) and their two boys. He is affluent and respected, but experiences a growing sensation that his lifestyle fails to satisfy him in any deep sense, though he cannot understand why. He manages his career with executive finesse, but feels that he has not fulfilled his creative potential, and now finds himself looking back wistfully to the war years (when he won a medal in combat) as the best time of his life.

But Larry does not take the experience of being a father lightly, and walks his boys to the school bus stop every morning. One day he strikes up a conversation with a beautiful blonde neighbor, Maggie Gault (Kim Novak), and reads between the lines of her nervous small-talk a confession that she is as unfulfilled as he. Almost immediately the two are drawn into an adulterous affair. At first, they are actually "high" on the experience, taking wild risks out of the thrilling feeling that they are "like kids again."

Shortly, though, they come back down to earth. Both care deeply about their spouses and their children. They begin taking greater precautions, meeting secretly at a motel that becomes their special retreat from the world. Each finds it is harder and harder to tolerate the small problems that surface at home and eventually they contemplate the possibility of divorce. But while Maggie is drawn ever further into desiring such a solution, Larry cannot face the idea of leaving his family.

Quickly the affair turns into a nightmare, an experience neither can do without but one that offers them almost no pleasure at all. When the two couples are matched together at a dinner party the hypocrisy is more than either Larry or Maggie can bear. In his need to talk about it, Larry speaks both to his bohemian novelist friend Roger (Ernie Kovacs), for whom he is building a house, and his neighbor Felix (Walter Matthau). Roger is envious of Larry's predicament, for though he has enjoyed success both as a writer and as a ladies' man, he has never experienced any deep, passionate feelings for a woman—and believes this is why his books are all sterile works, if stylishly written ones. Felix is sympathetic enough to help Larry realize that the affair, which at the moment of inception appeared to be the only possible means of curing Larry's lethargy, will only make him ever more miserable.

For a while Larry even prefers that to the vacuum his life has become. But as Maggie grows progressively more distraught over her compromising position, what once seemed to be "the love of the century" turns into a trap in which they hate one another but still cannot give the relationship

The Beatnik and The Executive: Ernie Kovacs and Kirk Douglas.

The lovers pretend to meet by accident when they take their children to an amusement park on the same day

up. When Eve learns of the situation, her shock and sense of betrayal make Larry aware that he will have to either leave his wife and family or end the affair. He makes his decision to break it off. He then tries, with Eve's help, to establish a relationship satisfying enough so that, coupled with a resurgence of creative interest in his work, his life will once again be meaningful—without resorting to the ego-gratifying excitement of other women.

Gidget

Columbia (1959)

Produced by Lewis J. Rachmil; directed by Paul Wendkos; screenplay by Gabrielle Upton, from a novel by Frederick Kohner.

CAST: *Gidget* (Sandra Dee); *Kahoona* (Cliff Robertson); *Moondoggie* (James Darren); *Mr. Lawrence* (Arthur O'Connell); *Mrs. Lawrence* (Mary La Roche); *Lover Boy* (Tom Laughlin); *Hot Shot* (Robert Ellis); *Lord Byron* (Burt Metcalfe); *B. L.* (Sue George)

Gidget made an overnight teenage idol out of Sandra Dee and began a shift in teenage fashions and fancies from the East Coast to the West. Based on a pleasantly innocuous little novel by Frederick Kohner which presented readers with a female equivalent to Max Shulman's typical teenage boy, Dobie Gillis, the movie was produced strictly as a youth exploitation film. But it did enjoy a respectable enough budget to feature both color photography and a number of highly respected actors. And unlike the rock 'n' roll sagas which featured greasers in black leather jackets, this story took place in Southern California and introduced to a country that had been hyped on Alan Freed's "big beat" style of music a far more easygoing complement to it called "the California sound." West Coast teenagers had for years been enjoying the beaches from Big Sur to Santa Monica, but no one had thought to commercialize their life-style on film before. In *Gidget*, Hollywood created an idyllic world of beach bums and bikini-clad surfer girls. These teenagers were tan, blond, and clean-cut, which came as a welcome relief to parents fed up with hoodlum heroes.

"Gidget"—short for "girl midget"—is a skinny young teenager (Sandra Dee) who receives her nickname from some clowning surfer boys, as she pales in comparison to the chesty bathing beauties who frequent the beaches. But Gidget's parents (Arthur O'Connell and Mary La Roche) understandingly explain to her that when she eventually reaches maturity, she'll be far happier than the girls who developed quickly. Deeply experiencing the difficulties of adolescence—feeling like a kid one minute and an adult the next—Gidget suddenly realizes her parents' prediction is true. The handsomest surfer boy of them all, Moondoggie (James Darren), takes an interest in her, as does Kahoona (Cliff Robertson), an older, individualistic surf bum whose affections for Gidget range somewhere between big-brotherly warmth and nostalgia for his own lost youth.

Good-looking James Darren became, for a short while, the heartthrob of teenage girls, then quickly disappeared from sight—but not before landing a role in one major movie, *The Guns of Navarone*. One of his fellow surfers, Tom Laughlin, failed to attract notoriety at all until a full fifteen years later, when his independently produced *Billy Jack* became the rage of the early seventies. Cliff Robertson moved into more mature roles, including his performance as John Kennedy in *PT 109* and his Oscar-winning *Charly* in 1968. His presence helped make the original *Gidget* far superior to the endless string of sequels and spin-offs; Kahoona gave a serious dimension to the story, through his struggle with the loneliness and cynicism a surfer eventually experiences if he doesn't give up the good life in time to make something of himself.

A few marketable songs were included, and despite the colorful glimpses of fun in the sun and a romantic portrayal of adolescent life and love, *Gidget* did manage to say something about the difficulty of being an affluent teenager. Sandra Dee at once became both a reflection of and an ideal for the teenage girls of America, as well as a pint-sized version of Doris Day for young boys to dream about. Previously she had appeared in dramatic films such as *Imitation of Life* with Lana Turner, but it was *Gidget* that made her a top-billed star, at least in youth-market movies.

James Darren (right) and friend carry Sandra Dee to the water

The All-American Girl: Sandra Dee

Ben Hur

Metro-Goldwyn-Mayer (1959)

Produced by Sam Zimbalist; directed by William Wyler; screenplay by Karl Tunberg, from the novel by General Lew Wallace.

CAST: *Judah Ben Hur* (Charlton Heston); *Quintus Arrius* (Jack Hawkins); *Messala* (Stephen Boyd); *Esther* (Haya Hayareet); *Sheik Ilderim* (Hugh Griffith); *Miriam* (Martha Scott); *Simonides* (Sam Jaffe); *Tirzah* (Cathy O'Donnell); *Balthasar* (Finlay Currie); *Pilate* (Frank Thring); *Drusus* (Terence Longden); *Sextus* (Andre Morell); *Flavia* (Marina Berti); *Emperor Tiberius* (George Relph); *Malluch* (Adi Berber); *Amrah* (Stella Vitelleschi) *Mary* (Jose Greci); *Joseph* (Laurence Payne); *Jesus* (Claude Heater)

By 1959 the wide screen had been filled with so many lavish spectaculars that it was in clear danger of going the way of 3-D and dying from overexposure. Then M-G-M provided what was at once recognized as a landmark in the religious epic genre, a type of film few critical moviegoers regard highly. Veteran director William Wyler departed radically from the traditional Cecil B. De Mille style of historical histrionics laced with moralizing that had reached its apotheosis with *The Ten Commandments*. Instead, Wyler approached his story with a striking modernity that balanced expansive action with human interplay, forsaking overt religiosity in favor of a believable human adventure with faith.

Too often, characters in films dealing with the ancient world, especially during the time of Jesus, seem remote from the everyday motivations and frustrations that we ourselves know and experience. But the story of Ben Hur, as adapted by screenwriter Karl Tunberg from the classic 1880 novel by General Lew Wallace, presented characters who, despite the exotic costumes, underwent personality and political crises not all that far removed from those of viewers.

Young Judah Ben Hur (Charlton Heston) is a member of the family of Judea that rebels against their state of virtual slavery under the Roman power of Emperor Tiberius (George Relph), depicted here as a clear Hitler figure who has convinced the Romans they are a master race. Ben Hur's refusal to conform to Rome's rule leads him into a series of diverse experiences: he wins the love of Esther (Haya Hayareet), a Hebrew maiden; is adopted by Quintus Arrius (Jack Hawkins), a stolid but well-meaning Roman citizen; and becomes a slave of Sheik Ilderim (Hugh Griffith), a

Jack Hawkins and Charlton Heston

Stephen Boyd and Charlton Heston

Cathy O'Donnell, Martha Scott
Charlton Heston and Haya Hay
areet

264

peddler of human flesh who matches Ben Hur in a chariot race against the cruel young Roman Messala (Stephen Boyd).

Though in summary the story sounds like a comic strip adventure, it was elevated by the intelligence of Tunberg's writing and the vast scope of Wyler's direction. The spectacular sequences were, strictly on the level of technical accomplishment, the most awesome of their kind since the Cinerama roller coaster ride—including a massive sea battle and the classic chariot race. Always, though, such moments were an organic part of the story of one man's journey through life. Furthermore, they occupied a relatively small portion of the film's three-and-a-half-hour running time. Most of the movie was given over to interesting interpersonal confrontations, which made the film continually fascinating and believable as melodrama. Best of all, Ben Hur's conversion to the teachings of Christ was not depicted in the usual manner, with a wildly staged moment of realization, but through a slow, continual change within him as he intellectually responds to Jesus' philosophies.

Never had the wide screen and stereophonic sound been so effectively integrated into a story to create a total cinematic experience in which the new techniques were inseparably combined with an old tale. *Ben Hur* was the film toward which Hollywood had been unconsciously moving since the beginning of the decade: the thinking person's spectacle.

The All American couple, circa 1959: Rock Hudson and Doris Day

Pillow Talk

Universal-International (1959)

Produced by Ross Hunter and Martin Melcher; directed by Michael Gordon; screenplay by Stanley Shapiro and Maurice Richlin, from a story by Russell Rouse and Clarence Greene.

CAST: *Brad Allen* (Rock Hudson); *Jann Morrow* (Doris Day); *Jonathan Forbes* (Tony Randall); *Alma* (Thelma Ritter); *Tony* (Nick Adams); *Marie* (Julia Meade); *Harry* (Allen Jenkins); *Pierot* (Marcel Dalio); *Mrs. Walters* (Lee Patrick); *Nurse Resnick* (Mary McCarty); *Dr. Maxwell* (Alex Gerry)

By the decade's end, Rock Hudson had proved to be too ruggedly immobile for contemporary drama but too perfectly chiseled for westerns, while his female counterpart Doris Day had attained full stardom yet failed to create any sort of clear-cut personal image. As luck would have it, both their careers were given a much-needed sense of direction when the two were cast together in the Ross Hunter production of *Pillow Talk*. Intended as a classy contemporary comedy laced with some sophisticated sexual innuendos, the film turned out to be that and more. The script provided ample laughs and the direction was fast-paced and bouncy, but in the end it was the casting that created the magic, helping the film to emerge as the fifties counterpart to that beloved romantic comedy of the thirties, *It Happened One Night*—with Hudson and Day established as the most popular screen couple since Clark Gable and Claudette Colbert.

The tone of the film was highly urbane, giving the entire country a glimpse of what life was supposedly like among the chic of Manhattan. A telephone party line rested at the heart of the slim plot, serving to propel the two central characters first into pure antipathy and, later, into love. Jann Morrow (Day) is a stylishly successful interior decorator, whose only real problem in life is that she can never use her phone when she needs to. She shares the party line with Brad Allen (Hudson), a wolfish songwriter-composer who is continuously monopolizing the wires, always luring another attractive young woman to his apartment under the pretense that he has written a new song "just for her."

When Jann begins breaking into his mushy conversations with sarcastic one-liners, hard feelings grow. He assumes she must be a stuffy old maid, but when he finally sees the "voice" and finds her highly attractive, it's necessary for him to woo her incognito—masked in the guise of an innocent Texan reminiscent of Hudson's own characterization in *Giant*. When Jann eventually learns that the man she's been falling for is actually her enemy from the telephone, she responds with venom.

Battle of the sexes comedies are always highly popular, and are usually highly effective at delivering popular mannerisms of speech, fashions of the day, and attitudes about sex of the period in which they are made. *Pillow Talk* was no exception. Tony Randall appeared in the part of a sullen suitor of Jann's, and his performance was so popular that he was invariably present in all of the film's sequels and spin-offs—even when the two original stars weren't around. Doris Day at last "found herself" on screen as the embodiment of the independent modern woman: wearing a complete wardrobe of Jean Louis garments, supporting herself in a creative career, falling but never sexually succumbing to the handsomest man in Manhattan. In the early moments of the movie, she and Hudson were seen together via a split screen; by the end, they had materialized as an important team.

The clinch: Doris Day and Rock Hudson

In *Pillow Talk*, Tony Randall created an effective caricature of the decade's executive hero

A new explicitness: Richard Egan confronts Constance Ford over daughter Sandra Dee's right to turn in her adolescent outfit for a more adult one

A Summer Place
Warner Bros. (1959)

Adapted, produced and directed by Delmer Daves, from the novel by Sloan Wilson.

CAST: *Ken Jorgenson* (Richard Egan); *Sylvia Hunter* (Dorothy McGuire); *Molly Jorgenson* (Sandra Dee); *Bart Hunter* (Arthur Kennedy); *Johnny Hunter* (Troy Donahue); *Helen Jorgenson* (Constance Ford); *Mrs. Hamble* (Beulah Bondi)

One way of understanding the changes in the American public's mores is to closely scrutinize the shifting styles of glossy soap opera-ish films. The content of such stories—how much is allowed to appear on the surface and how much must instead by suggested—provides a pretty good indication of what audiences either expect or will tolerate from Hollywood at any given time. And the mere thought that *A Summer Place* could be blandly released and quietly

consumed by moviegoers just two short years after *Peyton Place* created such a scandal is striking indeed.

That earlier film dealt both with marital infidelity of adults and the growing-pang passions of teenagers in the most cautious (indeed, almost discreet) of manners. Yet it brought down the wrath of various would-be censors. However, *A Summer Place* centered on those same issues so graphically—both in terms of the brutally frank dialogue and the romanticized visions of illicit lovers in each other's arms—that it made *Peyton Place* seem old-fashioned (and almost naively moralistic) by comparison. Yet when *A Summer Place* opened in New York, it was not at some downbeat art house but at that perennial home of the family picture, Radio City Music Hall!

The story begins as caustic, alcoholic Bart Hunter (Arthur Kennedy) opens his once-elegant home on Pine Island, Maine, to tourists for the summer, after his gentle wife Sylvia (Dorothy McGuire) protests about their growing need for money, especially since their son Johnny (Troy Donahue) is nearing college age. But she is shocked to learn that the people moving in are charmingly masculine Ken Jorgenson (Richard Egan), his nasty wife Helen (Constance Ford), and their impressionable daughter Molly (Sandra Dee)—for, twenty years earlier, Sylvia and Ken were lovers.

They never married because Sylvia belonged to high society and Ken was only a lifeguard, but in the last two decades, things have changed considerably: he is now a huge success, while she is broke. During the course of the summer, they quietly resume their affair out of the loneliness

The Generation Gap: Sandra Dee and Constance Ford

A Family Portrait: Sandra Dee, Troy Donahue, Constance Ford, Richard Egan, Dorothy McGuire, and Arthur Kennedy

and desperation they both experience with their cold, unresponsive mates. The two teenagers also fall in love, but when a sailboat they are in crashes in a storm, forcing them to spend the night together, a suspicious Helen forces Molly (in Ken's absence) to be examined by a doctor to determine if she is still a virgin.

When the adult affair finally comes out into the open, divorces are quickly arranged. The two former lovers are at long last married, but the teenagers are so upset by this development that they will not accept the older couple. Johnny and Molly each feel betrayed to learn their parents could be involved in such secretive doings. Finally, though, the adults and teenagers bridge the generation gap and accept one another when they are finally able to see that the values of the one generation are not those of the next—ex-

cept where love is concerned.

The film spared no details about the love affairs, the divorce, and, finally, Molly's pregnancy. While the movie-making itself, by veteran director Delmer Daves, was slick and colorful, the story line and dialogue were crude and obvious. The sophisticated socialites of New England talked like Hollywood back-lot performers. But in Troy Donahue, the motion picture industry found the perfect mate for Sandra Dee and, in time, her male equivalent. The balance between the two sentimental love stories—one for adults, one for teenagers—made the film highly popular with both audiences. And the ribbon tying up the package was the lovely title song, which became a standard that remained popular long after the film was forgotten.

Steve Reeves and Sylvia Koscina; the physical positioning of the women was often far more extreme than anything in the scandalous *Baby Doll*, but Hercules attracted little attention from the censors

Hercules

Warner Bros. (1959)

Produced by Federico Teti; an O. S. C. A. R. Film; presented by Joseph E. Levine; directed by Pietro Francisci; screenplay by Pietro Francisci, Ennio De Concini and Gaio Frattini.

CAST: *Hercules* (Steve Reeves); *Iole* (Silva Koscina); *Jason* (Fabrizio Mioni); *Pelias* (Ivo Garrani); *Eurysteus* (Arturo Dominici); *Iphitus* (Mimmo Palmara); *The Sybil* (Lidia Alfonsi); *Amazon* (Gina Rovera)

Two of the most popular film genres during the decade were costume spectaculars and imported foreign films. The colorful costume epics, though set in the ancient world and usually filmed on location in Europe, were invariably made by American companies with potent box-office stars like Charlton Heston; the black-and-white imported movies, made exclusively by Europeans, were either serious art films of the Fellini-Bergman mold or sexploitation pictures featuring an endless string of unclothed Brigitte Bardot imitators.

271

Steve Reeves

Though American audiences were oblivious to the fact, cheaply made costume epics were as popular in Italy as grade B westerns were in the States. Levine gambled that what was routine on the Continent might prove to be marketable as something new and different here; he selected *Hercules* as his initial entry simply because it featured a nominal American star-name theatre managers could put on the marquee. His exploitation project succeeded beyond his wildest dreams: *Hercules* reaped profits in the millions, turning Levine into an important producer who could afford to pick and choose his future films.

The story line was fundamentally different both from the heavy classical style of De Mille's *The Ten Commandments* and from the intelligent, modern spectacles such as *Ben Hur.* Wasting almost no time on dramatics, character development or moralizing, it jumped at a breakneck pace from one adventure to the next as the mighty Hercules and his wife Iole (Sylva Koscina) aid Jason (Fabrizio Mioni) with his search for the fabled Golden Fleece. Serious students of mythology were more than a bit concerned about the way the legends were jumbled, but adolescents were delighted to find an epic adventure that didn't waste time on talk.

Just as noticeable were the females: all the Greek maidens, Amazon warriors, and comely handmaidens were statuesque women of either the Sophia Loren or Anita Ekberg variety, alluringly draped in gauze-like costumes far more revealing than American filmmakers dared to employ. The abundance of sex, that managed to stay just within the bounds of popular morality, combined with comic book action, helped make the film immensely popular everywhere. But acceptance was especially impressive at drive-in movies, a phenomenon that spread like wildfire in the fifties. Previously, drive-ins had merely absorbed regular theatrical releases after they had fulfilled their potential in indoor houses. The success of *Hercules* helped distributors realize that the drive-in market could become considerably more lucrative if films were designed expressly for its more boisterous audience—de-emphasizing melodramatics and adding more sex and violence.

But the possibility of combining the two highly popular types by importing a foreign-made spectacle was largely overlooked—until Joseph E. Levine decided to give it a try. With Warner Brothers picking up the distribution tab, he created what came to be known as "saturation booking" with *Hercules:* spending a considerable amount of advertising money for this low-budget programmer (including many more radio and TV spots than newspaper ads), while opening it simultaneously in as many movie houses as possible across the country (it appeared in almost 150 cinemas in the New York and Long Island area alone), then pulling it after one week in case word of mouth was bad.

The film starred Steve Reeves, a former Mr. America who had failed to make any kind of an impression in domestic films. He became the first Hollywood has-been to drift to Rome and find a niche for himself in their low-budget, muscle-man movies—a syndrome that was soon to become highly prevalent with former stars of TV western series.

A conflict of lifestyles: Frank Sinatra and Martha Hyer withdraw from Arthur Kennedy's social circle

Metro-Goldwyn-Mayer (1959)

Produced by Sol C. Siegel; directed by Vincente Minnelli; screenplay by John Patrick and Arthur Sheekman, based on the novel by James Jones.

CAST: *Dave Hirsh* (Frank Sinatra); *Bama Dillert* (Dean Martin); *Ginny Moorhead* (Shirley MacLaine); *Gwen French* (Martha Hyer); *Frank Hirsh* (Arthur Kennedy); *Edith Barclay* (Nancy Gates); *Agnes Hirsh* (Leora Dana); *Dawn Hirsh* (Betty Lou Keim); *Professor Robert Haven French* (Larry Gates); *Raymond Lanchak* (Steven Peck); *Jane Barclay* (Connie Gilchrist); *Smitty* (Ned Wever)

The novels of James Jones deal with a single theme: Americans, when confronted with the threat of a powerful outside enemy, quickly form a tightly knit community able to withstand almost anything but, during times of peace, quickly slip into apathy and loneliness, venting frustrations on each other. In *From Here to Eternity* Jones presented the directionless lives of some men and women before the bombing of Pearl Harbor and their speedy redemption through courage at the outset of war; conversely, in *Some Came Running* Jones chronicled the speedy dissipation of that camaraderie following the armistice, and the sense of dislocation—more extreme, due to the ever-present threat of the Bomb, than ever before—that set in during the new decade.

The film made from this latter book is not, like the earlier one, a screen classic. It is, however, an often touching assessment of the way in which cynicism became the individual's only shield against social corruption during the period that witnessed the birth of modern suburbia. Dave Hirsh (Frank Sinatra) returns to his small Indiana home town after several years of aimless wandering following the war's end. His older brother Frank (Arthur Kennedy) is now a dishonest businessman and upstanding community leader, complete with wife (Leora Dana), daughter (Betty Lou Keim), and desirable secretary (Nancy Gates). Much to Frank's surprise, Dave has no desire to similarly "make something of himself" (amassing money and respectability though underhanded means). Instead, Dave drifts back and forth between the feminine companionship of Gwen French (Martha Hyer), an attractive schoolteacher who encourages him to develop his talent for writing poetry, and the masculine friendship of Bama Dillert (Dean Martin), the town's loud but likable professional gambler—who is, in his own way, an honest man, making no bones about presenting a socially respectable image.

Coming as it did at decade's end, the film served to summarize the American experience during the fifties. Its essential truth is inherent in a scene most people found confusing at the time: when Gwen spurns Dave's proposals, he without much trouble turns toward Ginny Moorhead (Shirley MacLaine), a young girl who's drifted in from Chicago, looking for excitement. Her amoral involvement with both Dave and Bama, and their unquestioning acceptance of each other's relationship with her, is important. The relationship between these three characters is, essentially, representative of what came to be called the Beat Generation—the post-World War II equivalent to the Lost Generation of the twenties.

Thus, we view Sinatra, first encountered jauntily sporting his service clothes (final vestige of the order and discipline that only recently ran his life) while a cigarette butt hangs cynically from his lower lip; Martin, sprawled out in a bathtub with his cowboy hat perched cockily upon his head; MacLaine, looking out through large, little girl eyes that belie her sexpot image.

Instead of playing the game of life according to the old, outdated rules they are social dropouts of the Atomic Age —endowing their desperate lives with meaning by living in their own unique style.

The birth of an alternative life style: Frank Sinatra and Dean Martin

Frank Sinatra and Shirley McLaine

275

John Wayne and Angie Dickinson

Rio Bravo

Warner Bros. (1959)

Produced and directed by Howard Hawks; screenplay by Jules Furthman and Leigh Brackett, from a short story by B. H. Campbell.

CAST: *John T. Chance* (John Wayne); *Dude* (Dean Martin); *Colorado* (Ricky Nelson); *Feathers* (Angie Dickinson); *Stumpy* (Walter Brennan); *Pat Wheeler* (Ward Bond); *Nathan Burdette* (John Russell); *Carlos* (Pedro Gonzalez-Gonzalez); *Consuela* (Estelita Rodriguez); *Joe Burdette* (Claude Akins); *Jake* (Malcolm Atterbury); *Harold* (Harry Carey, Jr.); *Matt Harris* (Bob Steele)

By the decade's end the adult western had run its course. *High Noon* had given birth to a cycle that included *The Fastest Gun Alive, Jubal,* and *The Tin Star*—all antiheroic in their treatment of the Old West. But as America began readying itself to leave the fifties behind, John Wayne and Howard Hawks assembled a massive movie-attack on all the "mature" cowboy pictures. *Rio Bravo* teamed the star and the director for the first time since *Red River,* the last of the great epic westerns of the forties. Their new effort was an attempt to turn American audiences away from the fascination with our own weaknesses and limitations, so lavishly

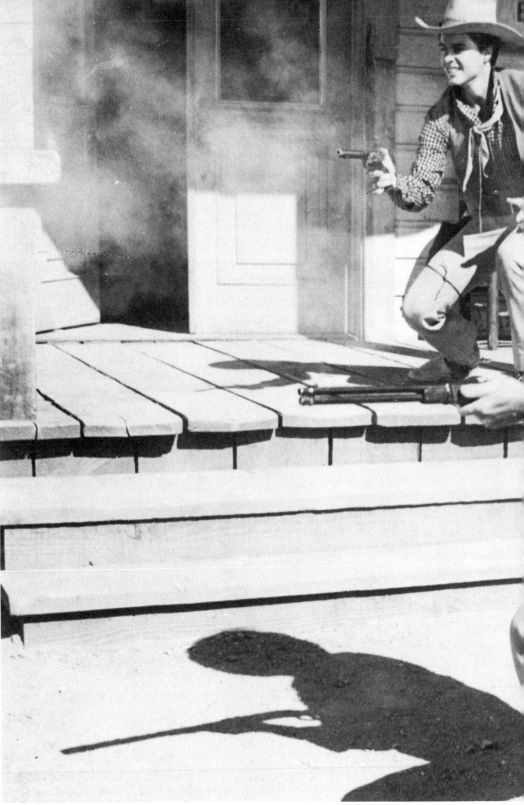

The Generation Gap bridged through violence: Ricky Nelson, John Wayne

fused to help him on the grounds of being worried about their families, struck the two men as absurd. In *Rio Bravo* they illustrated the alternative route of procedure. John T. Chance (Wayne), sheriff of the city that gives the film its title, becomes the target of a ruthless land baron, Nathan Burdette (John Russell), when he arrests the man's drunken brother Joe (Claude Akins). At one point Chance's old friend Pat Wheeler (Ward Bond) offers to lend him his drovers as deputies, and Chance refuses. In language clearly reminiscent of the *High Noon* confrontation, the sheriff flatly refuses such help on the grounds that these men would get themselves killed worrying about their wives and families, and ultimately be more of a hindrance than a help.

In *High Noon*, Gary Cooper rejected the aid of three men who did offer assistance—a drunk, an old man and a kid. In *Rio Bravo*, these are precisely the three figures Chance enlists. He creates a strong male community out of the alcoholic Duke (Dean Martin), the crippled, cackling Stumpy (Walter Brennan), and the callow Colorado (Ricky Nelson). Instead of letting his woman enter the fighting as Cooper's Will Kane did in the earlier film, Chance keeps his romantic relationship to the saloon girl Feathers (Angie Dickinson) in the background—and out of what are clearly a man's affairs.

It is no accident that all the leading characters have nicknames rather than Christian names, or that "Chance"—the only major figure whose proper name we know—*sounds* like a nickname.

This emphasizes the fact that they form the Hawks conception of a coterie of professionals, and exist out of the mainstream of life. *Rio Bravo* is very much a picture about being (or becoming) a man: Colorado grows to maturity, Dude redeems himself from his degenerate state, Stumpy proves he is still worthwhile, and when the shooting is over, Chance finally succumbs to the charms of his woman. Most important of all, nobody throws his star down in the dust at the end.

Critics were quick to criticize the film for its commercial concessions, and were unable to take seriously a western that included a singing sequence for Dean Martin and Ricky Nelson. But with the eventual reevaluation of Hawks' career, *Rio Bravo* came to be seen not just as a big, likable, silly western but as an artistically controlled work of personal expression by one of the most underrated of all American directors. Certainly its popularity helped to hasten the decline of the "adult" western, and to indicate that the end of an era was at hand.

displayed in the westerns of a self-searching decade, and revive a sense of national conviction in our powers and potentials.

Wayne and Hawks had been kicking around the idea of making an "answer" to *High Noon* for seven years, ever since they first saw—and intensely disliked—that film. The idea of a lawman who would try to enlist the aid of nonprofessionals, and then break out in tears when people re-

Some Like It Hot

United Artists (1959)

A Mirisch Company Presentation of an Ashton Picture, released by United Artists. Produced and directed by Billy Wilder. Screenplay by Billy Wilder and I. A. L. Diamond, suggested by a story by R. Thoeren and M. Logan. Photography by Charles Lang, Jr.

CAST: *Joe* (Tony Curtis); *Sugar Kane* (Marilyn Monroe); *Jerry* (Jack Lemmon); *Spats Colombo* (George Raft); *Osgood Fielding* (Joe E. Brown)

In 1950, screen comedy was most perfectly typified by *Francis, The Talking Mule*; for 1959, the logical choice would be *Some Like It Hot*. The disparity between the two pictures represents the drastic change in attitude America experienced during the intervening decade. In the fifties the country grew up, as evidenced by films like *From Here to Eternity, On the Waterfront,* and *Peyton Place,* all of which would have been quite impossible to produce even a decade earlier. And Billy Wilder's best film was both the end result

A hot band number on the train (Joan Shawlee as Sweet Sue at right)

Lemmon and Curtis play their instruments

Jack Lemmon carries Joe E. Brown

Tony Curtis and Jack Lemmon   A pensive Marilyn examines jewelry given by a suitor

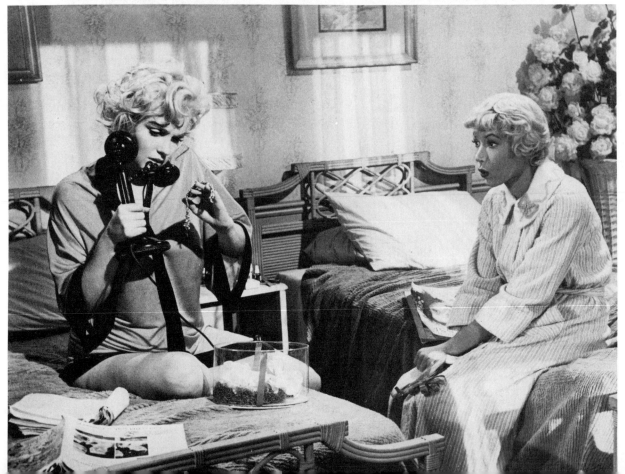

Lemmon and Marilyn in the upper berth

of that process, as well as the first milestone toward a new, racier style of comic pictures.

Today, *Some Like It Hot* may be shrouded in nostalgia for the fifties but in its day the film expressed a then existing nostalgia for an earlier era. The most popular television series of 1959 was *The Untouchables,* which dealt graphically with the gangster figures of the thirties. *Some Like It Hot* played off that fascination with the seamier side of the past by creating a comedy around two fictitious musicians who inadvertently witness the infamous St. Valentine's Day Massacre. Slick sharpie Joe (Tony Curtis) and his easygoing pal Jerry (Jack Lemmon) wander into a Chicago garage to get out of the cold, and happen to be present when ganglord Spats Colombo (George Raft) guns down seven members of a rival organization. Hysterically trying to escape, Joe and Jerry don women's clothing and join an all-female orchestra headed for Florida. All goes well enough until the boys meet Sugar Kane (Marilyn Monroe). Immediately, both fall madly in love with the irresistibly feminine singer. Upon arriving at the hotel, Joe/"Josephine" woos Sugar by donning yet another disguise, pretending to be a melancholy millionaire (Sugar adores millionaires),

while Jerry/"Daphne" is him/herself wooed by an aged millionaire named Osgood Fielding 3d (Joe E. Brown). The romantic problems, however, are temporarily shelved when Spats and his gang show up to attend a gangster convention.

Some Like It Hot sounds like a one-gag comedy: the protagonist's problem in winning the heroine because he must remain incognito. And certainly the film rests squarely in the tradition of classic romantic comedy, with all sorts of blocking characters arriving right on cue in order to postpone the seduction. But it is also a dark comedy, beginning with a mass murder and containing several other killings along the way. In addition, it works as a spoof of old movie clichés: Spats' dreaded enemy is Little Bonaparte (Nehemiah Persoff), a send-up of Edward G. Robinson's most famous characterization, while badguy George Raft and goodguy Pat O'Brien constantly caricature their stock screen images. There's plenty of slapstick too, with wild chases through the hotel lobby, and social satire on the entire business of sexual identity.

Most of all, though, *Some Like It Hot* is a condemnation of role playing as a way of life. The characters, afraid to re-

283

"Nobody's perfect": Joe E. Brown and Jack Lemmon

spond as people, find it easier to deal with one another as types. So to win Sugar, Joe must not only pretend to have a million dollars, but also act out an extended Hollywood stereotype by feigning a Cary Grant accent. Amazingly enough, with all the diverse types of comedy going on at once, the film never becomes cluttered or goes out of control. The box office returns proved to producers that the mass audience could be expected to enjoy such a highly complex comic film.

There was not even much problem over the extended drag situation. Of course, earlier screen comedies employed drag, from *Charley's Aunt* to *I Was a Male War Bride.* The difference was that, in those films, the male hero always appeared uncomfortable about being stuck in women's clothing. But in *Some Like It Hot,* Curtis and Lemmon very quickly take to the idea of being dressed up as Josephine and Daphne. Any embarrassment is short lived, and soon they are quite casual—at times, almost ecstatic—about running around in dresses. If drag was not new to movies, the attitude toward drag was.

For Marilyn Monroe, the film brought a very special kind of fulfillment. Pictures like *Niagara, River of No Return,*

and *Bus Stop* had long since established her as a leading box office star, but with the critics she remained declassè. In frustration over the situation, Monroe had gone so far as to form her own filmmaking company. She played opposite Sir Laurence Olivier in *The Prince and the Showgirl,* a lame effort to convince everyone she could hold her own against the best actor in the business. But it was by spoofing the dumb blonde image she had created that Monroe finally won the blessings of the press. *Variety* hailed her as "a comedienne with that combination of sex appeal and timing that just can't be beat"; Archer Winsten of the New York *Post* insisted "Marilyn does herself proud, giving a performance of . . . intrinsic quality"; A. H. Weiler of the New York *Times* called her a "talented comedienne."

At long last, Marilyn had arrived. But as with almost everything else in her career and life, it was too little, too late. The decade which she, more than anyone else, had come to symbolize was already over. Very shortly, Marilyn would be gone too. But not before starring with Clark Gable, last of the old Hollywood superstars and Montgomery Clift, first of filmdom's new breed, in a picture titled, aptly enough, *The Misfits.*

The submarine crew: Fred Astaire, Anthony Perkins and Gregory Peck

On the Beach

United Artists (1959)

Produced and directed by Stanley Kramer; screenplay by John Paxton, based on the book by Nevil Shute.

CAST: *Dwight Towers* (Gregory Peck); *Moira Davidson* (Ava Gardner); *Julian Osborn* (Fred Astaire); *Peter Holmes* (Anthony Perkins); *Mary Holmes* (Donna Anderson); *Admiral Birdie* (John Tate); *Lieutenant Hosgood* (Lola Brooks); *Ferrel* (Guy Doleman); *Swain* (John Meillon); *Sundstrom* (Harp McGuire); *Benson* (Ken Wayne); *Davis* (Richard Meikle); *Ackerman* (Joe McCormick); *Davidson* (Lou Vernon)

By decade's end the threat of atomic annihilation had been handled in such diverse styles as science fiction, screwball comedy, and racial "message" melodrama. The only untried avenue was a film illustrating what no one had so far shown the courage to come right out and depict: the total destruction of mankind due to nuclear irresponsibility. The perfect person for the job was Stanley Kramer, whose films had provided a consciousness for an entire era. In *On the Beach* he resolved the fears and tensions of the decade by at last putting on screen a vision of what everyone had, for a full ten years, lived with daily on a subconscious level, provid-

Ava Gardner and Fred Astaire

ing audiences all across America with a cinematic catharsis for their fears. After *On the Beach,* the number of films dealing with atomic destruction fell off drastically. There remained only one unexplored avenue, the spoof, which Stanley Kubrick would later provide in his 1964 opus, *Dr. Strangelove*—subtitled, most appropriately for that upcoming decade, "How I Learned to *Stop* Worrying, and *Love* the Bomb."

The last great film of the fifties was set five years in the future, in the very same year that *Dr. Strangelove* was released. It is 1964 and a number of survivors of World War III live comfortably enough in Australia, having missed the holocaust (significantly, the film never reveals who began the war). Gradually, they realize the fallout is drifting southward and will, in time, destroy them. Dwight Towers (Gregory Peck) clings to the hope that his beloved family in the States has somehow managed to survive. Moira Davidson (Ava Gardner) falls in love with Towers, hoping

that she can, by offering herself to him, make up for her tawdry and wasted life. Peter (Anthony Perkins) and Mary (Donna Anderson) Holmes are young marrieds who want to plan for a future family, while Julian Osborn (Fred Astaire) is the last embodiment of that fifties archetype, the scientist grown cynical from an understanding of what his profession unwittingly unleashed.

The film powerfully depicts man's unending struggle to survive, through a harried submarine journey to San Diego, California, to check on a strange radio signal heralding from that city. In a long wordless sequence that quickly became a classic, a single sailor, protected in an airtight suit, leaves the sub and wanders through the stark, empty city in search of the source of the message—only to find it comes from a pop bottle stuck in a window shade which, when battered by the wind, strikes against the wireless apparatus.

The haunting Australian folk song "Waltzing Matilda" was at first intended for use in only one scene. But director

Kramer found it so appropriate to the mood of his piece that he requested Ernest Gold to make it the dominant musical theme of the picture. Viewing the film, one begins to hope along with the characters that some means of salvation will be found, despite knowledge on a conscious level —through pre-release publicity and the popularity of the Nevil Shute novel—that no easy solution would be provided. Earlier films stirred up audiences by depicting the near-annihilation of mankind, but even they could not prepare us for the quite unforgettable experience of viewing a dramatization of our *total* annihilation.

As the situation grows bleak and the characters take their suicide pills, Kramer employs the film's final sequence in order to state, through a combination of the visual and the verbal, his last great message of the decade. In a succession of shots the camera shows us scenes of a world totally devoid of life, then at last comes to rest on a sign above a Salvation Army camp. Its slogan, previously aimed at the characters in the movie, is now turned directly at the audience: "There is still time, Brother!"